EGYPT

after the Pharaohs

Mummy portrait. A portrait of the early second century from Hawara, which shows a genuine attempt to capture the personality in the eyelids, brows and the lines of the face and neck.

Alan K Bowman

EGYPT
after the Pharaohs

332 BC–AD 642
from Alexander
to the Arab Conquest

BRITISH MUSEUM PRESS

© 1986 Alan K. Bowman

First published 1986
First published in paperback 1989
Second paperback edition 1996

First published in 1986 by British Museum Press
A division of the British Museum Company Ltd
46 Bloomsbury Street, London WC1B 3QQ

A catalogue for this book is available from the British Library

ISBN 0 7141 0992 4

Printed in Hong Kong

Contents

Acknowledgements

Acknowledgement is made to the following for permission to reproduce illustrations:

Antikenmuseum, Staatliche Museen, Preussischer Kulturbesitz, Berlin: 15
Ashmolean Museum, Oxford: 4, 67, 79, 139
Austrian National Library, Vienna: 3
Bodleian Library, Oxford: 48
British Museum: 2, 7, 12, 14, 16, 17, 19, 23, 37, 46, 58, 80, 84, 116, 119, 124, 126, 137, 138, 140, 145
British Library: 50, 94, 142
Dr R.A. Coles: 85, 91, 110
Coptic Museum, Cairo: 32, 121, 123
Deutsches archäologisches Institut, Cairo: 22, 31, 66, 72, 77
Deutsches archäologisches Institut, Rome: 40
Egypt Exploration Society: 8, 20, 27, 36, 41, 44, 63, 64, 68, 69, 70, 73, 76, 78, 90, 93, 96, 104
French Archaeological Delegation, Kabul: 128
Graeco-Roman Museum, Alexandria: 95, 106, 144
Kelsey Museum of Archaeology, University of Michigan: 55, 60, 61, 62, 75, 86, 87, 89, 92, 102, 103, 107, 109, 113
Metropolitan Museum of Art, New York: 114, 115

National Trust (The Calke Gardner Wilkinson Papers, Bodleian Library, Oxford): 10, 34, 52, 53, 82
Petrie Museum, University College, London: 6
Royal Scottish Museum, Edinburgh: 65
Scala, Florence: 1, 45, 71, 112
Dr H. Whitehouse: 54, 101, 105, 117, 136

The maps (Figs 1 and 2) were prepared by Paul Simmons of Oxford University Press.

Acknowledgement is made to the author and to Cambridge University Press for permission to quote extracts from M.M. Austin, *The Hellenistic World from Alexander to the Roman Conquest* (1981).

Preface

A book on the history of Egypt during a decisive period in its development stands in need of no elaborate justification. Viewed from the standpoint of the Egyptologist, the Graeco-roman period may seem to lack the grandeur and the romance which the relics of the Pharaohs possess, but it was during the millennium between the conquest by Alexander and the Arab invasion that Egypt made its most significant contribution to the classical world and itself absorbed its important influences. It is a period which is, by the standards of the ancient world, exceptionally well-documented. The historian can take advantage of a wide range of source material: the writings of historians, geographers and literary figures of classical antiquity, the archaeological remains and artefacts and, above all, the thousands of texts on papyrus which the climate and the environment of the Nile valley have preserved for posterity.

The attempt to write a general account based on a synthesis of an intimidating range and quantity of material might well appear foolhardy for a variety of reasons. Evidence may emerge tomorrow which will turn today's truth on its head – awareness of which tends to make documentary historians chary of committing themselves to sweeping generalities. I can claim only a layman's familiarity with the archaeological relics and the expertise necessary for critical analysis of those documents which are written in languages other than Latin and Greek is absent; hence I have had to rely on published editions and translations of demotic and Coptic material. But the attempt at synthesis is nonetheless worth making, it is hoped, because there is no recent account in English which tries to exploit both the written and the archaeological evidence in order to see the impact of the presence of the Greeks and Romans in Egypt against the backdrop of the Egyptian tradition. This is intended to be the essence of the book and the narrative is deliberately offered with only the bald citation of some exemplary items of evidence, avoiding the proliferation of footnotes replete with documentation, bibliography and argument.

My immense debts to friends and colleagues are impossible to enumerate, the more especially because many of them have been incurred in discussion or correspondence over a long period of time. Some of my creditors will recognise their contributions and will, I hope, take their appearance as a compliment. If I avoid the invidiousness of naming some and excluding others that is not intended to understate or obscure my acute consciousness either of my debt to them, or of my fundamental reliance on a sustained tradition of accurate and magnanimous scholarship in the field of papyrology and the history of Graeco-roman Egypt. But for these the book, such as it is, would not exist at all. It is, however, a pleasure to make one exception in thanking Jane Rowlandson who painstakingly read the whole text and rescued me from many errors and obscurities. For those which remain I alone am responsible. For this revised paperback edition, I have taken the opportunity to add a list of the locations of museum objects illustrated in the plates, to correct some errors (for assistance with which I am particularly grateful to Professor John Baines, Dr Willy Clarysse and Dr Susan Walker), to update the bibliography and to include an appendix with some additional notes.

Oxford

July 1995

Notes on conventions used in the text

NAMES

The transliteration of names is always problematic and complete consistency is impossible to achieve. I have generally contented myself with using the most familiar and recognisable forms of common personal and place-names; but some inconsistencies of practice remain. It should be noted that documents of the Roman period frequently use the name Caesar alone in referring to the current emperor. I have not attempted to expand these.

DATES

All dates are AD unless otherwise indicated. I have used the form '251/0 BC' to indicate that an event or document is to be placed at some point within the period and the form '251–0 BC' to indicate that events or items referred to cover the period between the dates. I have not attempted to provide Julian equivalents for month dates which occur in the quotations. The calculation of equivalents for dates in the Ptolemaic period is a complex matter because of the lack of correspondence between calendaric years of different lengths (see references in Appendix 1). After the Roman takeover, as a consequence of the Julian reform, the correspondences were stabilised as follows:

Egyptian month	Julian equivalent	Egyptian month	Julian equivalent
Thoth	Aug. 29 – Sep. 27	Pharmouthi	Mar. 27 – Apr. 25
Phaophi	Sep. 28 – Oct. 27	Pachon	Apr. 26 – May 25
Hathyr	Oct. 28 – Nov. 26	Payni	May 26 – Jun. 24
Choiak	Nov. 27 – Dec. 26	Epeiph	Jun. 25 – Jul. 24
Tybi	Dec. 27 – Jan. 25	Mesore	Jul. 25 – Aug. 23
Mecheir	Jan. 26 – Feb. 24	Epagomenal days	Aug. 24 – Aug. 28
Phamenoth	Feb. 25 – Mar. 26		

List of illustrations

9

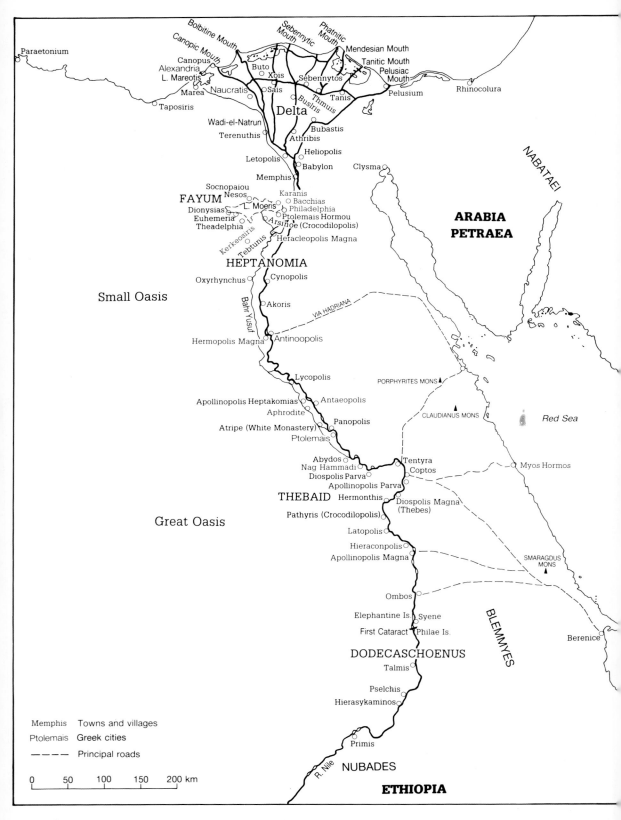

Paraetonium

Bolbitine Mouth
Canopic Mouth
Sebennytic Mouth
Phatnitic Mouth
Mendesian Mouth
Tanitic Mouth
Pelusiac Mouth

Canopus
Alexandria
L. Mareotis
Buto
Xois
Sebennytos
Tanis
Pelusium
Rhinocolura

Marea
Naucratis
Sais
Thmuis
Taposiris
Busiris

Delta

Wadi-el-Natrun
Terenuthis
Athribis
Bubastis

Letopolis
Heliopolis
Babylon
Clysma

Memphis

NABATAEI

Socnopaiou
Nesos
Karanis
FAYUM
Bacchias
Philadelphia
Dionysias
L. Moeris
Ptolemais Hormou
Euhemeria
Arsinoe (Crocodilopolis)
Theadelphia
Kerkeosiris
Tebtunis
Heracleopolis Magna

**ARABIA
PETRAEA**

HEPTANOMIA

Oxyrhynchus
Cynopolis

Small Oasis

Akoris

Bahr Yusuf
VIA HADRIANA

Hermopolis Magna
Antinoopolis

Lycopolis

PORPHYRITES MONS

Apollinopolis Heptakomias
Antaeopolis
Aphrodite
CLAUDIANUS MONS
Red Sea
Panopolis
Atripe (White Monastery)
Ptolemais

Abydos
Tentyra
Nag Hammadi
Coptos
Myos Hormos
Diospolis Parva
Apollinopolis Parva

THEBAID
Hermonthis
Diospolis Magna
(Thebes)
Pathyris (Crocodilopolis)

Great Oasis
Latopolis

Hieraconpolis
Apollinopolis Magna
SMARAGDUS
MONS

Ombos

Elephantine Is.
Syene
First Cataract
Philae Is.
Berenice

BLEMMYES

DODECASCHOENUS
Talmis

Pselchis
Hierasykaminos

Memphis   Towns and villages
Ptolemais   Greek cities
- - - - -   Principal roads

0   50   100   150   200 km

Primis

R. Nile   **NUBADES**

ETHIOPIA

Fig. 1.   Map of Egypt, 332 BC–AD 642.

I

The Gift of the Nile

Throughout its long history, the character and development of the land of Egypt has been dominated and dictated by the great river which flows through it. During the millennium in which it was controlled by a Greek monarchy and then by the Roman and Byzantine empires its territory stretched, with only minor temporary adjustments, from the Mediterranean coast in the north to the first cataract of the Nile, near Elephantine, in the south. On the western side, where the Libyan desert required no clear demarcation, its boundary was less clearly defined; the traveller from Cyrenaica would enter Egypt at the coastal town of Paraetonium. In the north-east, the divide between Egypt and the Arabian desert corresponded roughly to the line running between the gulf of Suez and the town of Rhinocoloura on the Mediterranean coast. Further south, the west coast of the Red Sea marked the natural limit of Egypt's territory.

The three major cultivable areas of Egypt were the valley and the delta of the river and the Fayum, a fertile depression some 100 kilometres to the south-west of the apex of the delta. The character and the existence of the Fayum depended upon the fact that it surrounded Lake Moeris which drained the water of the Bahr Yusuf (Joseph's Canal), a channel of the main river. These were the only inhabitable and cultivable areas of any size. To the east and west of the river valley lay inhospitable or mountainous deserts, sparsely and irregularly populated only by nomadic tribes. The western desert was punctuated by a series of oases, supporting a small population and accessible by tracks from the river valley; but their secure occupation was an important factor in controlling incursion or potential disruption by bands of desert nomads.

1 (previous page)   **The Palestrina mosaic**. This uniquely important mosaic originally formed part of the floor of a building in the Italian town of Praeneste (Palestrina). It perhaps dates to the early first century BC and gives a bird's-eye view of a Nilotic landscape. The exotic animals in the upper section must characterise the southern regions of the valley and the foreground will then represent the delta. A variety of boats is depicted on the river and its banks are lined with different kinds of religious and secular buildings. It has been presumed that the scene is intended to characterise the country at the time of the Nile flood. Apart from the intrinsic interest in the portrayal of the animals, structures and people, it exemplifies the early popularity of Egyptianising themes in works of art in the Roman world at large.

2   **Alexandrian coin**. The god Nilus crowned with lotus, holding a reed and cornucopia from which a genius emerges at the left holding a wreath to crown Nilus. In front is a Nilometer in the form of an obelisk up which a genius is climbing on left side. Reign of Severus Alexander (AD 222–235).

From the first cataract of the Nile at Aswan the valley itself extends for about 700 kilometres through Upper and Middle Egypt, varying in width between ten and twenty kilometres. A few kilometres to the north of Memphis lies the apex of the delta. The waters of the river are carried thence in three main branches (the Canopic, Sebennytic and Pelusiac) and several secondary channels to their points of discharge into the Mediterranean, almost 200 kilometres further north. The perennial flooding of the river, which was not controlled until the massive damming projects inaugurated in the twentieth century, has had a slow and constant effect in the valley and the delta, gradually raising the level of the land. The course of the river has changed too; in the valley it is now, on average, some three kilometres to the east of the course it followed 2000 years ago.

About a century before Egypt fell under the dominion of the Greeks, the historian Herodotus described and discussed what he thought the most amazing of its natural phenomena, the annual inundation of the Nile, and attempted to discern its causes. One of the speculative explanations he rejected was close to the truth and the geographer Strabo, writing in the reign of Augustus, was confident enough to affirm reports that the summer rains in Upper Ethiopia were responsible for the swelling of the river.[1] Although this failed to command universal acceptance in antiquity what was self-evident to all was that the prosperity, indeed the very existence, of this remarkable civilisation was entirely dependent upon the rich layer of silt which the waters of the river deposited in the floodplain and the delta. Strabo visited Egypt himself in the reign of the emperor Augustus and found the delta at floodtime a striking sight: 'the whole country is under water and becomes a lake, except the settlements and those are situated on natural hills or on artificial mounds and contain cities of considerable size and villages which, even when viewed from afar, resemble islands.'[2]

To Herodotus, agricultural production in these conditions seemed deceptively simple: 'they merely wait for the river of its own accord to flood their fields; then when the water has receded, each farmer sows his plot, turns the pigs into it to tread in the seed and then waits for the harvest.'[3] The river inevitably dictated the rhythm of life in all its aspects, and there was a good deal more to the survival of the mass of the population than met Herodotus' eye. For those who directed the nation's progress and stood to gain most from it 'the economic history of ancient Egypt was primarily one of continuous ecological adjustment to a variable water supply, combined with repeated efforts to intensify or expand land use in order to increase productivity.'[4] There is no doubt that the area of land under cultivation in antiquity reached its maximum in the Ptolemaic and Roman periods. Estimates of what that area was involve a degree of speculation and uncertainty. A total figure in the region of 25,000 square kilometres (about 9 million arourae) is probably a reasonable calculation and a modern estimate offers a breakdown, working with this order of magnitude, of approximately 16,000 square kilometres in the delta, 10,000 square kilometres in the valley and 1300 square kilometres in the Fayum.[5]

The natural resource base had, of course, a far wider potential than the products of conventional agricultural activity, though that was much the most important aspect of Egypt's economy.[6] The land was rich in flora, fauna and mineral resources. Many plant varieties offered nutrition or other profitable products without

3   The Peutinger map. A thirteenth-century copy of a late
Roman original, this map schematically depicts the known
world from India to Britain. In the section which shows Egypt
the major distortion in the projection is the fact that the flow of
the Nile is parallel to the Mediterranean coast. Towns and other
features are marked, with the distances between them, as in
other ancient Itineraries. One curious omission is the fact that
Rome and Constantinople are each emphasised by having a
pictogram, whereas Alexandria does not, although the Pharos
is represented.

systematic cultivation. Ancient writers noted that the root of a variety of wild bean
called colocasia was gathered and eaten raw or cooked and that a colewort yielded
grains like millet seeds which were crushed and made into loaves.[7] The abundant
growth of papyrus, particularly in the swamps of the delta, was exploited for the
production of writing material which Egypt was eventually able to export all over
the Mediterranean world; it was also a source of food, material for clothing and
fibre used in weaving mats. Reeds were put to many different uses. Balsam and
date-palms grew plentifully in their natural habitats; *persea*, acacia, sycamore, acan-
thus, oak and blackthorn were also to be found but sources of timber were in
general not overabundant and were carefully husbanded. *Persea* wood was used for
making statues, blackthorn for ships' ribs, acacia and sycamore were planted to
strengthen dykes and a variety of thorn yielded gum arabic which was used in the
manufacture of carbon-based ink.

Great numbers of species of wild animals were to be found, particularly in the
delta, offering entertainment for sportsmen or profit for professional hunters. Birds,
aquatic fowl, antelope, roebuck and wild boar were all regularly hunted. Ammianus
Marcellinus' catalogue of the fauna of Egypt, written in the fourth century AD,
includes a sad note about the southward retreat of the hippopotami, once plentiful
in the delta: 'but now they are nowhere to be found, since, as the inhabitants of

those regions conjecture, they became tired of the multitude that hunted them and were forced to take refuge in the land of the Blemmyes.'[8] Crocodiles were always of particular interest to the foreign observer and Ammianus also gives a fanciful version of the relationship between the crocodile and the ichneumon which preyed upon the female's eggs.[9] But there is, at least, no evidence for trade in crocodile skins and their survival was in any case ensured by the very great sanctity which they enjoyed as objects of religious veneration. The rivers and lakes also harboured many varieties of fish, some sacred, like the oxyrhynchus, others, like the silurus,

4   **Statuette of an Oxyrhynchus.** This votive object, probably dating to the late dynastic period, portrays the sacred fish, wearing a plumed crown and faced by a worshipper. It was particularly revered at the town to which it gave its name.

5   **Aswan, the granite quarries.** The source of many of the monumental obelisks. This example was evidently abandoned because of the crack which developed during the cutting process.

sufficiently prized to be exported to Rome as a delicacy; but fishing routinely played an important role in the local food supply.

Mineral resources were also of great value. The products of the red granite quarries at Aswan may still be seen, scattered in monumental buildings up and down the valley; huge obelisks were cut *in situ* and transported downriver by boat. The quarries at Mons Claudianus and Mons Porphyrites in the eastern desert yielded grey granite and porphyry respectively; alabaster, basalt, diorite, flint, granite, gypsum, limestone, marble, quartzite, sandstone, schist, serpentine and steatite were also to be found. The eastern desert, not fully exploited until Roman times, was also rich in ores – copper, iron and lead were mined there and in the southern region lay important gold-mines. The list of gems and semi-precious stones includes agate, onyx, sardonyx, amethyst, beryl, chalcite, chalcedony, cornelian, green felspar, garnet, quartz and turquoise. The natural oasis of Wadi-el-Natrun, to the south of Alexandria, a refuge for Egyptian Christians in ancient as well as modern times, was rich in deposits of nitre, which was used for fulling, as a

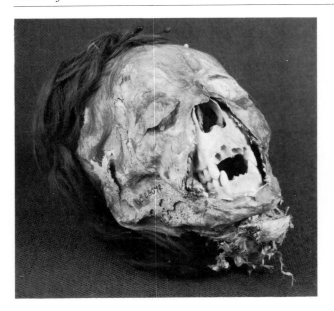

7 **Relief of a negro treading an Archimedean screw**. The screw thread is set inside a pipe and the negro treads the steps which rotate the pipe and raise the water. Vines are depicted in the background. From Alexandria, first century BC.

6 **Skull**. From the Roman period cemetery at Hawara in the Fayum, whose burials yielded many of the best mummy portraits. The excellent condition of the hair shows how effective techniques of preservation were.

preservative in mummification and in the manufacture of Egyptian glassware.

During the Pharaonic period, the ethnic characteristics of the population of Egypt were very heterogeneous. Recent studies by modern scholars have tended to be extremely cautious in the use of labels such as 'Semitic' or 'Negroid' and have been content with stating that the population mix reveals characteristics infused by the ethnic elements in the surrounding areas and undergoing relatively little modi-fication, despite repeated incursion and invasion by foreign peoples, during the whole of the pre-Dynastic and Pharaonic periods. The population of Upper Egypt in the pre-Dynastic period is described as typically small in stature, with long, narrow skulls, dark, wavy hair and brown skin, whilst that of the delta tends to be taller and more sturdy, with broader skulls.[10] Regional variation is to be expected through to much later periods and the preponderance of more strikingly African characteristics is still evident in the far south.

Ancient observers were not able to employ sophisticated analytical tools; for Ammianus Marcellinus the people of Egypt were 'as a rule somewhat swarthy and dark of complexion, rather gloomy looking, slender and wiry, excitable in all their movements, quarrelsome and most persistent in getting their way.'[11] By that time, the infusion of the Greek element into the population over a period of seven centuries must have made some impact. Intermarriage with Egyptians was certainly not uncommon, though some strata of the native population in the rural villages may have remained relatively unaffected by it. The mummy portraits of the Roman and early Byzantine period from the Fayum are our best guide to the facial characteristics of the people. But even these may be misleading: Sir Flinders Petrie, who first discovered and published them, remarked, perhaps under the influence of the clearly Greek ambience of the burials, that the Egyptian element was very poorly represented, but recent analysis of the skulls of the mummies reveals the same physical anthropology as that of the 'native' Egyptians of the Pharaonic period.[12]

The actual size of the population also poses some questions. Whatever estimate may be given for the Late Pharaonic period, there can be no doubt that there was considerable increase under the Ptolemies, and the population probably reached its maximum in the early Roman period. Josephus, writing in about AD 75, gives a figure of 7.5 million, excluding perhaps half a million residents of Alexandria, alleged to be based on the evidence of tax records, but some modern scholars consider this impossibly large.[13] Any trust which may be placed in it depends first, upon our assessment of whether a dramatic increase from, say, 3 million to 7.5 million is in itself plausible and second, upon the capacity of the land to support a population of this size. The increase from a Late Pharaonic population estimated at 3 million to one of 7.5 million would in fact take only about fifty years at an average annual increase of 20/1000 or 0.2 per cent, completely discounting any effects of immigration. As a useful analogy, an increase of this order can be documented for the years 1821–46, under the influence of political and economic improvements in the country brought by Mohammed Ali and although the rate of increase slowed thereafter, the census figures for 1882 record a population of 6.8 million.[14]

An estimate of the capacity of the land, published in 1836, reckoned that if all the land capable of cultivation were sown it could have supported an absolute maximum of 8 million.[15] Could Egypt have approached this level of productivity in ancient times? The simple answer is that we cannot be sure. But an oversimplified calculation in equivalence of wheat productivity over 9 million arourae of land and calorie requirements for 1.5 million families suggests that each aroura would need to return approximately the equivalent of a ten-fold yield in wheat to support such a

8 Crocodile mummies. Examples of mummified crocodiles of various sizes discovered by Grenfell and Hunt during their excavations in the villages of the southern Fayum in the 1890s.

population after taxes were paid.[16] Unfortunately, it is virtually impossible to be certain what average yields were, although there is no doubt that by ancient standards they were very high indeed. Ammianus Marcellinus claimed that under an ideal inundation the very best land would return a seventy-fold yield, but the average must be many times lower than this.[17] An average ten-fold yield is by no means impossible and may, indeed, be on the low side. Egypt was certainly the most populous country in the Hellenistic and Roman world and could well have supported a total population of the order of 8 million.

Apart from any question of an increase in population, there were other significant changes in the Ptolemaic and Roman periods of which we can be more confident. The political stability brought by the Ptolemies, and the foundation of a new capital at Alexandria, encouraged a shift of gravity towards the delta where many of the immigrants from the hellenised Mediterranean countries must have settled. They poured into the Fayum in great numbers too and this area underwent dramatic development in the early Ptolemaic period. The actual number of towns and villages in the valley will also have increased, as did the size of many of those already in existence. The use of the term 'urbanisation' might suggest something too sophisticated for the period and the area but there is no doubt that the towns grew in size and importance in harmony with their developing role as administrative, economic and cultural centres; and at the same time they will have encouraged the growth of villages in their sphere of influence.

Developments in the later Roman and Byzantine periods are more obscure. The population may well have declined somewhat – it is difficult to imagine that a

9 Mummy portrait. From the Fayum, probably late second or early third century AD. All the known examples of such painted panel portraits probably date to the first three centuries AD. The young boy portrayed here is holding a garland and a cup of wine, pagan funerary symbols; the latter may be connected with cult of Osiris.

10 Watercolour sketch. The great nineteenth-century pioneer Egyptologist, Sir John Gardner Wilkinson, spent a great deal of time in Egypt between 1821 and 1856, meticulously recording the monuments and inscriptions he observed. His artistic talent is evident in this sketch of an ox-driven sakkiyeh near Coptos. The machine itself, which consists of a waterwheel turned by cogs, is essentially identical to its ancient predecessor. See Plate 54.

devastating and widespread plague in the reign of Marcus Aurelius (161–80) did not make its effects felt. By the fourth century there are signs of decay and depopulation in some of the villages of the Fayum, although this may have been a purely local phenomenon which accelerated for particular reasons as the desert reclaimed once-fertile areas of land. If there was a decline in the valley and the delta, it was probably a very gradual one and perhaps ought not to overshadow the suspicion that under Greek, Roman and Byzantine rule Egypt as a whole attained a level of prosperity and development which was not matched again until the nineteenth century.

That prosperity was earned by labour and application, for growth and development depended upon the efficient use of the river's bounty. What underlay it was the maintenance of the irrigation system, which was certainly much improved under the Ptolemies. Irrigation was effected in one of two main ways, depending on the location and nature of the land. In the large areas which were open to natural flooding, the floodwaters were channeled into basins and retained by enclosing dykes, to be drained off when the river began to fall again. Areas which were not naturally inundated needed perennial inundation and this was accomplished by a variety of water-raising mechanisms, principally the shaduf, the sakkiyeh, or ox-driven water-wheel, and the Archimedean screw. Both the latter were Ptolemaic innovations and there is no doubt that the system of dykes and canals was greatly extended and improved as well. The most obvious large-scale development of the Ptolemaic period occurred in the Fayum, where the amount of land under cultivation was greatly increased by comparison with earlier periods. The maintenance of this

irrigation system was a constant and crucial preoccupation; dykes needed to be repaired annually, silted channels needed to be unclogged and machinery kept in good working order. Much of this was ensured through the imposition of compulsory labour obligations on the able-bodied males of the rural population. This is only one indicative aspect of the way in which manpower was systematically organised by the state to maximise efficiency of production.

The impact of Greek and Roman rule on the land of Egypt was felt in other ways too. The interlocking communication network of new roads and canals connecting with the river facilitated movement of goods and people all over the valley and the delta. Economic and trading interests may well have been an important stimulus, as for instance in the canal built by Ptolemy II Philadelphus and renovated under the Roman emperor Trajan, which ultimately linked the Nile to the Gulf of Suez. But better communications also ensured greater military security and a wider diffusion of new social and cultural patterns. It is the latter which reveal most clearly of all the effects of the Greek presence in Egypt and much of the remainder of this book is concerned with the relationship between the two major cultures, Greek and Egyptian, which coexisted in the land. The Greeks brought with them a level of literacy which had a gradual but ultimately massive impact. This was certainly an important feature of administrative, social and economic control by the government for it enabled it to record and control a mass of detailed bureaucratic operations. But its importance was not confined to the mundane and the routine. The Greeks up and down the Nile valley also bought books and read the works of many of the great classical authors of antiquity.

How far down the social scale this level of culture and literacy extended it is difficult to say. It might seem churlish to complain about this lack of precise knowledge when we know so much about Egyptian civilisation in this period, largely because of two factors – the habit of writing on papyrus and the role of the climate and the geographical environment in preserving the written record. The history which comes from this written record may be largely the history of the elite in the Nile valley, for the delta, which is too damp to allow the survival of papyri, is hardly represented at all. But it also offers a vivid and realistic picture of what life was like for the humbler inhabitants of the land in a period which was of surpassing importance not only in the history of Egypt itself, but in that of the whole of the Mediterranean world.

11   The temple of Ptah, Karnak. This small temple of the god whom the Greeks identified with Hephaestus lies within the complex of the great Temple of Amon at Karnak. It originated in the 18th Dynasty and is entered through a series of gates most of which date to the Late and Ptolemaic periods. The first gate includes scenes showing Ptolemy VI Philometor with a scribal tablet before Ptah and Ma'at and before Khonsu and Mut and, at the base, Ptolemy XII Auletes with fecundity figures, making offerings to various deities including Ptah.

2

The Ruling Power

When Alexander the Great entered Egypt in 332 BC he met with little resistance from the occupying Persian administration. Egypt was used to foreign domination but the oppressive Persians, whose second period of occupation (343–332 BC) probably had an important and lasting effect on the administrative organisation of the country, were hated by the native Egyptians of the fourth century BC no less than by their descendants almost one thousand years later. Alexander was therefore welcomed by the Egyptians. Greeks and Greek influence in Egypt were well known: under Psamtik I (664–610 BC) the Ionian city of Miletus had founded a Greek colony and trading post in the delta, called Naukratis; groups of resident Ionians and Carians are known elsewhere in Egypt as well, notably at Memphis. Herodotus provides the best-known, but by no means the only, testimony to the Greek interest in and veneration for the wisdom and antiquities of Egypt.[1]

The facts of Alexander's visit are as hard to disentangle as any in the romantic tradition which has recorded his achievement. He visited the Oracle of Amon at Siwah Oasis, renowned in the Greek world – and it disclosed the information that Alexander was the son of Amon. It is certain that he initiated the foundation, on the site of the insignificant village of Rhakotis, of the great city which was to bear his name. There may also have been a ceremonial coronation at Memphis which, if it occurred, will have placed him firmly in the tradition of the native Pharaohs. More obviously romantic, and explicable in the same terms, is the myth of his parentage through a liaison of his mother Olympias with the last Egyptian Pharaoh, Nectanebo II.

A king of Egypt who was to wield power from within the land would find it necessary to locate himself more securely in the local tradition than Alexander did. He would need clearly to be seen to hold the reins of civil, military and religious authority; above and beyond that, he would be closely identified with the great god Horus on whose divine throne the crowned Pharaoh would sit. But Alexander left in 331 BC. Egypt was only part of the Empire which he had wrested from the Persian King, to be ruled by a viceroy with the Persian title of satrap, heading the civil administration; the first was a certain Cleomenes of Naukratis.

This was the position claimed by Ptolemy, son of Lagos, when, at Alexander's death in 323 BC, his generals divided up the empire. Perdiccas, the holder of Alexander's royal seal, might well have regretted his failure to take Egypt, as his unsuccessful invasion in 321 BC shows; Ptolemy had Alexander's body, Perdiccas' army was only lukewarm in support of its leader and the Nile crocodiles made a good meal from the flesh of the invaders. Until the day on which he officially and openly assumed an independent kingship as Ptolemy I Soter (November 7, 305 BC), he was nominally the satrap, first of Alexander's half-brother, Philip Arrhidaeus and then of his son, Alexander IV. But the great hieroglyphic 'Satrap Stele' which he had inscribed in 311 BC indicates a degree of self-confidence transcending his viceregal role: 'I, Ptolemy, the satrap, I restore to Horus, the avenger of his father, the lord of Pe and to Buto, the lady of Pe and Tep, the territory of Patanut, from this day forth for ever, with all its villages, all its towns, all its inhabitants, all its fields'.[2] The inscription emphasises Ptolemy's own role in wresting the land from the hated Persians and links him firmly with a mysterious Khabbash who seems to have led a native insurrection against the Persians in about 338 BC.

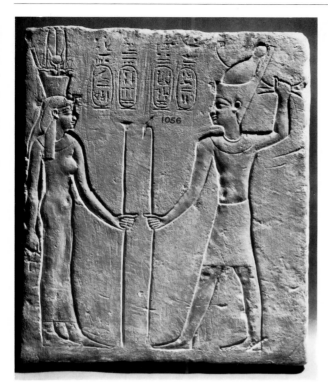

12 Bas-relief from Tanis.
The relief shows Ptolemy II
Philadelphus facing his wife and
sister Arsinoe II. Both are
deified. He wears the traditional
double red and white crown of
Upper and Lower Egypt and
carries a sceptre in his right hand.
Arsinoe wears the red crown
with the plumes of Isis, the cow-
horns of Hathor round the sun-
disk and the ram-horns of Amon
with the uraeus; in her hands she
carries a papyriform sceptre and
the *ankh* (symbol of life).

Egypt was ruled by Ptolemy's descendants until the death of Cleopatra VII on
August 12, 30 BC. The kingdom was merely one of several which emerged in the
aftermath of Alexander's death and the struggles of his successors, but it was the
wealthiest and, for much of the next three hundred years, the most powerful
politically and culturally; and the last to fall directly under Roman dominion. The
character of the Ptolemaic monarchy in Egypt set a style, in many respects, for
other Hellenistic kingdoms; this style emerged from the response of the Graeco-
macedonian political awareness of the need to dominate Egypt, its resources and its
people and at the same time to turn the power of Egypt firmly towards the context
of a Mediterranean world which was becoming steadily more hellenised.

The monarchy was very much a family affair, its internal harmony emphasised by
names and titles: Philadelphus ('Brother-/Sister-loving'), Philopator ('Father-loving'),
Philometor ('Mother-loving'). The benevolent aspect of the monarchs towards
their subjects was stressed in the titles Euergetes ('Benefactor'), Soter ('Saviour') –
which actually originates as an honour from Rhodes to Ptolemy I in gratitude for
his having relieved them from a siege – Epiphanes ('God-manifest'). Finally, the
Macedonian identity was preserved, although Plutarch alleges that it was all but
forgotten at the end, in the repeated use of the traditional names and, especially
later on, of the addition of 'Alexander'.[3]

From the earliest period, the stability of the royal family was reinforced by the
practice of associating a son and heir in the reign of his father before the latter's

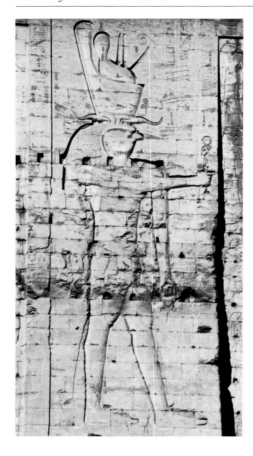

13 The Temple of Horus, Apollinopolis Magna (Edfu). The god Horus, depicted on the right-hand side of the great pylon of the temple, wearing the traditional double crown of Upper and Lower Egypt with two plumes added in the middle and ram's horns.

14 Coin of Ptolemy II Philadelphus. The obverse of a gold coin with busts of Ptolemy II Philadelphus diademed and wearing a Greek chlamys, and Arsinoe II.

death, as was the case with Philadelphus and Soter at the end of 285 BC, and by the introduction of consanguineous marriage. The first was the marriage between Philadelphus and his full sister Arsinoe II and the practice was maintained until the end of the dynasty. It is doubtful whether this was an imitation of a habit common in the Egyptian royal houses, though there may be isolated Pharaonic precedents. Arsinoe had previously been married to her half-brother, Ptolemy Keraunos, and the further step of marriage to a full brother might have seemed unlikely to cause difficulties. Arsinoe was a powerful, resolute and ambitious woman. Perhaps the Macedonian rulers were indifferent to possible outrage, perhaps they misunderstood the Egyptian habit of using 'brother' and 'sister' as a form of address between husband and wife, as Christians in the Roman world were later to be misunderstood and accused of incest, and assumed there would be no reaction. In the event, they were correct – the habit seems to have caused remarkably few raised eyebrows.

   The Macedonian court in Alexandria was marked by extravagant display. We have a description of the procession at the Ptolemaieia, a four-yearly celebration instituted by Ptolemy II Philadelphus in honour of his father and intended to enjoy a status equal to that of the Olympic games. It included a mechanical float carrying a statue almost four metres high which stood up and sat down again after pouring a libation of milk from a golden vessel and another which contained a wine-press measuring 11 by 7 metres with sixty people dressed as satyrs trampling grapes![4] This is all very much in keeping with the Graeco-macedonian atmosphere of the court. A birthday inscription for Philadelphus in 267 BC shows similar practices in middle Egypt; it contains a list of victors with Greek names in contests of a distinctively Greek type, musical, gymnastic, equestrian.[5] Even the actual divinisation of the living rulers as 'Benefactor Gods', which first happened in the reign of Euergetes and Berenike, does not appear to be a direct assumption of a native Egyptian practice.

In fact, no monarch until the last, Cleopatra VII, learned to speak Egyptian and even then it was only one of several languages in which she could converse without an interpreter. But the ideals of the monarchy were firmly and emphatically expressed in an Egyptian context as well, in a changing and developing pattern. It was surely

15 Cleopatra VII. A bust of Greek marble made for a statue just under life-size. The portrayal of the queen suggests her great physical beauty and contrasts sharply with the rather unflattering coin-portraits.

not simply an antiquarian interest which induced the Ptolemaic court to offer patronage to the learned Egyptian priest Manetho of Sebennytos; the concrete result of which was an orderly account, written in Greek, of the history of the Egyptian Pharaohs, which is still the basis of our conventional enumeration of the dynasties.[6] A decree of a synod of Egyptian priests which met at Canopus in the delta in 238 BC to honour Ptolemy III and Berenike notes their benefactions to the temples throughout the land and their constant care, in particular, for the sacred Apis and Mnevis bulls.[7]

16   **Coin of Ptolemy IV Philopator.**

17   **Coin of Ptolemy III Euergetes.** A silver coin, perhaps from Crete, showing Ptolemy I Soter diademed and with an aegis.

After the first century of Ptolemaic rule court intrigues and rivalries began to loom larger, sometimes fomented by high-ranking Greeks outside the immediate family. Two courtiers, Agathocles and Sosibius, managed the succession of the boy-king Ptolemy V Epiphanes and the murder of his mother Arsinoe, according to Polybius, in a staged ceremony in Alexandria at which they produced two silver urns allegedly containing the bones of Ptolemy IV Philopator and Arsinoe III (though the latter in fact was full of spices!) and a forged will appointing themselves as guardians of the under-age king.[8] Some forty years later the struggles between Ptolemy VI Philometor, a man of pious and magnanimous character, and his brother, later Ptolemy VIII Euergetes, ended with the latter ruling Cyrene. The character of this man, nicknamed Physcon, or 'Pot-belly', was well suited to ruthless intrigue; on a later occasion he is said to have murdered a son whom he had by his sister and served the dismembered body to the sister at a meal! Physcon eventually succeeded his brother in Egypt but his own reign was disturbed by internal conflict with his sister and his niece (both of whom he also married) which did not end until 124 BC. Some six years later there followed in the names of the three monarchs a long and detailed Amnesty Decree which was undoubtedly intended as a sign of strength, indicating reconciliation, unity and consequent benefactions for the subjects; these come in the form of a long series of administrative measures and reforms, affecting both Greeks and Egyptians – a demonstration of a kind which may well go back to

Pharaonic precedents.[9] The example of 118 BC is the longest such Amnesty Decree but it is by no means the only one.

The strength of the Ptolemaic monarchy was forcefully demonstrated outside Egypt. From the earliest days of his rule as satrap Ptolemy I Soter had engaged in an intense and serious struggle for power, prestige and territory in the wider context of the Mediterranean world. These struggles were conducted partly through acts of diplomacy, partly through acts of military aggression or outright war. There was never any question, especially in the first century of their rule, of the Ptolemies being content to barricade themselves in Egypt and if their horizons were more restricted thereafter that was a matter of political necessity rather than choice. However we interpret the complex relationship between Cleopatra VII and Marcus Antonius at the end of the period, it would be a serious omission to ignore Cleopatra's ambition to use Antonius to help restore the great imperialist days of her ancestors.

Family connections and dynastic alliances played a large part in imperial ambitions and the family is as important outside Egypt as within, its tentacles stretching far and wide. In about 300 BC Ptolemy Magas, son of Berenike I and stepson of Soter, was installed as governor of Cyrene; his daughter, Berenike II, married Ptolemy III Euergetes. Another Berenike, daughter of Ptolemy II Philadelphus, married the Seleucid Antiochus I. The first of the Cleopatras, who married Ptolemy V Epiphanes, was the daughter of a later Seleucid monarch, Antiochus III. Illegitimate children also have a role to play. Ptolemy Apion, bastard son of Physcon, ruled Cyrene until his death in 96 BC. An illegitimate son of Ptolemy IX ruled Cyprus from 80 until 58 BC. It would be absurd to suppose that such links preserved harmony between the ruling houses – this was far from the reality and perhaps far from the intention. But their real effect was to keep the ruling houses relatively compact, interconnected and more identifiably true to their Graeco-macedonian origins. This was a significant element in the nature of hellenistic monarchy.

The wealth of Egypt under the early Ptolemies was immense. St Jerome, writing over six hundred years later, quotes figures of 14,800 talents in money and 1.5 million artabs of wheat as the annual revenue; the figures may well be unreliable – particularly the wheat which seems far too low – and it is any case difficult to see what they represent.[10] A recent estimate suggests that the money would pay for three quarters of a million years of manpower at the basic labour rates![11] At any rate, the use to which such wealth could be put is vividly demonstrated by a grandiloquent inscription recording the career of a certain Kallias of Sphettos, evidently a man with a talent for 'fixing'.[12] His services to Athens in the late 280s BC included arranging a gift from Ptolemy II Philadelphus to Athens of 50 talents of silver and 20,000 *medimnoi* of wheat. He was also the leader of an Athenian delegation to the first celebration of the Ptolemaieia in 279/8 BC and by 270/69 BC he is found as a military and civil administrator in the service of Ptolemy in the Carian coastal city of Halicarnassus. One very important detail emerges concerning the gift of wheat; it was transferred to Athens through a depot, evidently under Ptolemaic control, on the island of Delos. We know also that since a treaty of 315 BC the Ptolemies had made extensive use of the island of Rhodes as a mercantile base. These are important hints about the way in which the economic power of the Ptolemaic kingdom was made effective in the Greek world.

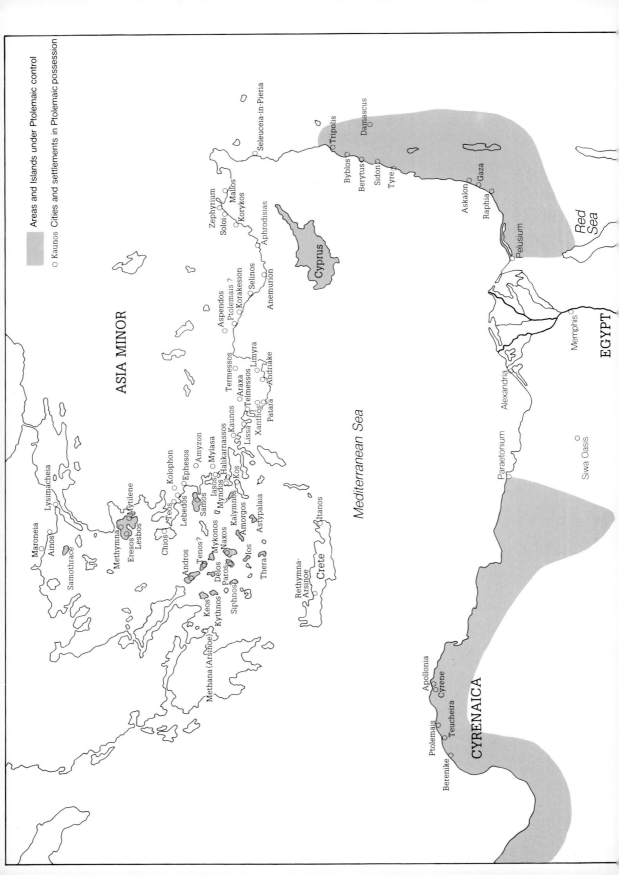

Areas and Islands under Ptolemaic control

○ Kaunos Cities and settlements in Ptolemaic possession

ASIA MINOR

Maroneia
Ainos
Lysimacheia
Samothrace
Methymna
Eresos
Lesbos
Mytilene
Chios
Teos
Lebedos
Kolophon
Ephesos
Amyzon
Mylasa
Iasos
Halikarnassos
Samos
Myndos
Kos
Andros
Tenos?
Mykonos
Delos
Naxos
Paros
Amorgos
Ios
Astypalaia
Keos
Kythnos
Siphnos
Thera
Rethymna-Arsinoe
Itanos
Crete
Methana (Arsinoe)

Kalymnos

Termessos
Araxa
Telmessos
Kaunos
Lissa
Xanthos
Patara
Limyra
Andriake

Aspendos
Ptolemais ?
Korakesion
Selinos
Anemurion

Zephyrion
Soloi
Mallos
Korykos
Aphrodisias
Seleuceia-in-Pieria

Cyprus

Mediterranean Sea

Tripolis
Damascus
Byblos
Berytus
Sidon
Tyre
Askalon
Gaza
Raphia
Pelusium

Red
Sea

Alexandria
Paraetonium
Memphis

EGYPT

Siwa Oasis

CYRENAICA

Berenike
Ptolemais
Teucheira
Cyrene
Apollonia

The political map of the Mediterranean world in the third century BC shows that the Ptolemies controlled an extensive empire. It had been gained by military and diplomatic power and was maintained by a powerful army and navy, the former regularly stocked with African elephants. But it was not easy. Possession of territory in Syria and the Levant was a constant bone of contention and five wars were fought with Seleucid monarchs between 274 and 200 BC. A few years after the end of the Fifth Syrian War (202–200 BC) the Ptolemaic empire outside Egypt had been effectively reduced to Cyprus and Cyrene (though there was perhaps a revival in the Aegean islands in about 165–45 BC). But loss of control of territory in Ionia and the Aegean to Antiochus III in about 197–5 BC was a serious blow to Ptolemaic prestige, perhaps even a threat to the stability of the dynasty.

18 The Temple of Horus, Apollinopolis Magna (Edfu). Ptolemy VIII crowned by Buto and Nekhbet, the goddesses symbolising Lower Egypt (red crown, left) and Upper Egypt (white crown, right). The reigning monarch was traditionally regarded as the incarnation of Horus on earth and the important annual Festival of the Coronation took place in this temple. Despite his unsavoury reputation Ptolemy VIII Euergetes Physcon was an important and generous benefactor of Egyptian temples.

So it is perhaps not mere coincidence that at just about this time the royal court introduced a series of grandiloquent titles for its administrative officers, honorific and loosely linked to function:

KINSMAN
OF THE ORDER OF FIRST FRIENDS
LEADER OF THE BODYGUARD
OF THE ORDER OF FRIENDS
OF THE ORDER OF SUCCESSORS
OF THE ORDER OF BODYGUARDS

and later on:

OF RANK EQUIVALENT TO KINSMAN
OF RANK EQUAL TO FIRST FRIEND

Fig. 2 Ptolemaic overseas possessions. The Ptolemaic empire was held not in the form of blocks of territory delimited by frontiers but by control of cities. Control for varying periods and in various areas of Thrace, Asia Minor and Syria was a phenomenon of the third century BC, as was that in the Greek Islands with the possibility of a revival *c.* 165–45 BC. Cyprus was a Ptolemaic possession from 312–30 BC except for the period 58–?48 BC; Cyrenaica from 322–96 BC.

19 The Rosetta Stone. This famous trilingual inscription in black basalt was found in 1798. It records, in hieroglyphic, demotic and Greek, a decree passed by a council of priests at Memphis on the first anniversary of the coronation of Ptolemy V Epiphanes (March 27, 196 BC) bestowing honours on the king in return for his benefits to Egypt.

This must have been a device to reinforce the loyalty of the officers at a difficult time; perhaps also through the use of pseudo-familial titles like Kinsman and Successor to give the impression of strength and numbers in the royal family and to advertise this strength in what was left of the overseas dominions.

The holders of these titles were almost all Greeks, but there are also clear signs of a serious move to conciliate native Egyptian feelings. The inscription on the famous Rosetta stone, issued on March 27, 196 BC, proclaims clearly and for the first time that we know for certain the coronation of the king at Memphis, the traditional Egyptian capital, and decrees measures which will secure the loyalty and support of the native priesthood:

'Since King Ptolemy, the ever-living, beloved of Ptah, the god Manifest and Beneficent, born of King Ptolemy and Queen Arsinoe, Father-loving gods, has conferred many benefits on the temples and those who dwell in them and on all the subjects in his kingdom, being a god born of a god and goddess – just as Horus son of Isis and Osiris who avenged his father Osiris . . .'

The reference to Horus avenging his father has some point:

'When he came to Memphis to avenge his father and his own royalty, he punished in a fitting way all the leaders of those who rebelled in his father's time, who had disturbed the country and done harm to the temples, at the time when he was there for the performance of the appropriate ceremonies for his reception of royalty'.[13]

As we might expect, this is not a full account of the relevant facts. We know of serious revolts, based on the city of Thebes, beginning in 207/6 BC. Two native 'Pharaohs' were proclaimed in succession, Haronnophris (or Hurgonaphor) and Chaonnophris, and the disaffection of a large area around Thebes persisted through the 190s, despite some temporary gain of ground by the government in 199/8 BC. It is usual to regard these revolts as evidence of native Egypt flexing its new-found muscle after the contribution made by larger contingents of native troops to the victory of Ptolemy IV over Antiochus III at the battle of Raphia in 217 BC. But so-called native unrest had caused the recall of Ptolemy III from the Third Syrian War (246–1 BC) and native Egyptian contingents had been used by Ptolemy I as early as the battle of Gaza in 312 BC. Nor did native unrest end with the re-establishment of control in the south under Ptolemy V; further outbreaks are known later in the century and again undermined royal control, particularly in the 160s and 130s BC.

A different expression of such feelings can surely be seen in demotic Egyptian 'nationalist' or 'propagandist' literature. In about the middle of the third century the *Demotic Chronicle* was composed; this was a collection of romantic tales of earlier Pharaohs which clearly emphasises the pre-Ptolemaic native tradition.[14] Obviously, one of the significant things about it is the fact that it was compiled and circulated in the early Ptolemaic period. Again, from the period between about 130 and 115 BC we have an apocalyptic piece called the *Oracle of the Potter*, which is known only from Greek versions still in circulation in the second and third centuries AD:

'And then the Guardian Spirit will desert the city which they founded and will go to god-bearing Memphis and it will be deserted . . . That will be the end of our evils when Egypt shall see the foreigners fall like leaves from the branch. The city by the sea will be a drying-place for the fishermen's catch because the Guardian Spirit has gone to Memphis, so that passers-by will say, "This was the all-nurturing city in which all the races of mankind live."'[15]

The message is clear: the foreigners are the Macedonian rulers, their city is Alexandria, Memphis will rise again.

Thus the preservation of the native traditions of kingship found verbal expression in a very lively demotic literary tradition which was probably pervasive, outside Alexandria, and necessarily focused its attention on the Egyptian religious establishment. It found a different and more forceful expression, from time to time, in native revolt, though it must be borne in mind that little is known of the practical effects of such revolts beyond the proclamation of native Pharaohs. The Rosetta stone inscription, in the Greek, hieroglyphic and demotic languages, shows Ptolemy V looking inwards, trying to appease the native Egyptian tradition at a time when it was particularly threatening to the stability of the royal house and when Ptolemaic power and prestige outside Egypt was in the process of virtual annihilation.

Twenty-five years later Egypt had to face the presence of an invader from outside, for the first time since Perdiccas. The Seleucid king Antiochus IV invaded twice in the reign of Ptolemy VI, first in late 170 BC when he established a 'protectorate' over the young king and a second time in 168 BC when, more ominously, he left a Seleucid governor at Memphis after accepting coronation in the traditional Egyptian fashion. In the summer of 168 BC a Roman ambassador, Popillius Laenas, arrived in Egypt, met Antiochus at Eleusis near Alexandria and staged a spine-chilling display of Roman power, vividly described by Polybius.[16] He ordered Antiochus to withdraw from Egypt. Antiochus asked for time to consult his advisers. Laenas drew a circle around the king with his stick and told him to give an answer before he stepped out of the circle. Only one answer was possible; by the end of July Antiochus had left Egypt. A month later, on August 29, a scribe and priest named Hor of Sebennytos had an audience at Alexandria in which he described, in the form of a prophetic dream, his earlier premonition of the salvation of Alexandria. A remarkable archive of documents, found at Saqqara preserves his account, written in demotic:

20 Demotic ostrakon. This belongs to the archive of the priest Hor of Sebennytos, who was involved in the administration of the ibis-cult at Memphis, and records Hor's dream prophesying the departure of the invading Seleucid king Antiochus IV in 168 BC.

'The dream which was told to me of the safety of Alexandria and the journeyings of Antiochus, namely that he would go by sail from Egypt by year 2, Payni, final day. I reported the said matter to Eirenaios who was strategos in year 2, Payni, day 11 . . . From Hor, the man of the town of Isis, lady of the cavern, the great goddess in the nome of Sebennytos. Eirenaios sent within the hour (?). Account of a letter: I gave it to the Pharaohs in the great Serapeum which is in Alexandria . . . I read out the salvation of Alexandria and every man who was within it which happened through the good disposition of the Pharaohs.'[17]

A native priest might, then, use his own language and tradition (in which the interpretation of dreams and oracles is a strong feature) in the service of Greek Alexandria as well as Egyptian Memphis.

The episode showed how much the power of Rome was to be reckoned with. A century earlier Ptolemy II Philadelphus had taken the initiative in sending an embassy to Rome. In 211 or 210 BC the Romans had requested grain supplies from Ptolemy IV. In 201 BC a Roman embassy had mediated in the Fifth Syrian War. Such exchanges had been conducted in the polite diplomatic language of friendship and alliance. After 168 BC the language did not change but the reality did. For the rest of the Ptolemaic period Egypt's independence was exercised, in effect, at Rome's discretion and under her protection. The first of the hellenistic kings to plan to bequeath his kingdom to Rome was Ptolemy VIII Euergetes Physcon, as king of Cyrene where he was installed by Rome after his struggles with his brother Philometor – the statement of intent was provoked by an alleged attempt upon his life in 155 BC and refers to his sincere preservation of the 'friendship and alliance' with Rome.[18]

The last century of Ptolemaic rule is usually depicted as a rather gloomy stalemate, a period of decline in which the kings were merely puppets of Rome. This is an over-simplification of several aspects of the relationship between Rome and a client-kingdom and perhaps relies partly on the assumption that the dependence itself indicates decline. But for much of the period Rome was content to support a dynasty which had no overseas possession except Cyprus after 96 BC and no ambitions which would directly threaten Roman interests or security. Interference and influence was such that in many cases it made comparatively little difference to freedom of action whether an area was a free client state or a province. Egypt's wealth certainly attracted Roman politicians. In 65 BC Crassus and Julius Caesar showed interest in the idea of making Egypt a province, but nothing came of it. Ptolemy XII Auletes (the 'Flute-player') fled from Egypt in 58 BC and Pompey got his friend Gabinius to restore him in 55 BC. For a time thereafter Ptolemy's financial affairs were managed by a Roman of equestrian rank, Rabirius Postumus, whom Cicero later defended against charges of bribery arising from this management.

In short, Roman commanders, their associates and their troops were playing their traditional and profitable 'advisory' role in the military and civilian affairs of Rome's clients. It is fascinating to observe the way in which the Roman government could officially sanction such chicanery in the name of 'friendship and alliance'. When Auletes died his will was deposited in the Roman public treasury, Pompey took charge of it and late in 49 BC was appointed by the senate as the legal guardian of Ptolemy XIII after the expulsion of his sister and co-regent Cleopatra. This must have involved control of the young king's property.

21 The Temple of Sobek and Horus, Ombos (Kom Ombo). In this relief on the west face of the enclosure wall, the emperor Caracalla presents a ceremonial collar to the goddess Tasenetnefret.

22 Statue of (?) Marcus Antonius. A high-ranking Roman is portrayed in this excellent sculpture of the late Ptolemaic period. The modelling of the torso and the royal headdress are in the Egyptian style; the absence of the uraeus is taken to indicate that the subject may be the non-royal consort of the queen.

The last and most famous of the Ptolemaic line, Cleopatra VII, was a vigorous and exceptionally able queen whose ambitions certainly included the intention to revive the prestige of the dynasty by using the Roman's capacity to aggrandise their clients and allies. Her effect on Roman generals was, to say the least, powerful. The first victim of her charm was Julius Caesar who pursued Pompey to Egypt and, after his treacherous murder at the hands of Egyptian courtiers, reinstated her as queen late in 48 BC. He stayed long enough to enjoy the delights of a sight-seeing journey up the Nile in her company in the early summer of 47 BC, although no ancient source describes the trip in any detail. But when Caesar left Egypt Cleopatra was pregnant with a son said to be Caesar's and to be named Ptolemy Caesarion. After Caesar's death Cleopatra provided a gift of ships and money for Cornelius Dolabella which secured Roman authorisation for the temporary association of Caesarion as co-regent with his mother.

The longer and more serious liaison with Marcus Antonius in the following decade must also be put firmly in the context of their political aspirations but the truth about the affair is not easy to discern. This is largely because Octavian's victory over Antonius and Cleopatra was to a considerable extent due to a clever and successful propaganda campaign which he waged against them between 35 and 30 BC and which has certainly coloured our ancient accounts of the episode. But Antonius should not be regarded simply as a besotted drunkard; he was an astute statesman and general who might reasonably hope that his control of the east in the 30s would give him power, prestige and wealth on the scale that Pompey had enjoyed after his eastern campaigns of 66–63 BC which had, in effect, made him master of the Roman world and had increased official Roman revenues by about 60 per cent. Antonius could legitimately manage the affairs of clients and allies – indeed, it was expected of him – and that was probably his primary intention in summoning Cleopatra to meet him in Cilicia. In the event her spectacular arrival may have temporarily overshadowed matters of state. She came up the river Cydnus in a barge decked out with a gilded poop, purple sails and silver oars, dressed as Venus reclining beneath a gold-spangled canopy and surrounded by Cupids, the whole atmosphere drenched with exotic perfumes and the music of flute and lute.[19]

By 34 BC Ptolemy Caesarion was officially co-ruler with Cleopatra, clearly an attempt to exploit the popularity of Caesar's memory. In the autumn Antonius and Cleopatra staged an extravagant ceremony in Alexandria at which they made dispo-

23 Coin of Cleopatra VII. The queen is represented as the goddess Aphrodite, holding her illegitimate son Ptolemy Caesarion, represented as Eros, in her arms; behind her shoulder is a sceptre.

sitions in favour of their own children. Cleopatra herself was to be queen of Egypt, Cyprus, Libya and Coele Syria, Alexander Helios was given Armenia, Media and Parthia, somewhat optimistically in view of the fact that only in Armenia could a degree of control be claimed with any plausibility at all; Ptolemy was to have Phoenicia, Syria and Cilicia; Cleopatra Selene, the daughter, would get Cyrene. However realistic the intentions were, they certainly promised the restoration of the old Ptolemaic empire, and more. The grand gesture involving Parthia and Armenia would recall the achievement of Alexander the Great as would the name of Alexander Helios. Antonius might justify all this to the senate and people of Rome by claiming merely to be disposing of Roman territory to clients. The treatment of Herod the Great in Judaea, whom Cleopatra had constantly attempted to keep in Antonius' bad books, was not different in principle.

That public opinion in Rome could throw up its hands in pious outrage at the evil influence of the foreign queen may be attributable to the skill with which Octavian had out-manoeuvred Antonius psychologically as well as strategically. The Romans were probably content to believe that Antonius was accustomed to appear in public with Cleopatra in the garb of an eastern potentate, or that the lovers would pose for artists in the guise of Dionysus and Isis and while away their evenings in rowdy and decadent banquets which kept the citizens of Alexandria awake all night. Antonius certainly took the charges seriously enough to write a pamphlet in his own defence, entitled '*De sua ebrietate*' ('*On his drunkenness*')!

The propaganda war was the prelude to armed conflict. The issue between Octavian and Antonius was finally settled at the naval battle fought at Actium in western Greece in September of 31 BC. It proved to be the swan-song of the once-great Ptolemaic navy. In fact, Cleopatra and her squadron withdrew, for some unexplained reason, when the battle was at its height and Antonius eventually followed suit. But even if Antonius and Cleopatra had won that battle they would probably still have lost the war for Octavian's power base was in Italy and the west and he never put it at real risk. Antonius and Cleopatra fled to Alexandria but they could do little more than await the arrival of the victorious Octavian, ten months later. Alexandria was captured and Cleopatra died on August 12. Ptolemy Caesarion, as an illegitimate son of Julius Caesar, was too dangerous and embarrassing to be allowed to live. The children of Antonius and Cleopatra did live – the daughter later married another Roman client, King Juba of Mauretania – and were probably

24 Stela of Augustus. The cult of the sacred Buchis bulls at Hermonthis is known from the excavation of their necropolis and reveals the same general character as the better-known cult of the Apis bulls at Memphis. Tradition demanded that when a bull died its successor was 'installed' by the monarch and this stela from the Bucheum, with the figure of Augustus at the right, facing the bull, shows the form in which this fiction was preserved for the Roman emperors until the reign of Diocletian (although Titus, son of the emperor Vespasian (69–79) is said to have attended an installation of an Apis bull in person in 70).

credited with a nominal 'reign' of eighteen days which allowed Octavian's takeover to be dated from the first day of the Egyptian new year (corresponding to August 31, 30 BC). Octavian was in Egypt for the first and last time. He saw and touched the corpse of Alexander the Great, causing a piece of the nose to fall off. He refused to gaze upon the remains of the Ptolemies: 'I wished to see a king, not corpses,' he said.[20]

'I added Egypt to the empire of the Roman people'.[21] With these words the emperor Augustus (as Octavian was to be known from 27 BC onwards) summarised the subjection of Egypt to Rome in the great inscription which records his achievements. In an epigram inscribed on the base of a statue of Apollo erected at Alexandria to commemorate the victory at Actium an anonymous local poet proclaimed more fulsomely that 'Caesar calmed the storm of war and the clash of shields . . . and came rejoicing to the land of the Nile, heavy laden with the cargo of law and order and prosperity's abundant riches, like Zeus, the god of freedom.'[22] The coming of the new age is presented to us very much through the eyes and the languages of the Greeks and Romans, but the passing of Ptolemaic rule was probably unmourned, perhaps even largely unnoticed, by the majority of the inhabitants of the Nile valley for whom the replacement of a Macedonian monarch by a Roman emperor heralded no obvious or dramatic change.

But there were changes and important ones at that. Augustus wished to announce a sharp break from his Ptolemaic predecessors and documents from the first few years of the reign refer to it as the '*kratēsis*' of Caesar, a strong term for which the best translation might be 'dominion'.[23] For over three hundred years the dominion of Roman emperors effectively ensured peace and significantly changed the articulation of Egypt's role in the Mediterranean world. At the same time we can observe the beginning of a process of internal change in many social, legal and governmental institutions which profoundly affected all aspects of life and society in Egypt. It has become an accepted truth that when Rome took over new provinces she was content to make very little change if the existing institutions worked well but in the case of Egypt this is very misleading. Other eastern provinces had been created from kingdoms which were essentially based on political structures evolved in city-states (*poleis*) of the Greek and Hellenistic type but this was not the case with Egypt where the few Greek cities were late additions. From the start, therefore, the Romans treated it carefully and differently in important respects and took some steps which helped introduce some of the features of the Greek *poleis* as convenient instruments of administration.[24]

Augustus' own words are a more accurate representation of the general situation than the common notion that Egypt was treated as a kind of personal domain of the emperor. Egypt did indeed differ from the other major Roman provinces which were all governed by members of the Roman senate appointed, from 27 BC onwards, either by the senate directly or by the emperor as his legates, responsible through him to the Senate and People of Rome. Augustus created something different for Egypt, a viceregal governor with the title of prefect, normally of equestrian rank (that is, possessing a minimum property qualification of 400,000 sesterces), but in any case never a senator, appointed directly by and always responsible to the emperor. His position was ratified by a law which stipulated that his powers and decisions were to be as valid as those of any governor of senatorial rank. This curious formula is very important for it had the effect of obscuring the issue of the prefect's accountability to the state. On closer scrutiny it turns out to imply, as the exiled poet Ovid candidly and acerbically stated, that 'Caesar is the state' ('*res est publica Caesar*').[25] In fact, senators and leading equestrians were forbidden to enter Egypt without the emperor's express permission. Prominent figures might be too dangerous in a wealthy province and Augustus learned the lessons of history more thoroughly than most. Amongst the few people in Egypt who were put to death after the defeat of Antonius and Cleopatra had been a senator named Ovinius who was in charge of Cleopatra's woollen and textile factories. So, although there were revolts and usurpations in Egypt, no-one could anticipate or emulate Sulpicius Galba, who, as governor in Spain in 68, proclaimed his allegiance to a higher and more legitimate authority than the emperor Nero by styling himself 'Legate of the Senate and People of Rome'.

For over 350 years, until the foundation of Constantinople, one of the most important aspects of Egypt's role in the Roman empire was as the supplier of a considerable proportion of the grain needed to feed the populace of the city of Rome. A fourth-century writer puts the contribution at 20 million *modii* of wheat under Augustus.[26] The arrival of the huge ships of the Alexandrian grain fleet in Italy was a political event of some significance – though not nearly as significant as the threat of their absence. It is perhaps in a tone of portentous traditionalism that

25   The Temple of Khnum, Latopolis (Esna). The relief, on the north side wall of the temple, portrays the Roman emperor Trajan (98–117) in a traditional pose, subduing the enemies of Egypt.

26   The Temple of Isis, Philae. The temple was built in the Ptolemaic and Roman periods and is one of the best preserved in Egypt. The complex also contains a chapel of the Nubian deity, Mandulis. The temple retained its importance until the mid-sixth century as the object of an annual pilgrimage of tribes from beyond the southern frontier and there are many signs of subsequent occupation by Christians in the Coptic crosses and inscriptions carved on the walls.

the Roman historian Tacitus refers to imperial Rome's preference for cultivating Africa and Egypt and for committing the lifeline of the Roman people to ships and all their risks, but the risks were real.[27] The sailing season was short and these maritime monsters were liable to run into trouble, as we know from St Paul's vivid account of his shipwreck in Malta when the precious grain was dumped in the sea just before the ship ran aground.[28] The fates of emperors and their ministers might depend on control of the grain supply – in 189 Cleander, a freedman of the detested emperor Commodus, incurred great unpopularity by buying up and controlling supplies of grain and his downfall was engineered by the ability of the Prefect of the Grain Supply to exacerbate the effects of a shortage.

But the grain trade, which exploited the most obvious and abundant of Egypt's resources, is only one example of the way in which the province was for over three centuries oriented towards the consuming nucleus of the empire. The most conspicuous of her resources are neatly illustrated in a story told of a wealthy Alexandrian merchant of the early 270s named Firmus who is said to have been proclaimed emperor in the aftermath of the defeat of the Palmyrene Queen Zenobia by the emperor Aurelian.[29] Firmus was immensely rich, had such huge physical appetites that he could consume a whole ostrich in a single day and drain two buckets of wine at a sitting in a drinking contest. The visible signs of his wealth were the fact that the windows in his house were fitted with panes of glass set in pitch, that he owned so many books that he could supply an army on paper (which says something about

the amount of paperwork generated by the military bureaucracy!) and that his vessels sailed to India, as a result of which he owned two legendary twelve-foot elephant tusks. Papyrus, glass and luxury goods: Firmus epitomises the wealth of Egypt. The whole personality and his usurpation may well be a fiction but the details do not lose their general significance. We could add that Egypt supplied Rome with fine masonry (the quarry at Mons Claudianus on the western shore of the Red Sea was the source of columns in the Pantheon), exported goods of Alexandrian manufacture all over the Mediterranean and enriched emperors and private individuals both inside and outside the province. The economic importance is thus obvious, even though we cannot fully understand the way in which the closed monetary system, operated through the Alexandrian mint until 296, interfaced with the world outside.[30]

The stability brought by Roman rule was important in the sense that it depoliticised Egypt and created the conditions for increase of such economic activity. Economic development accelerated from the reign of Augustus and was intimately linked to Rome's general policy regarding the extension of control in the east. Security, both internal and external, was of primary importance. Egypt could be effectively defended by a very small force against attack from the Mediterranean. Three Roman legions provided the basis of a security network normally sufficient to ensure peace after the first prefect, Cornelius Gallus, had dealt with disaffection in the area around Thebes. Nicopolis near Alexandria, Babylon and Thebes were their stations at first. With increasing security they were reduced to two and concentrated at Nicopolis, sending detachments up-river as and when necessary.

The spirit of Augustan imperialism also looked further afield in the first decade of Roman rule. Provincial boundaries were not inflexible lines of demarcation; they were fringed with obliging (if they knew what was good for them) clients whose independence of action could be curtailed if necessary. Expansion was tried, to the east and the south. A great expedition to Arabia under the prefect Aelius Gallus (26–25 BC) might have succeeded but for the treachery of the Nabataean king's minister Syllaeus who led the Roman fleet astray in uncharted waters. Arabia remained an independent and friendly client until Trajan took it over in 106, completing Roman occupation of the area and making it possible to reopen the canal from the head of the gulf to the Nile. Henceforth the border between Egypt and Arabia was unclear; when the Arab forces under 'Amr ibn al 'Aṣî invaded in 639 they stopped at the easternmost town in Egypt, Rhinocoloura, and asked, 'Is this place in Syria or Egypt?'[31]

The Meroitic people beyond the southern border had taken advantage of the absence of Gallus and mounted an attack on the Thebaid. The next prefect, Petronius, led two expeditions into the Meroitic kingdom, captured several towns, received the submission of the formidable one-eyed Queen Candace and left a Roman garrison at Primis (Qasr Ibrim). But not for long. The potential revenue from the area did not justify the expense of maintaining a permanent military presence and within a year or two the limits of Roman occupation had been set at Hiera Sykaminos some eighty kilometres south of the First Cataract. But there are few things which so strikingly indicate the mixed character of the region than the great popularity of the cult of the goddess Isis among the people of Meroe and the foundation of a temple by Augustus at Kalabsha (Talmis) dedicated to the local god Mandulis. Roman contacts through the region and to the south continued, as we know from the accounts of an expedition under Nero which collected geographical and anthropological information in East Africa.[32]

Hence the strategic importance of Egypt and its resources justified Augustus' firm view that its prefects must be exemplary. The first, Cornelius Gallus, had led the army in from the west in the invasion of 30 BC. Soon afterwards he pacified the Thebaid but boasted too vaingloriously of his achievement in carrying arms further south.[33] He was removed from office ignominiously and his successors watched their step, or at least their public image. Some were suspicious of their environment. Galerius, a prefect for sixteen years in the reign of Tiberius, had his wife with him but she never set foot outside the official residence or admitted a provincial into it. Better to be unknown than notorious, remarked Seneca, her stepsister's son, for the province was rancorous and adept at insulting its governors.[34]

But the political potential of the prefecture was realised in bids for imperial power from outsiders who well knew the strategic value of getting a foothold in Egypt through the support of its prefect. The emperor Vespasian was first proclaimed at Alexandria on July 1, 69 by the prefect Tiberius Julius Alexander; perhaps significantly, the first prefect from the city of Alexandria itself, a member of a great Jewish family which included the theologian and philosopher Philo. The creation of an emperor involved a great propaganda campaign, the convening of congratulatory embassies and the mounting of popular demonstrations. Late in 69 Vespasian came to Egypt and played the appropriate role, accepting acclamation in

27 Papyrus letter. The text of this letter, found at Oxyrhynchus, appears to reflect the propaganda of the usurper of AD 175, Avidius Cassius.

the hippodrome at Alexandria as benefactor, son of Amon, Sarapis incarnate. In the latter capacity he is alleged to have performed miracle cures of cases of blindness and a crippled leg![35] In somewhat similar circumstances over a century later Avidius Cassius, the son of a prefect who had probably been born in Alexandria, was proclaimed emperor in 175, stimulated by what turned out to be false rumours of the death of Marcus Aurelius. His recognition in Egypt lasted only three months and his rashness prompted a pithy letter from the famous Athenian sophist and millionaire, Herodes Atticus: 'Herodes to Cassius. You have gone mad.'[36] Avidius Cassius had seen action in Egypt a few years earlier in 172 when he had been sent to quell a mysterious uprising in the delta, known as the revolt of the Boukoloi (the word means 'herdsmen' – but it is not clear whether it was religious or rural in character). The reaction shows that such events were taken seriously. The most violent and threatening episode in the second century was undoubtedly the Jewish Revolt of 115–7 which was sparked off by the appearance of a 'Messiah' in Cyrene and spread first to Egypt and then to Cyprus and Mesopotamia. There was exceptionally fierce fighting all over Egypt and considerable bloodshed and loss of property, as we know from the vivid descriptions in a dossier of correspondence of a certain Apollonius, a local official of the district of Apollinopolis – Heptakomias in Upper

28   The Colossi in the Theban Plain. These colossal sandstone figures of Amenhotep III, with smaller statues of his wife and mother to right and left, are more than 21 m in height and originally sat in front of the Pharaoh's mortuary temple, now completely destroyed. The name given to the right-hand figure by the Greeks originates in an identification with the Trojan hero Memnon, the son of Eos, who was killed by Achilles. The crack in the structure which probably caused one of the figures to 'sing' when struck by the rays of the sun at dawn was repaired late in the Roman imperial period and it has remained silent ever since. See Plate 30.

29 Trajan's Kiosk, Philae. David Roberts' watercolour of the small but
beautifully proportioned unroofed temple, built early in the second century AD.
The temple is easily visible from the approach to Philae by boat. David Roberts was
a Royal Academician and one of the first professional artists to visit Egypt. *Sketches
in Egypt and Nubia* was published in 1846 and is important not merely for its
intrinsic merits but also for its record of the condition of many important
monuments before systematic excavation and research began.

Egypt.[37] The Jewish community in Egypt may have been all but annihilated, though
it recovered somewhat in the course of the third century. The defeat was certainly
long commemorated for its anniversary is mentioned in a letter of *c.* 200.[38]

This revolt undoubtedly sprang from general hostility to the Roman rulers. Our
other main expression of such feelings comes from aristocratic Greek circles in
Alexandria in a tradition which has its roots in the enmity between the Alexandrian
Greek and Jews in the time of the Julio-Claudians. By the late second century it had
assumed in addition a tone of more general antipathy to the Roman emperors, as is
clear from the words of a certain Appianus at his 'trial' before the emperor Commodus:
'The divine Antoninus your father (i.e Marcus Aurelius) was fit to be emperor for
he was first of all a philosopher, secondly had no love of money and thirdly was a
lover of goodness. But you are the opposite – tyrannical, boorish and uncultured.'[39]
Such accounts are probably largely fictional but the fact that they were in circulation
in the late second and early third centuries tells us something important about
current attitudes in Alexandria.

Sometimes the hostility was justified. During a visit in 215 the emperor Caracalla dismissed all 'Egyptians' from Alexandria save those on legitimate business, removed the prefect from office and issued orders from the temple of Sarapis for indiscriminate slaughter of the youth of the city; the Alexandrians had offended Caracalla by alleging that he was implicated in the murder of his brother Geta.

But such a reaction was exceptional. Imperial visits to Egypt were normally more peaceful affairs. Noisy demonstrations might occur, as they did for Germanicus, the nephew and adopted son of the emperor Tiberius, in the Alexandrian hippodrome in AD 19. The greetings of the magistrates and populace are preserved in a vivid documentary account: 'The crowd called out "Bravo, may you live all the longer." The General: "I am mindful of what is common knowledge and also of the way in which I have found your greetings multiplied through being stored in your prayers."'[40] Sometimes the written record is more workmanlike and mundane: among the results of a visit by the emperor Septimius Severus in 199–200 is a series of administrative reforms and a collection of legal judgements on rather routine cases issued by the emperor in response to plaintiffs from Alexandria and the country.[41]

The visit which is known in most detail is that of Hadrian, the most widely-travelled of emperors, who spent eight or ten months in Egypt in 130–1. The notable events of his tour included a great lion-hunt in the Libyan region to the west of the delta, the drowning of Hadrian's friend and lover Antinous in the Nile, the foundation of a Greek city called Antinoopolis in commemoration of the dead youth and a visit by Hadrian and his retinue to the famous singing Colossus of Memnon in the Theban plain. The great statue, which emitted a sound like a lyre when struck by the rays of the rising sun, failed to perform for the emperor on his first day but made amends the following morning. A document from Oxyrhynchus dated almost a year before Hadrian's arrival indicates the extent to which such visits could burden the local populace; the items requisitioned include 200 artabs of barley, 3000 bundles of hay, 372 suckling pigs and 200 sheep.[42]

Later emperors had, of necessity, to be more concerned with asserting the control of the central authority. The mid-third century saw a general weakening of the grip of the Roman emperors on their empire and the east suffered heavily from the aggression of the Sassanian kings of Persia. For a number of years the only real resistance to the Persians was offered by the wealthy dynasts of the Syrian caravan city of Palmyra, first Odenathus and later his widow Zenobia and their son Vaballathus. The latter are acknowledged as joint holders of imperial power in Egyptian documents dated between 270 and 272, but by the summer of 272 the emperor in the west, Aurelian, had defeated them in battle and regained control of Egypt.[43] We know that this event was marked by the presentation of a golden statue of Victory to him by the town of Oxyrhynchus because we have a copy of the minutes of a council meeting at which the resolution to make this presentation is mentioned.[44]

Whether or not this was followed by the attempted revolt of the Alexandrian merchant Firmus, we have, in any event, reliable information about more serious internal revolts in the 290s. First in 293/4, when the emperor Galerius was present in person to reduce and destroy the town of Coptos, and later in 297/8 when a mysterious figure named Lucius Domitius Domitianus was proclaimed emperor and, with the assistance of a deputy or *corrector* named Achilleus, controlled Egypt for almost a year. This time the senior emperor Diocletian appeared on the scene and was present in person at the fall of Alexandria after a siege of eight months. After the capitulation Diocletian is alleged to have vowed to continue the slaughter of the populace until the blood reached his horse's knees, a promise which was mitigated by the fact that his mount stumbled and fell as he entered the city; the grateful citizens of Alexandria erected a statue of the horse.[45]

After the siege of Alexandria Diocletian travelled up-river to the southern frontier. The trip to the border appears to have had a serious military and political aim for we are told by the historian Procopius that Diocletian re-established and refortified the island of Philae as a frontier post (thus withdrawing some seventy miles from the earlier post of Hiera Sykaminos) and came to an accommodation with the tribes which inhabited the border region.[46] Probably in the course of his return down-river he visited Panopolis in the Thebaid and a lengthy document from the town contains copies of the correspondence of local officials and their superiors concerning the details of a massive and somewhat badly-managed bureaucratic operation which was mounted to make the necessary arrangements for the accommodation of the emperor and his retinue in 298.[47]

30 The Colossus of Memnon. The left foot of the northern-most figure contains several inscriptions recording the visits of tourists who came to hear the statue 'sing', including one commemorating the presence of the empress Sabina with her husband Hadrian in AD 130. See Plate 28.

Four years later Diocletian was in Alexandria again, just before the beginning of the 'Great Persecution' of the Christians, for which he was so detested by Egyptian Christians that the Church later dated its 'Era of Martyrs' retrospectively from the first year of his reign, 284. Egypt might in fact have suffered more heavily than other areas because one of the fanatical persecutors of the age, a certain Sossianus Hierocles, held the post of prefect in 310. But in 302 the Alexandrian populace was probably gratified to receive a distribution of free bread organised by the emperor. It was perhaps more indifferent to the edict which Diocletian probably issued at this time against the practice of the Persian religion of Manichaeism in the Roman empire and this may well be another aspect of a general desire to re-establish the strength of the traditional Roman religion.[48]

Diocletian was the last reigning Roman emperor to visit Egypt. Constantine seems to have planned a visit in 325 but there is no clear evidence that it took place. A decade or so after the visit of Diocletian, the cessation of the persecution of

Christians took place and had such far-reaching effects that from this point on it is necessary to think of the political history of Egypt in a very different framework.

It would be absurd to imagine that we could identify one single turning point which marked the watershed between what are conventionally called the Roman and Byzantine periods in Egypt. Many have put the break in 284, with the accession of Diocletian or, to put it another way, the transition from 'Principate' to 'Dominate', from the peace, culture and prosperity of the high Empire through the chaos of the third-century anarchy to the darker age which is supposedly characterised by a more oppressive state machinery in the throes of decline and fall. But for Egypt it is more useful to focus on the crucial years around 312.

The years 311 and 313 saw the cessation of official persecution of Christians by the Roman state, first through the Edict of Toleration issued by the emperor Galerius and then through the so-called Edict of Milan which restored the property of the Church.[49] In 313 a new system of calculating and collecting taxes in Egypt was introduced with fifteen-year tax-cycles called indictions, inaugurated retrospectively from the year 312. From about 308 Egypt almost uniformly abandoned its idiosyncratic custom of dating documents only by the regnal years of emperors and began to convert to the more standard method of dating by the Roman consuls. Many important administrative changes had already taken place in the reign of Diocletian.[50] In 296 the separation of the Egyptian coinage from the rest of the empire had come to an end when the Alexandrian mint stopped producing its tetradrachms which had been the basis of the closed currency system. These changes certainly had the cumulative effect of knitting Egypt more uniformly into the administrative structure of the Empire. This makes it easier to understand one aspect of the way in which Egypt came, in the Byzantine period, to play again a more central role in the political history of the Mediterranean world.

One other event which clearly did have an enormous effect on the position of Egypt was the foundation of Constantinople. Constantine marked out the perimeter of his new city on November 8, 324 not long after he had taken control of the east, including Egypt, from his rival Licinius; the formal foundation took place on May 11, 330. This was to affect the role of Egypt in two respects. First, as Constantine undoubtedly intended, it established Constantinople as an imperial capital and an eastern counterpart to Rome itself, thus undermining Alexandria's traditional position as the first city of the Greek-speaking east. Secondly, it diverted the resources of Egypt away from Rome and the west for henceforth part of the surplus of the Egyptian grain supply, which is put at eight million artabs in an edict of the emperor Justinian, went to feed the growing population of the city of Constantinople.[51] This created, as we shall see, a physical and politico-economic link of some importance.

These facts by themselves will not entirely account for the change in Egypt's political role, which brought it more into the centre stage of Mediterranean politics. They are part of a nexus of developments in the early fourth century which gave to the political or quasi-political institutions of Egypt a role which extended beyond the borders of the land. The principal changes concern the growth of Christianity.

During and after the reign of Constantine the country gradually became more Christianised, the Church more and more powerful. In order to understand the full significance of this in its various aspects we need first to discard the idea

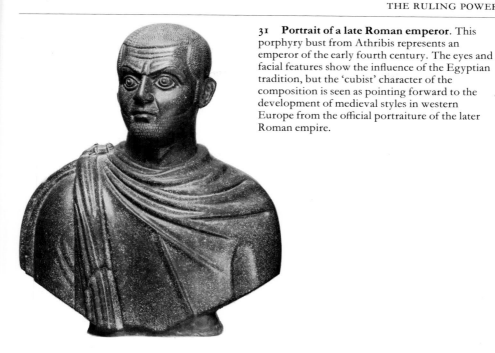

31 Portrait of a late Roman emperor. This porphyry bust from Athribis represents an emperor of the early fourth century. The eyes and facial features show the influence of the Egyptian tradition, but the 'cubist' character of the composition is seen as pointing forward to the development of medieval styles in western Europe from the official portraiture of the later Roman empire.

that we are considering only an element in the religious history of Egypt or the religious experience of its people. A distinguished historian of Byzantium has recently observed, in writing of the sixth century, that 'religion, that is Christianity, had come to occupy every aspect of thought and life, every mode of reasoning and every activity. It worked as a power structure itself and through the existing power structure.'[52] This could certainly also be said for Egypt and we might emphasise its effect even more by showing that it also changed the existing power structure to its own ends.

But before we do so we should again refer briefly to the process of Christianisation and ask by what date Egypt had become a fully Christian country. It is difficult to provide an unequivocal answer. We might take a recent estimate which suggests that in the reign of Constantine between 318 and 330 it reached the 50 per cent mark and that in the latter half of the fourth century it advanced to encompass between 80 and 90 per cent of the populace.[53] But if we accept these figures, which are based on an attempt to quantify the evidence for Christian nomenclature and may be biassed towards too rapid a Christianisation, we must recognise that there were undoubtedly degrees of commitment and belief; that important elements of paganism survived, as such, into the sixth century and beyond and that pagan influences infused and affected Christianity in a specifically Egyptian context. This can more profitably be discussed later as part of the social and religious history of Byzantine Egypt. For the present it is sufficient to say that our estimate of the political power and influence of the Church cannot be gauged merely by reference to the numerical superiority of its adherents.

The key to understanding lies in seeing how the Church in Egypt dominated secular as well as religious institutions and acquired a powerful interest and role in every political issue during the three centuries which elapsed between the death of Constantine and the arrival of the Islamic army; and how the over-arching persona of the Christian Church made it inevitable that that role could not be confined to Egypt. What, then, and when were the changes? There can be no doubt that the restoration of Church property in 313 was the first important step, but this was not all. Constantine encouraged the repair or building of churches from public funds through the civil authorities in the provinces. Money was made available for charitable donations. Financial incentives were also provided for Christian clergy in the form of tax exemptions and immunity from compulsory public services. But it was the wealth and power of the Church as an institution which needs emphasis here and we should be under no illusion about the political nature of its role and the struggles within it.

Two developments stand out. First, the power of the Patriarchy of Alexandria in the Egyptian Church and secondly its position *vis-à-vis* the eastern Empire as a whole and Constantinople in particular. The Bishop, or Patriarch of Alexandria was, quite simply, by far the most powerful figure in Egypt. We need only reflect that he was directly responsible for the appointment of bishops throughout his patriarchy, and thus indirectly for appointments at lower levels too, to understand the power of patronage within the structure of the church which this gave him. In short, he could decide who was and who was not politically and theologically acceptable. Further, at the important Council of Nicaea in 325 where the consubstantiality of the Father and the Son was established as orthodox doctrine, it was made clear that the Patriarchy of Alexandria included not only Egypt but Libya and the Pentapolis as well. Richard Pococke, an eighteenth century visitor to Egypt, claimed to have seen a map in the possession of the then Patriarch of the Coptic Church which showed all the bishoprics under the sway of the Patriarch of Alexandria. They numbered one hundred and thirty-six.[54] When Egypt was divided for administrative purposes into a number of smaller units the Patriarchy was not and its power thus far outweighed that of any local administrative official. Only the governors of groups of provinces (*vicarii* of dioceses) were equivalent, the praetorian prefects and emperors superior, and when a Patriarch of Alexandria was given civil authority too, as happened in the case of Cyrus, the last Patriarch under Byzantine rule, the combination was very powerful indeed.

It is therefore hardly surprising that the Patriarchy of Alexandria should be the focus of political struggles from the fourth century onwards. At first it was the supreme position in the east but the challenge of Constantinople was patent. The Third Canon of the Council of Constantinople which met in 381 threw down the gauntlet and undermined the primacy of Alexandria in the east by stating that the Bishop of Constantinople stood second only to the Bishop of Rome.[55]

A good deal of the turbulent history of Egypt in the fourth, fifth and sixth centuries can be understood in terms of the struggles of the successive (or, after 570, co-existing) Patriarchs of Alexandria to maintain their position both within their Patriarchy and outside it, in relation to Constantinople. But the two areas are not by any means always distinct and separate. What links them is the way in which the imperial authorities, when strong (as, for instance in the reign of Justinian), tried to manage or control the Egyptian Church from Constantinople, whilst at the same time assuring the capital's food supply from Egypt and, as often as not, conducting wars to keep their empire intact. Conversely, when weak, they failed to control it. For the Patriarchs of Alexandria it turned out that trying to secure the support and approval of both the imperial authorities in Constantinople and their own power base in Egypt was like trying to square the circle. The two made quite different demands and this emerged ultimately as a social, political and cultural gulf between Alexandria and Egypt, between Hellenism and native culture. The two strains had always existed, partly intermixed, partly distinct. The Church as a political institution created a medium through which the differences were emphasised.

Within Egypt, the fourth century saw internal divisions in the Church which were sometimes expressed in terms of doctrine; challenges to the position of the establishment which often reacted violently and perhaps made orthodoxy seem more solid and tangible than it was. The great fourth-century Patriarch Athanasius, champion of orthodoxy, who was a native of Marea near Alexandria, fought bitterly to suppress the Arian doctrine, a conflict overtly concerning the nature of the Father and the Son and the relationship between them. Athanasius was exiled for his continual refusal to admit Arius to communion, represented as an undermining of the unity of the Church. He also faced the more localised challenge of the Meletian schism whose origin was not doctrinal but concerned the treatment of those who had temporarily renounced their Christian faith in the pressure of the Great Persecution under Diocletian. A letter written by a Meletian named Callistus at Nicopolis near Alexandria in about 335 vividly illustrates the means used to combat it:

'Isaac, the Bishop of Latopolis came to Heraiscus at Alexandria and he desired to dine with the Bishop in the Camp. So the adherents of Athanasius, hearing of it, came bringing with them soldiers of the Duke and of the Camp; they came in a drunken state at the ninth hour, having shut the Camp, wishing to seize both him and the brethren. So certain soldiers who were in the Camp and had the fear of God in their hearts, hearing of it, took them and hid them in the store-chambers in the Camp; and when they could not be found they went out and found four brethren coming into the Camp; and they beat them and made them all bloody so that they were in danger of death, and cast them forth outside Nicopolis.'[56]

This kind of partisanship, whether expressed through doctrinal dispute, social division or both, became a significant thread in the fabric of Egyptian politics from the reign of Constantine and the Patriarchy of Athanasius. The combative personality of the great Athanasius played an important role in the period from 328 to 373, during which the balance of power shifted with Athanasius' periods of exile and the appointment of Arian bishops. Athanasius may have been accused of undermining the unity of the Church but it looks very much as if such divisions and disputes were endemic and that Church unity was a convenient fiction which could be invoked when useful. The political importance of such divisions depended on the personalities involved and the ways in which they created *causes célèbres*.

Patriarchs had various ways of enforcing their will whether inside Egypt or abroad: control of a corps of five or six hundred Parabolani, a kind of ecclesiastical private army of layman orderlies whose nominal task was to tend the sick; strong influence over the attitudes and actions of sailors and ships' captains, which might cause blockage of the route of the river boats bringing grain to Alexandria, as happened in the reign of the emperor Maurice (582–602), or emerge in popular demonstration in the Alexandrian docks; or at Constantinople when Egyptian bishops might come *en masse* to impose their will on the imperial authority. Then there is the organisation of popular violence through the factions attached to the circus – the Blues and the Greens, identified by their support for the rival charioteers – which might be mobilised either by the Church against the civil authorities or by one churchman against another.[57] An example of the former occurred after the installation of the Patriarch Dioscorus II in 516 when there were riots and demonstrations in favour of a more popular and spectacular enthronement and the Augustal Prefect was killed. Violence was the *lingua franca*, its mobilisation a matter of political muscle.

This forms the essential background to our understanding of the important events of the mid-fifth century which followed the bitter struggles between rival Patriarchs, Theophilus, Cyril and Dioscorus at Alexandria and Chrysostom and Nestorius at Constantinople, for political supremacy in the eastern Church. The momentous events of the Council of Chalcedon were decisive in one sense. Its declaration of October 25, 451 stated as official doctrine that Christ was to be acknowledged as existing in two natures, inseparably united, and is usually seen as a turning point against the power of Alexandria, a watershed which sent the Egyptian church off on its own path of Monophysitism, centred around an insistence on the singularity of the nature of Christ.[58] This is a little misleading from two points of

32 Stela of the Byzantine period. The stela carries a Greek inscription and juxtaposes the Coptic cross and the traditional Egyptian *ankh* (symbol of life).

view. For one thing, it underestimates the strength of Monophysitism outside Egypt – among its powerful adherents were Justinian's Empress Theodora and the Patriarch Severus of Antioch. For another, it fails to give enough emphasis to the divisions within Egypt, where the Patriarchy of Alexandria became the bone of contention between rival Coptic (that is, Monophysite) contenders and Chalcedonians favoured by the imperial authority at Constantinople. The latter were, consequently, Egypt's best means of contact with the imperial authority.

Some thirty years after the Council of Chalcedon the Emperor Zeno produced a formula for harmony, the *Henōtikon* which attempted to put the doctrine of Chalcedon in a way which would look acceptable to Monophysites. It is an exercise in hair-splitting doctrinal gymnastics which looks merely absurd if we try to understand it only in theological or philosophical terms. Half a century later when the imperial authority was strong in the person of Justinian, who tried to exert political control over the Church, the distinction was emphasised by the preference of the notorious empress Theodora for Monophysite doctrine. The rivalry is illustrated in a bizarre way by the official attempts to convert the Nubades on the southern frontier in the 540s; Justinian sent a Chalcedonian mission, Theodora a Monophysite one and the former experienced some mysterious delay which was put down to Theodora's influence with the Duke of the Thebaid! From 570 we find coexistent series of Coptic and Chalcedonian Patriarchs, the former confined to areas outside Alexandria, the latter installed outside Egypt before being sent to Alexandria and none of them native Egyptians.

What lay behind Justinian's policy was certainly the need to emphasise the role of Egypt as part of the fabric of the eastern empire, an empire whose integrity was more and more threatened by external as well as internal forces. In Egypt there had been a long struggle to maintain control in the south against the tribes inhabiting the region of the Cataracts, the Blemmyes and Nubades. The former, identified with the Beja, occupied the Eastern Desert between the Nile and the Red Sea, where there were important emerald mines. The historian Olympiodorus of Thebes visited them in about 421 and reported on their occupation of Talmis, Primis and other important towns. Their potential threat to southern Egypt can be gauged from an appeal by a Bishop of Syene who sought protection from them for his Churches and from the fact that the famous White Monastery of Shenute is said to have maintained for a period of three months a total of 20,000 refugees whom the Blemmyes had taken prisoner.[59] Trouble may well have been endemic since the reign of Diocletian. A one hundred-year treaty, struck in 453, proved very short-lived, but their capacity for causing trouble was reduced somewhat by victories of the neighbouring Nubades who deprived them of some of their territory. In the sixth century, according to the contemporary historian Procopius, they were receiving subsidies and grants of land and were converted to Christianity in the 530s (an event no doubt connected with Justinian's closing of the Temple of Isis at Philae), as were the Nubades in the following decade.[60]

The holders of imperial power could still be threatened by the strength of Egypt, properly harnessed. The last striking example is the case of Phocas, a monstrous tyrant, brought down in 609/10 by Nicetas, the general of the future emperor Heraclius, who made for Alexandria from Cyrene intending to use Egypt as his main power base and cut off Constantinople's corn supply. By the spring of 610 the struggle with Bonosus, the general of Phocas, for control of Egypt was won and the fall of the tyrant duly followed. The episode well illustrates how difficult it could be to defend Egypt from a power base in Constantinople.

The same was to prove the case against threats from outside powers in the next forty years. First, with the appearance of the old enemy, the Persians. The thread of undying hostility in Egypt to the Persians is amply expressed by the fact that there exists a Coptic account of the first Persian conquest by Cambyses.[61] The spread of Persian power through Syria culminated in the conquest of Jerusalem and Persian hostility to the Christians, which is heavily emphasised in our Christian sources, thrust many Christian refugees westwards to Alexandria. By 618 the Persians had advanced to the Nile delta and captured Alexandria. Our documents show the final subjection of Egypt early in 619 for a period of occupation which was concluded by a peace treaty and Persian withdrawal in 628.[62] This was, if we are to believe our sources, a period of violent hostility to the Egyptian Coptic Christians. We are told that the Persians refused to allow the normal ordination of bishops and that they massacred seven hundred wealthy monks in their cave monasteries.[63] Our most vivid evidence comes from the *Life of Pisentius* who was Bishop of Coptos in the first three decades of the seventh century. He referred to them as 'that pitiless folk' and in a threatening exhortation to his flock warned them 'Let God be wroth with you and give you over into the hands of the barbarians and they humble you.' He evidently had little hope for better treatment for himself – when he heard of the impending Persian invasion he distributed all his possessions to the poor.[64]

The Persian withdrawal can hardly be heralded as the return of peace in Egypt. Events were already in train which were to bring momentous changes to the Nile valley – events which have conditioned both the history of the region until the present day and the attitudes of the west to it. The chain of events began with the flight of Mohammed from Mecca to Medina and his declaration in 632 of a holy Islamic war against Byzantium. Ten years later, by September 29, 642, the last remnants of Byzantine forces had left Egypt, the fleet having departed for Cyprus twelve days earlier. The Arab general 'Amr ibn al 'Aṣî was able to march into Alexandria and the Arab conquest of Egypt which had begun with an invasion three years earlier ended in peaceful capitulation after an eleven-month armistice. The invasion had apparently been preceded by several years of vicious persecution of the Coptic Christians by the Chalcedonian Patriarch Cyrus and it is he who, under the guise of 'Al Mukaukas' in the Arabic sources is said to have betrayed Egypt to the forces of Islam.

The view of our ancient sources is not entirely uniform. But Cyrus does not come out well, particularly in the eyes of the Coptic tradition which sees its adherents as a beleaguered and persecuted minority surviving under Arab rule. Certainly some parts of the delta, for instance, remained quite heavily Christian for several centuries. During the three-year period of the conquest there had been some apostasy to Islam – its uncomplicated propaganda must have seemed attractive and drawn attention to the political and religious rifts which successive and rival Patriarchs of the Christian Church had so violently created and exploited. Perhaps many of the civilian populace of the Nile valley were relatively indifferent and capitulated with little resistance to the Islamic presence, which certainly does not seem to have excited violent political and military opposition.

Not that the conquest was bloodless. Fighting there certainly was; desultory at first in the eastern delta, then the defence of the Fayum in 640; in July a great battle at Heliopolis in which 15,000 Arabs are said to have engaged 20,000 defenders. The storming and capture of Trajan's old fortress at Babylon on April 6, 641 was crucial. By September 14 Cyrus, who had been recalled from Egypt ten months earlier by the emperor Heraclius, was back with authorisation to conclude a peace. Byzantium signed Egypt away on November 8, 641, with provision for an eleven-month armistice to allow ratification of the treaty of surrender by the emperor and the Caliph. The emotional impact of the end of Graeco-roman civilisation is very great on modern heirs to the western tradition. The despatch of tribute and gold in heavily laden ships in December 641, the departure of the Alexandrian fleet to Cyprus, Rhodes, Byzantium – all this emphasises the discontinuity and the end of an era. Even if it is valid, it should not lightly be taken to imply that Graeco-roman civilisation in Egypt had been harmonious and homogeneous. But politically speaking, domination by the theocratic Islamic Caliphate was more strikingly different than anything that had happened in Egypt since the arrival of Alexander the Great almost a thousand years earlier.

33 Trajan's fortress, Babylon. Remains of the fortress as published in the voluminous *Description de l'Egypte* (1809–30), which recorded the antiquities and phenomena observed by the team of scholars and scientists who accompanied the Napoleonic expedition in 1798. The surviving great gate of the fortress is now incorporated in the Coptic Museum in Old Cairo.

34   The temple of Amon, Thebes (Luxor); fresco. The
watercolour sketches made in the nineteenth century by
Gardner Wilkinson are the only record of what must have a
magnificent series of paintings on plaster in the temple. The
plaster was later removed to reveal the Pharaonic reliefs
beneath. The temple lay at the centre of a Roman camp in the
period *c*. AD 300 and the paintings show a procession of Roman
soldiers wearing short tunics, leading their horses and armed
with lances and circular shields. In the niche are the four
emperors – Diocletian and Maximian in the centre, Galerius
and Constantius at the sides – dressed in purple gowns with
yellow haloes.

3

State and Subject

The catalyst which welded the natural resources of Egypt and its population into an effective foundation of political power was the governmental system which began its development under the early Ptolemies. The Ptolemaic government is usually characterised as one of the most efficiently run and most rigidly hierarchical bureaucracies ever devised; an administrative machine whose *raison d'être* was the enrichment of the monarchy through a highly organised and tightly controlled economy. This seems at first sight to be supported by what we know of the main features of the system. The administration was staffed by a host of officials and bureaucrats, recording and regulating the activities and obligations of the king's subjects, down to the last detail of the requisitioned labour and surveillance of irrigation works, cultivation and transport which was drafted in order to ensure maximum efficiency of production and profit. The ubiquitous tax-collector enforced harsh demands in the form of a bewildering variety of imposts. The land itself was in royal ownership, for the most part granted in modest parcels to tenants whose security of tenure was ultimately subject to the overriding power of the king. The other productive industries, most notably papyrus and oil, were minutely monitored in every aspect by government officials, as is shown by an extraordinarily detailed set of Revenue Laws promulgated under Ptolemy II Philadelphus.[1] These industries are usually described as royal monopolies but the term is something of a

35　The Island of Philae. David Roberts' sketch shows the spectacular complex of buildings as it stood in the mid-nineteenth century on the island which lay close to Egypt's southern border. The building of the Aswan High Dam necessitated the removal of the ancient structures, stone by stone, and their reconstruction on the neighbouring island of Agilqiyyah.

misnomer; certainly the crown owned some such enterprises but many were privately owned and operated under strict supervision and conditions. The Ptolemies also operated a closed and carefully controlled monetary system, an example which the Romans followed until the end of the third century AD. The higher degree of royal organisation and secular control was complemented by a decline in the wealth and power of the native Egyptian temples.

The general picture is strikingly illustrated by a remarkable text in demotic from the year 258 BC referring to orders for a complete census of the kingdom, the ultimate responsibility for which lay with the chief finance minister.[2] Detailed returns were submitted by the scribes and district officials of the nomes from Elephantine in the south to the Mediterranean coast; the sources of water, the position, quality, irrigation potential of the land, its state of cultivation, specification of the crops grown, the extent of priestly and royal holdings – all were to be recorded in detail. The operation was surely envisaged as a real one, even if the pompous tone of the text carries a hint of propaganda on the part of Philadelphus as 'the king who triumphed over the pro-Persian king at the time of the Syrian journey'.

But this outline hardly does justice to the complexity of the Ptolemaic system in Egypt and it runs the risk of identifying the end – accumulation of wealth in the royal coffers – as the only feature of importance in the eyes of the rulers, ignoring or understating the significance of the methods and institutions by which the society was managed, the social and cultural patterns which they supported. It also tends to underplay the economic complexity and sophistication of a society for which a simple model of subsistence agriculture will hardly suffice. The picture of oppression of a poor and ignorant peasantry which grew almost everything it consumed and consumed (after rents and taxes were paid) almost everything it grew might suit some modern historical tastes but it does violence to the evidence for the diversity of economic activity in the towns and villages, for the high degree of monetisation, for commerce and transportation, for manufacture of raw products into goods without which the heavily dominant agricultural economic base could not have been converted into usable wealth. We might characterise this aspect of the Ptolemaic achievement as the creation of the means to use that economic base to great social and political effect and it is arguable that in the Ptolemaic, Roman and Byzantine periods, as a consequence, the Egyptian society and economy achieved a higher level of sophistication and complexity than we are accustomed to find in the ancient Mediterranean world.[3]

36 Order of Peukestas.
When Alexander left Egypt in 331 BC the command was divided between Balakros, son of Amyntas and Peukestas, son of Makartatos. This, the earliest known Greek documentary papyrus, contains a notice posted at Memphis which reads: 'Order of Peukestas. No-one is to pass. The chamber is that of a priest.'

An analysis of the Ptolemaic machinery of government brings out the essential character of the administration very clearly. To begin with, we have the monarch who stood at the head of government as much more than a mere figurehead; he was the chief executive, his authority acted as a control on the conduct of his officials and, in concept at least, he was accessible to his subjects in a very direct relationship. The tone of numerous royal decrees of the Ptolemaic period gives the firm impression of the monarch making decisions and policies which his officials would implement, even on apparently trivial matters.[4] One petition, for instance, cites a letter of Ptolemy II Philadelphus to one of his chief ministers regulating the conduct of lawyers in accepting cases which involve issues affecting the royal revenues.[5] Control of malpractice by officials is a frequent source of concern, as a letter of the reign of Ptolemy VIII vividly demonstrates:

'The king and the queen attach great importance to justice being done to all the subjects in their kingdom. Now many people are . . . lodging complaints against you, your subordinates and especially the tax-farmers for abuses of power and fraudulent exactions and some even allege blackmail. We wish you not to lose sight of the fact that all this is incompatible with our rule of conduct and no less with your safety'.[6]

This splendid example of the power of suggestion resulted from complaints made at court, but it might equally come from the monarch's own journeys of inspection round the kingdom or from reports submitted by other officials hoping to curry favour and gain promotion.

It is more difficult to know what to make of the matter-of-fact way in which even a very humble person might petition the king:

'To King Ptolemy greeting from Ctesicles. I am being wronged by Dionysius and my daughter Nike. For though I had nurtured her, being my own daughter, and educated her and brought her up to womanhood, when I was stricken with bodily infirmity and my eyesight became enfeebled she would not furnish me with the necessaries of life. And when I wished to obtain justice from her in Alexandria . . . she gave me a written oath by the king that she would pay me twenty drachmae every month by means of her own bodily labour . . . Now, however, corrupted by that bugger (*sic*) Dionysius, she is not keeping any of her engagements to me, in contempt of my old age and my present infirmity.'[7]

Undoubtedly such a petition would not normally be dealt with directly by the king and the petitioner asks that a local official be instructed to handle the matter. But we know that the more influential could, with persistence, reach the king directly, if they needed, and it is of some importance that the letter of the aggrieved father reflects that theoretical possibility.

Arrayed beneath the monarch was a handful of powerful officials whose competence extended over the whole land – a chief finance minister, a chief accountant and a chancery of ministers in charge of records, letters and decrees. Beneath them again, the broadening base of a pyramid of subordinate officials with competence in geographically limited areas, right down to the chief administrator of each individual village (komarch). About half-way between the chief ministers and the village officials stood those such as the nome-steward (*oikonomos*) whose competence extended over one of the more than thirty nome divisions of Egypt. The nomes, of varying size and population, had been the established geographical divisions from time immemorial, with their own local and religious traditions; though there were changes in the number and areas of the nomes they retained their importance as administrative units until the early Byzantine period and their local characteristics much longer.

The Ptolemaic bureaucracy certainly involved careful definition of duties and functions, but we must beware of identifying a rigid civil service mentality, involving clear demarcation of departments; in practice specific functions might well be performed according to local need and the availability of an official competent to

37 **Coin from Hermopolis**. A standing figure of the god Thoth (identified by Greeks with Hermes), bearded and wearing an *atef*-crown, *chiton* and *himation*, carrying a small squatting cynocephalus on right hand. These so-called nome coins of the Roman period reflect particular local associations and traditions.

take the appropriate action. It is particularly important to appreciate that there were no rigid lines of separation between military and civil, secular and religious, administrative and legal matters. The same person might perform duties in any or all of these areas and the law in particular pervades every aspect of society, regulates every activity to an extent which the use of the terms 'legal' and 'judicial' tends to hide. This is why, in some cases, we find it difficult to specify the precise area of competence of a particular official or to explain why he is doing something apparently outside what we take to be his proper sphere.

In fact, the issuance of general guidelines and instructions to officials was a Pharaonic tradition, which is still found in the Ptolemaic period. The following general exhortation is part of a long text from the late third century BC, which probably originated in the office of the chief finance minister and contains detailed instructions on the duties of an oikonomos:

'During your tour of inspection try, as you go about, to encourage everybody and make them feel happier; not only should you do this by words but also, should any of them have a complaint against the village-scribes or the village-chiefs about anything to do with agriculture, you should investigate the matter and as far as possible put an end to such incidents.'[8]

The text goes on to much more specific detail about duties in connection with the sowing schedule for crops, records of the numbers of livestock, checking the production of linen and auditing the revenue accounts and so on. It is striking that the whole tone of the document is one of positive exhortation rather than negative restriction.

Such official posts were evidently well worth having and people were prepared to act unscrupulously in order to get them or help others to get them. A report of the year 117 BC points the finger at people who 'have been appointed without the knowledge of the chief finance minister, and some have wormed their way into positions of steward of the nome, district-chief, collector of wheat, village-chief and other offices inconsistent with their own work and others have transferred their duties to their sons who are quite young men and sometimes to other persons altogether'.[9] Legal penalties against such behaviour could be very severe but the advantages to be derived from the posts, especially at the highest levels, meant that there were always some people willing to take the risk. An extreme example of a successful official with personal interests not easily distinguishable from his public duties is Apollonius, the chief finance minister under Ptolemy II Philadelphus, an enormously influential courtier who was personally enriched by the royal gift of a very large estate at Philadelphia in the Fayum. This was the centre of Apollonius' sizeable business enterprises which involved import and export on a considerable scale, many details of which are known from the surviving archive of the papers of his estate manager, Zenon.[10]

Such activities ought properly to be classed as private but the distinction between public and private is not quite so clear cut as in some modern political systems; for instance, one of the minor apparent oddities in the Ptolemaic machinery is the existence of the king's 'Special Account', which suggests that we should not think of the whole kingdom as the private possession of the monarch in a straightforward sense, but rather of the monarch as in some aspects an institution, in others an individual. As far as administrators and officials were concerned, the distinction was not easy to maintain in a system where the collection of taxes and the operation

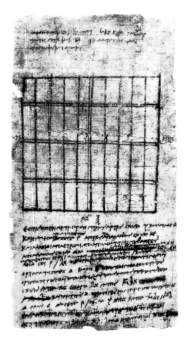

38 Plan of irrigation works. The papyrus illustrates the irrigation system on the estate of Apollonius at Philadelphia and contains an estimate for the cost of digging out canals and moving earth. The area is divided into 40 plots of 250 arourae each by a system of 4 main irrigation channels, represented by double lines, and transverse dykes. The Greek text was written with a rush pen by an Egyptian and the compass directions are given in both Greek and demotic.

of banks was contracted out to private businessmen and there was no regular salary structure for the administrators and officials themselves. This striking fact in itself does much to account for corruption and malpractice. The idea that magistrates and officials should be the kind of people who could afford to fill offices without pay was a distinctively Greek one – democratic Athens was a rare exception – and reflects the values and traditions of aristocratic society.

It also makes a contrast with Egypt in the late Pharaonic period, when the tendency went against compartmentalisation of function, favoured hereditary transmission of office and placed considerable power in the hands of the army of scribes who could write demotic Egyptian (first attested in use in 643/2 BC). In fact, in the Ptolemaic period demotic was still much used and the scribes still appear, especially in connection with native Egyptian temples. But the government administration was conducted in Greek, at first the officials at the upper levels were all appointed from the Greek-speaking elite. If Egyptians wanted an entrée into the bureaucracy at the lower levels they had to hellenise and learn Greek. Many did so but the absorption of the Egyptian element into this powerful Greek overlay was a slow, uneven and ambiguous process. Certainly in the Ptolemaic period there are striking signs of consciousness of the distinction. 'They have treated me with contempt because I am a barbarian ... I do not know how to behave like a Greek'; this from a camel-contractor demanding unpaid salary.[11] 'Some of them had stones in their hands and others sticks and they tried to force their way in, in order to seize the opportunity to plunder the temple and to put me to death because I am a Greek'; this from a religious detainee in the Serapeum at Memphis, demanding legal redress against attacks made on him by Egyptian temple-cleaners.[12]

But cultural and linguistic differences, even though they may give rise to hostility and favour one group against another, do not necessarily imply an institutionalised 'apartheid'. Such implications have sometimes been identified in the legal system, with a higher-level judiciary (*chrēmatistai*) for the Greeks and a lower counterpart (*laokritai*) for the native Egyptians; but these were not exclusive legal systems operating different bodies of law for different sectors of the population. They were interlocking institutions which existed to meet the different needs of, on the one hand, a native Egyptian populace whose internal social and economic relationships (marriage contracts, divisions of property and the like) were largely conducted in the demotic Egyptian language, and on the other a Greek elite, politically and economically dominant, which operated roughly in the framework of traditional Greek law, gradually adapting to its new environment.

This is precisely the significance of a regulation which we find in the Amnesty Decree of Ptolemy VIII and the two Cleopatras issued in 118 BC:

'And they have decreed concerning suits brought by Egyptians against Greeks, viz. by Greeks against Egyptians or by Egyptians against Greeks, with regard to all categories of people except those cultivating royal land, the workers in government monopolies and the others who are involved with the revenues, that the Egyptians who have made contracts in Greek with Greeks shall give and receive satisfaction before the *chrēmatistai*, while the Greeks who have concluded contracts in Egyptian (i.e. with Egyptians) shall give satisfaction before the *laokritai* in accordance with the laws of the country (i.e. Egyptian laws). The suits of Egyptians against Egyptians shall not be taken by the *chrēmatistai* to their own courts, but they shall allow them to be decided before the *laokritai* in accordance with the laws of the country.'[13]

The Greeks were certainly favoured by the governmental and legal system – that is what being the dominant elite means – but there are many areas (including the law) in which the term 'Graeco-egyptian' has real meaning. There could scarcely be a more vivid illustration of this than the fact that one of our main sources of knowledge of the traditional Egyptian laws is a demotic papyrus from the reign of Ptolemy II Philadelphus and that there survives, from the second century AD, about half a millennium later, a fragment of a Greek translation of this text.[14]

The gradual erosion of some aspects of the superiority gap can also be seen in the Ptolemaic handling of the army and the land, both vital aspects of the whole organisation of the state. Although the army was a visibly distinct entity when it was assembled as a fighting force, its regular soldiers, as opposed to mercenaries which the Ptolemies also used, were socially integrated when they were not on active service. As favoured holders of allotments of land (cleruchs) in many communities they formed an elite group among the small to moderate landholders. The rentals were low and although the grants were personal they came gradually almost to have

39 Elephantine Island. The island, in the Nile opposite Aswan, was a crucial site for the defence of the southern frontier. Its ancient name derives either from the shape of the rocks at the right or from its involvement in the ivory trade. The quay dates to the Roman period.

the status of hereditable private property. These soldier-cleruchs were at first drawn exclusively from the Greek-speaking elite and the less favoured royal tenants (*basilikoi geōrgoi*) were mainly native Egyptians. But at the battle of Raphia in 217 BC large numbers of native Egyptian soldiers were used in the army for the first time since the battle of Gaza in 312 BC and thus became eligible for such grants of land.

It remains to ask how this apparatus of government worked in practice. One way to answer this is by pointing to the great body of royal ordinances and regulations which tell us how it was supposed to work. Or we can look at the petitions and complaints, evidence of official malpractice or government repression, which tell us when things did not work the way they were supposed to. Between the evidence for the theoretical ideal and the possibly untypical malfunction there must lie a great deal of routine which is, for that very reason, unremarkable. Egypt is practically the only place in the classical world from which evidence of this routine kind has survived in significant quantity. Thus for instance, we can follow the operations of the office of Menches, village scribe of Kerkeosiris in the Fayum, in compiling a topographical survey of the area registered around the village in about 115 BC; and we can see that, despite mistakes and falsification, the complicated system of classification and registration did work, on the whole, even if it was less accurate in practice than in theory.[15]

But perhaps a more vivid impression is to be gained by looking at the ways in which the everyday lives of individuals were affected by their government. Such a worm's eye view comes from a marvellously informative archive of papers belonging to a man named Dionysius, son of Kephalas, who lived in a village called Akoris in Middle Egypt towards the end of the second century BC.[16] Dionysius is an excellent example of a man of modest status who straddled the Egyptian and the Greek worlds. The archive itself contains documents in demotic and Greek (Dionysius was capable of writing both) and gives information about his family, many of whom bore both Greek and Egyptian names, like Dionysius himself, whose Egyptian name was Plenis (which actually means 'smith', although it is not certain that it also indicates his engagement in a trade). The Greek name Dionysius will have been adopted to bring him into the world of the Greeks, but at the same time he also appears in some documents under a third name, also demotic, which indicates a particular priestly or religious office in connection with a local deity, perhaps connected with the ibis-cult, very popular in the Hermopolite Nome where he lived.

So here we have a man who held a priesthood in a traditional Egyptian religious cult, but who entered the more privileged milieu through military service as his father Kephalas had also done, at around thirty years of age; it is worth noting that the father's status had not automatically taken the son entirely out of the Egyptian milieu. As well as being a soldier, Dionysius appears in the guise of a royal tenant, his main source of livelihood as a civilian before he entered military service. So he was priest, farmer and soldier, perhaps all three simultaneously at some time in his life.

Many of the documents in the archive refer to economic transactions. It is fascinating to see that in some of the demotic documents Dionysius appears as the economically dominant force, selling livestock, letting small parcels of land, tenure of which was presumably connected with his priesthood, whereas his predominant role in the Greek contracts is as a borrower of commodities at 50 per cent interest; but this may not necessarily reflect a lower standing in the Greek world so much as a respectable credit-worthiness in a bigger pond. The people from whom Dionysius borrowed belonged mainly to the class of soldier-farmers which Dionysius had himself joined.

So we can grasp the nature of the social, economic and occupational institutions within which such a Graeco-egyptian family was able to manoeuvre. What happened when they got into difficulties? Naturally they turned to the government and its officials for help. We have a petition to the king from Dionysius' father Kephalas, complaining of the behaviour of a certain Lysikrates, one of the Greek military elite, which is threatening he says, to reduce him to the status of a slave.[17] Kephalas had bought some wine on credit from Lysikrates, paid the debt in two instalments but had failed to obtain a receipt for the second, with the predictable result that Lysikrates was claiming that it was still owed. Kephalas asks that Apollodorus, one of the 'First Friends', president (*epistatēs*) and scribe of the cavalry landholders (*katoikoi hippeis*), be instructed to investigate the matter and make sure that, if Kephalas' version is accepted, Lysikrates is allowed no claim against Kephalas' property.

Dionysius' problems, thirty years later, were not dissimilar and related to a loan of 150 artabs of wheat (a very large quantity, perhaps intended for resale at a profit) which Dionysius and his mother had contracted. The creditor was harassing them and Dionysius petitioned first the governor of the nome and then the royal scribes, asking to be left in peace and using the argument that he was a royal cultivator, it was the sowing season and if he was not left to get on with it the land would be left idle. The point was effective and the nome governor docketed the petition: 'If he is a royal cultivator see to it that he is left in peace until he has completed the sowing.' Similarly, the royal scribes passed down the instruction to the *epistatēs* of the village not to distrain on his person until the land was sown.[18] The conclusion of this particular episode is not recorded but Dionysius' papers show him taking further loans soon afterwards, perhaps to pay off the first debt; but we do not know where this chain ended.

The case of Dionysius and his family suggests clearly that, however rigorous was the framework of rules which prescribed royal control of all aspects of the economy, there was a large area within which the small man could behave as if he enjoyed a good deal of freedom of manoeuvre, socially and economically. He might improve his social status, better himself professionally and economically, behave as if he really owned and controlled goods and property. The autocratic rules by which his actions were constrained and restricted were perhaps not more oppressive than, for example, tax law in a modern capitalist state. If he got into trouble he could ask the government for help. If that did not work he could defy the law and run away from home, perhaps to become a brigand; there is evidence, even from the prosperous reign of Ptolemy II Philadelphus, of serious attempts to stamp this out.[19] But freedom of manoeuvre was limited because, in the final analysis we come up against the hard fact that Dionysius and his like were powerless to choose, challenge or change the governmental system which ruled their lives. What they conspicuously lacked was any degree of political freedom.

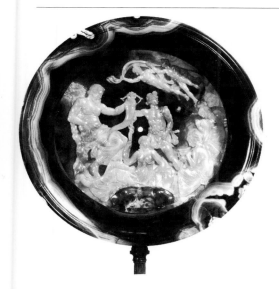

40   The Tazza Farnese. This dish, dating to the first century BC, is a masterpiece of Alexandrian artistry, magnificently carved from sardonyx in the cameo technique. Seated against the tree to the left is the god Nilus holding a cornucopia, below him Isis reclining on the head of a sphinx. The central figure is Horus-Triptolemus, depicted as the 'sower' carrying a knife and a bag of seed. The significance of the scene has been much debated – some have seen it as a comment, after the battle of Actium, on the passing of an era and an expression of hope for a new order.

This system of government is best known from the early Ptolemaic period in Egypt and, although there were changes in detail, it continued to work in much the same way until the coming of the Romans. If Dionysius had lived seventy or eighty years later he would probably not have seen much difference in the general level of prosperity or security experienced by people of his class. There are suggestions that the administrative system was running down in the later Ptolemaic period, that corruption and oppression were more rife than earlier, that when Octavian made his brief tour of Egypt he found the canals and waterways clogged, the dykes collapsing and the irrigation system in a general state of neglect and disrepair, a situation which the Roman soldiers were set to work to remedy.[20] It is true that a petition of village priests in 51/0 BC refers to the decline and desertion of their village but it is difficult to know how widespread this kind of thing was.[21] And there may well be an element of propaganda at work in our Roman sources, designed to set off the decadence of the last of the Ptolemies against the workmanlike efficiency of the Roman administration.

The pattern of government which was established in Egypt under Augustus was to last, in all its essential features, for over three centuries. And even then, the changes which occurred in the Byzantine period were subtle and gradual rather than radical and sudden. Many have seen its basis as the Ptolemaic legacy, which indeed it was in some important respects, but despite the similarity of titles and terminology, the innovations were far more significant and the notion that the Romans merely took over the institutions which they found, with minimal adaptation, cannot be applied to Egypt. If nothing else, the advent of Roman law will have guaranteed the inevitability of far-reaching changes.

Who, then, made the new rules? There might at first sight appear to be little difference between the writ of a Ptolemaic king and that of a Roman emperor. The emperor and his officials imposed their will by issuing decrees and edicts, writing letters, responding to requests and petitions. The effect of all this was cumulative, not simply replacing, but adding to and modifying what was there before and adapting to circumstance. Thus an official in the middle of the second century writes:

'I have appended for you a summary of the sections in current use of the code of regulations which the deified Augustus established for the administration of the Special Account and of additions made to it from time to time either by the emperors or the senate or the various prefects or those in charge of the Special Account, so that by applying your memory to the condensed form of the exposition you may readily master the topics.'[22]

Usually such a convenient codification was not available to simplify the bewildering state of the law as is vividly shown by an interchange between the lawyers and a prefect of Egypt at a hearing which took place in 250:

'I read the law of the Emperor Severus to the effect that villagers must not be impressed into compulsory service in the metropolis . . . and after Severus all the prefects have judged thus. The laws are indeed to be esteemed and revered . . . what do you say to the law of Severus and the decisions of the prefects? Severus promulgated his law in Egypt when the towns were still prosperous . . . the argument of prosperity, or rather decline in prosperity, is the same for the villages and the towns . . . the force of the laws increases with the passage of time.'[23]

41 Poems of Gallus. The earliest known manuscript of Latin literature was discovered at Qasr Ibrim (Primis), where it was presumably left by a member of the Roman military garrison established there towards the end of the 20s BC. It contains previously unknown elegiac poems written by Cornelius Gallus, the first Roman prefect of Egypt.

It might seem natural that the officials appointed to administer Egypt, whose affairs were, as Philo of Alexandria put it, 'intricate and diversified, hardly grasped even by those who have made a business of studying them from their earliest years',[24] should be carefully trained for the job, but oddly enough this does not appear to be the case in the higher echelons. The prefect of Egypt, and his immediate subordinates, almost always outsiders of equestrian rank, normally lacked specialist training for the peculiarities of Egypt's administrative system and were not usually in office for more than three or four years. What they invariably did possess, however, was a broad training in the principles of Roman administration which they obtained through experience in the law and military service.

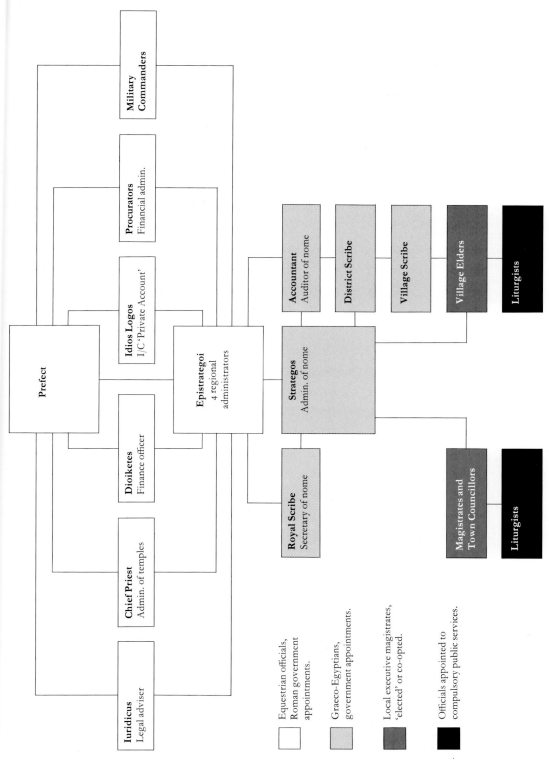

Fig. 3   The bureaucracy of Roman Egypt.

The chart (Fig. 3) presents a somewhat idealised picture of the structure of the bureaucracy – idealised in the sense that not all of the elements shown existed at all times during the first three centuries AD, nor does it include all known officials. It is intended to show levels and areas of responsibility and routes of contact, not to suggest either that departmental responsibilities were defined and demarcated without ambiguity and overlap, or that officials could communicate with each other only through these hierarchically ordered channels. The top three tiers are staffed by people of equestrian status. The prefect is the emperor's deputy ruling from the old Ptolemaic palace and served by subordinates with various areas of responsibility. Beneath them the *epistratēgoi* served in areas which were geographically defined. Then, at the nome level, appointees from the upper stratum of the Graeco-egyptian populace, but appointed to serve only outside their home district. One important innovation is that these people and the equestrians above them were paid bureaucrats, with a regular salary structure. These officials at the nome and district level were the broad base of the pyramid of career administrators upon whom the efficient functioning of the system depended. Indeed, the nome strategos in particular is the key to our understanding of the way in which the central government secured or enforced the co-operation of the local officials in the towns and villages.

It was precisely in the nome capitals that the most significant innovations under Roman rule appear with the gradual introduction of institutions of local government. These are basically imitations of the traditional oligarchic organs of government of the hellenistic Greek cities grafted into the Egyptian towns. The councils, whose

42 Antinoopolis. The drawings by Jomard and Cécile in the Napoleonic *Description de l'Egypte* show how the Greek character of the foundation of Antinoopolis was reflected in the distinctive style of its architecture. The drawing records a general view of the remains of a magnificent colonnaded main street.

members were co-opted for life, were not created until 200/1 but there had been developments in that direction earlier with the introduction of executive magistrates, elected (however nominally) for short periods of office. And along with this, and much more important, a massive network of liturgies – public services and enforced labour, in concept voluntary display of public munificence, in practice compulsory exaction of personal service or financial contribution, based upon property qualification and spreading all the way down the social and economic scale. This was quite different from anything which had existed in the Ptolemaic period. The range of tasks performed by such liturgists was huge: work on the dykes, supervision of irrigation and sowing, collection and delivery of the harvest to the state threshing-floors and granaries, collection of money taxes, supervision of building works, festivals and public facilities of all kinds. Magistracies and liturgies were in principle different kinds of posts, the former much more prestigious, theoretically desirable and open to competitive election, but there are clear signs that by the late second century these were so burdensome as to be regarded in the same light as liturgies. Some notion of the oppressiveness of the latter can be gained from the fact that an official of the town of Oxyrhynchus reported in 147/8, at a time when the empire is traditionally seen as enjoying its greatest period of prosperity, the confiscation of the remaining property of 120 liturgists who had literally fled from their responsibilities because they had not sufficient resources to fill them.[25]

The intended role of this growing local administration was clear enough. It was supposed to take some of the weight off the government-appointed officials by

43   Stela of C. Julius Valerius. Epitaph of the baby son of a Roman soldier in Egypt (*c.* AD 225–50). The inscription reads: 'C. Julius Valerius, son of C. Julius Severus, a soldier of the second legion Traiana. He lived 3 years.' The monument is an interesting mixture of elements. The inscription is Latin, the boy's tunic is Roman, the jackal of Anubis, the falcon of Horus, the sidelock and the griffin of Isis/Nemesis are Egyptian.

being responsible for ensuring that the towns and villages met their obligations to the government in the form of tax; and on the other hand for conducting internal administration of facilities in the towns and villages themselves. So this was an attempt to shift some of the burden of government on to the real amateurs, the local moneyed classes, the descendants of those privileged Greeks of the Ptolemaic period, whose fitness to serve lay primarily in their ability to afford the time and the money essential to the job. In the event it failed because the burdens were too great. The local magisterial classes were, except for the very wealthiest stratum at the top, ruined by the effects of responsibility without power. But the failure was a gradual process and the system did have important and beneficial consequences. The most important was the effect on the nome-capitals, the metropoleis, administrative, economic and social centres on a far grander scale than in the Ptolemaic period – the counterparts of the myriad towns in the Roman west and east which were the most vital and thriving signs of the Roman imperial peace.

The Roman empire at its height has been described as an aggregate of self-governing communities. Whilst this reflects only one of its many aspects, it is nevertheless true that this degree of local self-government in the communities was a hallmark of Roman rule and, particularly in Egypt, represented a real change from what had preceded. A detailed description of how this worked in one particular community will therefore tell us a good deal about Roman administration in Egypt. The town of Oxyrhynchus, some 200 kilometres south of the apex of the delta, provides more detailed information than any of the other nome-capitals and the evidence from the late third century both reflects the institutions of self-government in their most developed form in Egypt and sharply highlights the problems which prevented them from functioning efficiently.

The principal organ of government after AD 200 was the council, consisting of

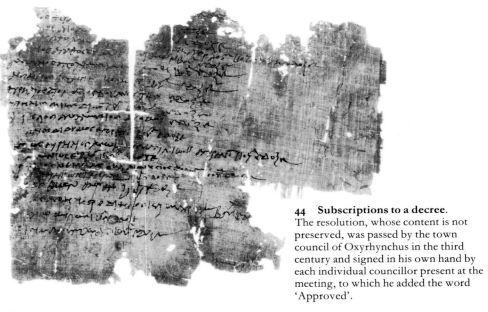

44 Subscriptions to a decree.
The resolution, whose content is not preserved, was passed by the town council of Oxyrhynchus in the third century and signed in his own hand by each individual councillor present at the meeting, to which he added the word 'Approved'.

45 Palestrina Mosaic (detail). The mosaic depicts several
temples with Greek architectural features. Egyptian elements
include the papyrus boats, the procession of priests and the dog
on a pedestal, illustrating animal cult.

perhaps as many as one hundred councillors, all of the Greek 'gymnasial' class, with
a property qualification (which naturally tended to make membership hereditary),
who were co-opted for life. The presidency of the council changed hands annually
and was held by distinguished members who had previously served in the other
colleges of magistrates. Other minor administrative tasks were performed by a
secretary and treasurer of the council fund (probably fed by the entrance fees exacted
from members on election). The council normally met monthly, though extra
meetings could be specially summoned as and when necessary. It could make re-
commendations to the assembly of the citizens of Oxyrhynchus, membership of
which was probably restricted to adult males. This might have convened from time
to time in the theatre, but it was a body with virtually no real power – an account of
a noisy meeting suggests that it could do little more than the honorific, making
public acclamations of emperors or prefects, voting statues and the like.[26]

The corporate responsibilities of the council show clearly that it was supposed,
on the one hand, to guarantee that the town and the villages in the nome met their
tax-obligations to the government and, on the other, that the local administration
of the town itself (excluding the villages, which had their own authorities) was
carried out without recourse to government officials. In fact, of course, it did this
by appointing and supervising the liturgical officials in both these spheres, some
from its own membership, some not, depending on the nature of the task. But in
the matter of tax-collection it was itself carefully watched by central government

officials such as the strategos of the nome. If things went wrong in local adminis-tration, it might have to solicit their assistance; if this was a chronic problem, an imperial delegate might be appointed over its head to sort things out (one such is known at Hermopolis in the 260s).

Its role *vis-à-vis* the central government was not confined to the collection and delivery of taxes, important though that was – it had also to keep property records which were the basis of individual liability and, within limits, it probably had some discretion in dividing up the tax-assessment on the town among individuals and groups. It would also deal with extraordinary levies such as those made to meet the needs of a visiting emperor or prefect with his retinue. Additional levies for military supplies were also made with increasing frequency in the later third century and were perhaps the principal feature in the failure of the councils to cope properly with their responsibilities. An extract from the minutes of a meeting held at some time in the late third century brings this out forcibly:

'Two communications from the strategos having been read, one concerning the appointment of a substitute for Actiasion, convoying collectors of wine, who had absconded . . . after reading the president said "Appoint persons to do the duty in order that the carriage of the *annona* for the most excellent soldiers may not be hindered." The councillors said "Let . . . not be nominated beforehand lest they run away." The president said "On this point we will refer to his excellency the *epistratēgos*."'[27]

On the local front, the council and its officials had overall control of the city funds and supervised the letting of such property as belonged to the town. It looked after organisation of festivals, the running of the gymnasium and the baths, administration of the local markets and the town's food supply which involved collecting market dues, regulating quantities of commodities for sale, and general supervision of local commerce. Buildings and their upkeep were an important responsibility and the council's officers determined what needed doing and contracted the work out, from leaking roofs to new colonnades. The welfare of individual members of the community was also a concern; the council was responsible for the administration of the free distributions of wheat made to a restricted number of privileged citizens, organised very much along the same lines as the so-called corn-dole at Rome, and for admitting persons of the Greek class to the Association of Elders (*gerousia*) which, amongst other things, gave them the privilege of maintenance at the public expense.

The following extract from the agenda for a council meeting in about 299 gives a good idea of the range of functions which such a body performed in a large and busy town:

'Concerning the appointment of someone to invite the *epistratēgos* to the festival.
Concerning the making of an advance from the council funds for certain posts.
Concerning the urging of one of the nominees to offices to become steward of the games.
Concerning the urging of . . . to be gymnasiarch on certain dates.
Concerning the postponement of the petition of the priests until the next meeting.
Concerning the election of a *kosmētēs* in place of Silvanus.'[28]

The multifarious and complex responsibilities of the career bureaucrats might at least seem to justify this relatively minor attempt at decentralisation. The task of the prefect of Egypt, even with his staff of subordinates, was daunting. Best described as a combination of legal, military and financial responsibilities, in practice frequently inseparable, it required considerable skill and conferred great power. Sometimes the sheer volume of business was awesome:

'The most illustrious prefect Subatianus Aquila has ordered, according to his all-embracing foresight, that the petitions handed in to him in Arsinoe on the 26, 27 and part of the 28 of Phamenoth (209), 1804 in number, having been published also in Alexandria for sufficient days, are also to be published on the spot for three whole days and to be made clear to those in the nome in order that those wishing to get a copy of what answers pertain to themselves may be able'.[29]

The prefect and the lower officials administered a huge corpus of laws: on the one hand an accretion of codes, edicts, rescripts and the like which embodied what might amount to an ever-changing reference book of decision- and policy-making. On the other hand there were the 'laws of the land', survivals from Ptolemaic Egypt of both Greek and native Egyptian law (which we would call broadly civil), as well as special arrangements affecting groups such as the Jewish community in Alexandria. On top of all this came the Roman *ius civile*, the body of law which defined the privileges and obligations of, as well as the relationships between, Roman citizens. This was inevitably to become, with the spread of Roman citizenship itself, more important and more pervasive and might justifiably be regarded as the very essence of the process of romanisation.

For the administration of these laws there existed courts in Alexandria to which people could bring their cases and, in addition, the prefect made an annual tour (the *conventus*) of the assize centres, accompanied by some of his immediate subordinates and using the local officials' expertise on the spot. Although it might prove time-consuming and tedious to wait for a hearing (or even require a touch of graft to jump the queue), much routine business could be dealt with in this way, a great deal of it simply by written reply from a subordinate official. The system itself shows great flexibility and warns us not to put too modern an interpretation on the notion of judicial functions. The prefect handled petitions, lawsuits and administrative matters; we might be tempted not to think of the latter as legal matters but the fact is that the decisions made about such things did, for all practical purposes, have the force of law. Thus, in local courts of various kinds and statuses even the lowlier officials at the nome level administered the law in this broad sense when they decided, for instance, whether a person might be entitled to exemption from an office or had been illegally treated or overtaxed.

Thus there is, in practice and probably even in principle, very little distinction between administration and jurisdiction. Various factors, separately or in combination, determined how a person or an issue was handled; the nature of the issue, the status of the people involved, the competence of the official dealing with it (from a centurion or nome secretary, right up to the prefect himself) and cases could be pushed up the hierarchy or delegated down it. Such activity can cover a very wide range of deliberative procedure, from informal examination and decision to a full-dress trial. This is strikingly illustrated by an episode which occurred in 63, when the prefect encountered a delegation of veteran soldiers complaining about their rights as Roman citizens being overridden. First they accosted him in the street of their camp, then handed in written documents at the headquarters, then met him again at some other location and finally appeared at his tribunal where he sat in full session with his council of advisers, only to be told that they must go to their homes and not be idle![30]

The episode highlights the importance of military personnel in Egypt. The number of serving soldiers in Roman Egypt was at first probably of the order of 20,000 (three legions, reduced to two by AD 23, nine infantry cohorts and three cavalry units). In comparison with the Ptolemaic period the degree of social integration of serving soldiers will have been smaller because most will have been recruits from elsewhere (conversely most Egyptian recruits will have served in other provinces) and soldiers were expressly prevented from acquiring land in Egypt during their service. But, even so, the army as an institution was more closely integrated into the civil life of the province than modern experience would suggest. It played an important role in policing the province, especially the transportation of wheat down the Nile, supervising the working of mines and quarries by companies of contractors; officers appear as arbitrators in disputes, soldiers are assigned to duties in factories. The less pleasant side of the picture emerges occasionally in reports of

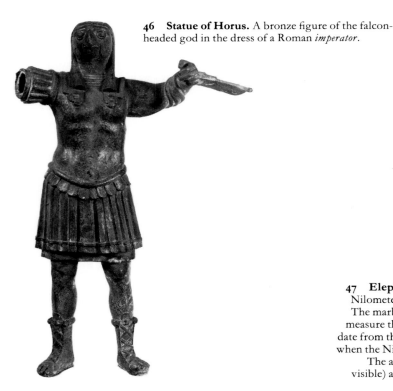

46 Statue of Horus. A bronze figure of the falcon-headed god in the dress of a Roman *imperator*.

47 Elephantine Island. The Nilometer built into the quay. The marble slabs calibrated to measure the height of the flood date from the nineteenth century when the Nilometer was re-used. The ancient markings (not visible) are on the facing wall.

the extent to which the civilian populace was burdened, indeed often terrorised, by billeting and requisitions. Another and more sinister dimension of this aspect becomes clearer in the course of the third century, when local officials are repeatedly bombarded with orders to collect foodstuffs and clothing in the form of irregular levies and requisitions (*annona militaris*) and transport them directly to military units. The increase in demands of this sort was an important contributory factor in the breakdown of the system of local government in the latter part of the third century, perhaps less because of shortage of goods than because of the difficulties inherent in the administration of the supply-system.

In fact, Egypt produced an overall surplus of considerable size and, as during the Ptolemaic monarchy, the administration was largely geared to the exaction of revenue in the form of tax. Some of this was ploughed back into the province, much was despatched to Rome, both in kind and cash. Fundamental to the taxation system was the census, instituted under Augustus as a fourteen-year cycle, with provision for interim amendments of individual returns. Records of the ownership of land and other property, the status of individuals and their occupations, occupancy of houses were maintained by local record offices in the nome-capitals. The procedure was not without its difficulties, as a prefect's edict of 89 shows:

'Neither public nor private business is receiving proper treatment owing to the fact that for many years the abstracts in the property record office have not been kept in the manner required . . . Therefore I command all owners to register their personal property at the record office within six months and all lenders the mortgages which they hold and all other persons the claims which they possess.'[31]

The main constituent of the revenue was the land-tax paid in kind, but there was also a huge variety of small money taxes payable by individuals – a poll-tax assessed at more favourable rates for the higher classes and, until the early third century, exempting Roman citizens altogether, taxes on traders, manufacturers and artisans such as weavers and potters, customs and market dues, and from the middle of the third century an increasing quantity of irregular exactions. Almost all taxes were collected for the imperial government – examples of local taxes raised by the towns for their own purposes are few. To this list should be added the very wide financial interests and powers of the emperors' Special Account, another example of a Ptolemaic institution which was radically changed in character. It acquired revenue in the form of property of intestates or criminals, imposed fines or confiscation for various offences against marriage laws or rules of inheritance – in short, it functioned as an instrument of public finance.

Methods of tax-collection varied: some taxes were contracted out to private collectors, most were collected by appointed officials who had to work in liaison with the government administrators, principally the nome strategos. The officials and their communities were given strong incentives to make sure that their quotas were filled because it was they themselves who were liable to make good any deficits from their own assets.

It is difficult to be quite sure how burdensome this system was for the taxpayers. People complained, naturally, as the prefect Tiberius Julius Alexander noted in his edict of 68: 'For often the farmers throughout the whole country have petitioned me and revealed that they have been condemned to pay many unprecedented charges . . . through payments in kind and money, although it is not open to any who wish to introduce recklessly some general innovation.'[32] Sometimes they ran away to avoid their obligations; a document of the year 55 lists the names of 105 such fugitives from the small village of Philadelphia (probably about 12 per cent of the taxpayers).[33] Later it became increasingly common for the government to try to keep them legally bound to their place of work. On the other hand, the total assessment could be lowered in years when the flood was too high or too low and the fertility was affected. Sometimes emperors beneficently remitted arrears or suspended collections of particular imposts, especially at the beginning of a reign, and it must be said that the evidence which we have for tax rates does suggest that the basic tax on agricultural land was quite low for those people who owned private land, perhaps as little as about 10 per cent of the yield. The introduction of genuine private ownership of land on a significant scale had been another important innovation under Roman rule and provided incentives for the wealthier inhabitants, especially in view of the low tax rates. The military allotments of the Ptolemaic period also effectively moved into private ownership.

But alongside these categories there survived considerable quantities of state-owned land, designated as 'royal' or 'public' which was leased out to 'public tenants'. In yet another category fell imperial land, which was in some genuine sense owned by the emperor, members of his family or his court and administered through the Special Account. Tenancy of royal, public and imperial land cost far more in rent than did ownership of private land in tax; tenants might surrender between 30 and 60 per cent of their yield. Land in these categories, of course, required more from the government in the way of supervisory officials and other overheads. The relative proportions of such land varied greatly from place to place and it is impossible to make any generally valid estimate. In 167 the Fayum village of Hiera Nesos administered an area containing roughly 38 per cent imperial land, 29 per cent private and 33 per cent public. In the early second century the area of the village of Naboo in Apollinopolis-Heptakomias, about 670 arourae in all, comprised 33 per cent public land, 63 per cent private and 4 per cent temple land.[34]

In the late third century there is unequivocal evidence for difficulties in administration. A file of letters of the year 298, relating to the visit of the Emperor Diocletian to the Thebaid, contains the following missive from one official to his immediate superior:

'Upon your orders, my lord, that the ships of the Treasury . . . should be repaired and refitted . . . for the service of the auspiciously impending visit of our ruler the emperor Diocletian, the ever-victorious Senior Augustus, I have commanded the president of the town council to select a surveyor . . . and also an overseer of the same ships to receive the money from the public bank and account for the expenditure incurred . . . but he in contempt for his most honourable duty had the audacity to reply that the city ought not to be troubled. How then, is it possible when this man shows such contempt for my Mediocrity, for the repair of the ships to be carried out . . . ? And not only this, but there is the appointment of receivers and overseers of the supplies of the commodities which have been ordered to be reviewed in different localities in readiness for those who are expected to arrive with our ruler Diocletian, the Senior Augustus. Concerning all which matters I have of necessity been pressing him ... and have also commanded him in writing not once but many times. And since he has not even yet nominated the receivers and overseers, I have found it necessary to report to your universal Solicitude, enclosing copies not only of my letters to him but also of his replies . . . For if this man makes a beginning of disobeying orders, others may try to do the same thing, and through this and his unparalleled insolence the whole administration is endangered.'[35]

There could scarcely be a more eloquent testimony to the problem. It was not one of shortage of supplies, or even money, in conventional terms, but the fact that the governmental machinery, particularly at the local level, was simply not working properly at that time. But it is a striking fact that, over three hundred years later first the Persians and then the Arabs were able to take over, with relatively few immediate changes, a province in which the administration did still function. This needs to be stressed, for the documents tend to spotlight occasions when things went wrong or the imperial authority tried to put them right.

For most of the time, then, in the three centuries of Roman rule, the administration remained more or less in working order but there were very important changes which made the world of Byzantine Egypt much different from what had preceded. A great many of these were introduced in the period between 293 and the foundation of Constantinople (330) and yet more in the reign of the emperor Justinian who, in a long edict issued in about 537/8, effected a thorough-going reorganisation of many of the principal features of the government of Egypt.[36] At first sight Justinian's terms of reference look like the traditional ones and an overriding concern is still the collection of taxes – Egypt's ability to feed Constantinople as well as itself. But the foundation of Constantinople had meant that from the early fourth century Egypt faced eastwards again and found itself part of a different, more restricted and, in many ways more natural, context.

The general reorganisation of the structure of provincial government which began in the reign of Diocletian eventually gave overall control in the east to the Praetorian Prefects as deputies of the emperor, and beneath them, *vicarii* in charge of groups of provinces (dioceses), with the governors of the individual provinces next in the hierarchy. From about 293/4, when the Thebaid was separated, Egypt went through various forms of subdivision into smaller individual provinces and eventually, perhaps by 371, the Egyptian group became a diocese on its own, though exceptionally the official in overall charge was not called a vicar but an Augustal prefect (Fig. 4). Given these developments towards a more integrated structure, it is not surprising that from the fourth century onwards the administration of Egypt began to look less idiosyncratic and more like that of other provinces.

The formal structure is, however, only one easily defined aspect of a great complex of subtle changes which took place in Egypt. Most of them centred around the identity and nature of the sources of authority and the ways in which they interacted and conflicted. The overall scenario has to be seen in terms of the imperial authority at the top, adjusting and modifying its methods and agents of control in order to achieve balance between, on the one hand, a rigid and hierarchical central

THE DIVISIONS OF EGYPT

AD 295	AD 314/5–325	AD 325–41	AD 341–395/408	AD 395/408	AD 560
Aegyptus	Aegyptus Herculia	Aegyptus	Aegyptus	Aegyptus	Aegyptus I / Aegyptus II
	Aegyptus Iovia		Augustamnica (Arcadia, perhaps from 386)	Augustamnica	Augustamnica I / Augustamnica II
				Arcadia	Arcadia
Thebaid	Thebaid	Thebaid	Thebaid	Thebaid	Lower Thebaid / Upper Thebaid
Lower Libya	Lower Libya	Lower Libya	Lower Libya	Lower Libya	Lower Libya
Upper Libya	Upper Libya	Upper Libya	Upper Libya	Upper Libya	Upper Libya

Fig. 4   The administrative divisions of Byzantine Egypt.
From the early fourth century until (?) 371 the Egyptian provinces were part of the Diocese of the Orient, thereafter they formed a diocese on their own.

FIG. 4

control which could not be effectively enforced without the co-operation of the local authorities and, on the other, allowance of too much power to any of the individual elements.

These elements are easily identified in broad terms – the civil, the military and the ecclesiastical authorities, each of which wielded political and economic power in fluctuating degrees. From the point of view of the Egyptian subject, it perhaps did not make a great deal of difference whether he made obeisance to bureaucrat, churchman or soldier and he could and did play one off against the other. This striking phenomenon is more characteristic of the Byzantine period perhaps because the dilution of power that had been vested in the Roman prefect allowed for a greater degree of direct contact between subject and sovereign. Though a well-placed individual might petition the emperor in the Roman period, as did Lollianus, the public teacher at Oxyrhynchus,[37] more routine matters normally landed on the prefect's desk. But in the Byzantine period, for instance, the villagers of Aphrodite petitioned Justinian directly more than once about their tax privileges; Dioscorus and his brother added something to one such petition regarding their loss of property and the emperor intervened directly through the governor of the Thebaid.[38] Or, more astonishingly, the villagers could complain about the behaviour of an official named Theodosius and in reply Justinian could candidly confess that 'his intrigues proved stronger than our commands'.[39]

Equally striking is the language in which such communications are expressed. Gone is the brusque simplicity of an earlier age to be replaced by hyperbole, often florid and abstract, as in this example to the governor of the Thebaid in 567:

'Petition and supplication from your most pitiable slaves, the wretched small owners and inhabitants of the all-miserable village of Aphrodite . . . We humbly recall your all-wise, most famous and good-loving intelligence, but it reaches such a height of wisdom and comprehension (beyond the limited range of words to express) as to grasp the whole with complete knowledge and amendment; whence without fear we are come to grovel in the track of your immaculate footsteps and inform you of the state of our affairs . . . All justice and just dealing illuminate the proceedings of your excellent and magnificent authority . . . we set all our hopes of salvation upon your Highness . . . to help us in all our emergencies, to deliver us from the assault of unjust men, to snatch us out of the unspeakable sufferings'.[40]

Such a tone is normally taken as an indication of the abject servility to which subjects had been reduced by the heavy hand of an oppressive government, but it pervades the writings of the powerful and wealthy as well as the humble. The moral dimension is also strong, as in this case, often involving an appeal to natural (or artificial) justice. But we perhaps ought not to jump too lightly from this to the conclusion that the whole society was pervaded by 'unspeakable sufferings', especially bearing in mind that the admittedly serious complaints of theft, imprisonment and torture made against an official in this petition were only one side of the story!

The nature and development of government in Byzantine Egypt can best be described in detail by observing the interaction of the various limbs of authority – civil, military, ecclesiastical – in relation to the subjects governed in the specific areas of government, the bureaucracy, the role and use of the army, the dispensation of justice, the financial administration. But none of these areas is the exclusive preserve of one department of government – there is a perpetual tug-of-war and a balance is maintained precariously at best.

The reorganisation of the bureaucracy in the reigns of Diocletian and Constantine was fundamental. First the division of Egypt into several provinces, which underwent various modifications (Fig.4). More important was the fact that civil and military authority was divided for the first time within each province between a civil governor (*praeses*) and a military one (*dux*). In the long term this proved unsatisfactory because it ignored the role of the ecclesiastical authority which could ultimately outgun both. Hence, Justinian eventually combined the civil and military power in the hands of the Duke, with a civil deputy (the *praeses*), as a counterweight to the power of the church authorities. But thereafter they were not always separated – the most celebrated example is the infamous Patriarch Cyrus who held both secular and ecclesiastical offices and wore alternately the red and black shoes which were the symbol of the different powers.

On the smaller scale, the nomes lost their major importance as administrative units; from 307/8 this was taken over by smaller subdivisions called *pagi*, which eventually (perhaps in the late fifth or early sixth century) brought into being a powerful district officer, made more powerful by Justinian's reorganisation, called a pagarch, whose main function was financial – the collection of taxes – though some later pagarchs seem to have combined military powers as well. This was a high level appointment which carried direct responsibility to officials as high as the Praetorian Prefect or even the emperor, but it is significant that many of the pagarchs whom we know held office in their home regions and were often wealthy and influential landowners. Obviously the opportunities for corruption, favouritism, extortion or maltreatment inherent in such an office do not need to be underlined.

Such a development had long been foreshadowed by the breakdown of the Roman system of local government which has already been described. By the early fourth century, as we have seen, the local councils were not functioning properly. The remedy was to create a number of executive posts at the local level, probably nominated by the town councils but with direct responsibility to the officials of the central government: president of the council, finance officer, exactor of taxes, legal officer. The effect of this was to separate off the top layer of the local elite and weld it more securely into the structure of the central bureaucracy. The consequence was that the remainder of the local councillor class (the *curiales*) became simply tax-collectors, their burdens and responsibilities thrust on them by their wealthier and more powerful fellow-citizens whose tenure of these executive posts made them the more able to avoid such things themselves. By the end of the fourth century the

48 **The Notitia Dignitatum**. The register of civil and military offices of the Roman/Byzantine empire was compiled in the mid-390s. This illustrated manuscript is a fifteenth-century copy of a Carolingian manuscript. The insignia of the officials are depicted as a book with a formula on its cover and scrolls. In the region under the 'Count of the Egyptian Frontier' the towns of the delta are schematically represented and from them the traditional symbols of the various nome divisions emerge.

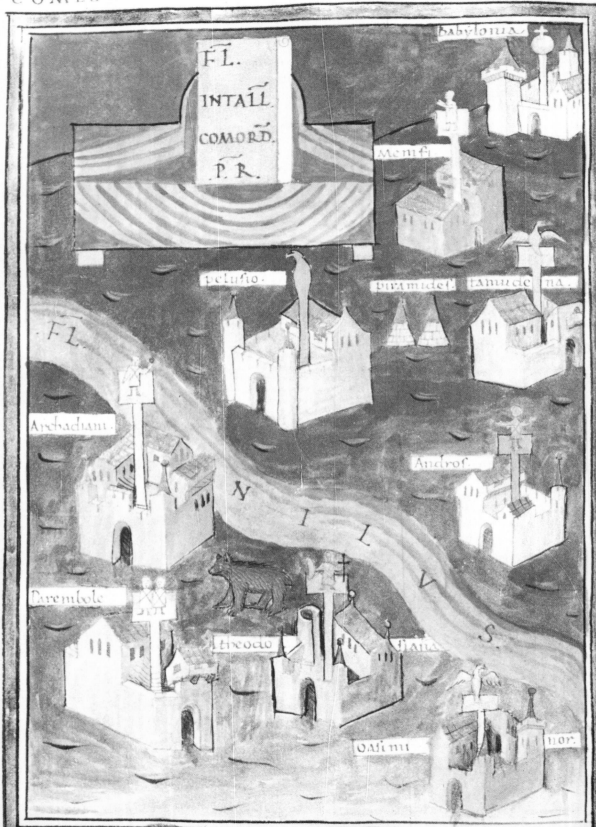

FL.
INTALL
COMORD.
P.R.

babylonia

Menfi

FL.

pelusio

piramidef. tamuderna.

Archadiam.

Androf.

NILUS

Darembole

theodo

fiana

Oasimi

Hor.

councils had ceased to function as administrative units – the majority of the *curiales* formed simply a pool of administrative dogsbodies.

Promotion and preferment in the higher governmental posts depended very much on having good contacts at the imperial court in Constantinople and often rested ultimately on the capriciousness of imperial favour. Some Egyptians were able to obtain it. Much the most spectacular and unusual example is the wealthy family of the Apiones from Oxyrhynchus, members of which in three generations between about 500 and 580 held the offices of quartermaster-general in the Persian war of 503–5, praetorian prefect, Augustal prefect of the diocese of Egypt, Count of the Sacred Largesses and consul. Again, there is a striking contrast with the Roman imperial period when very few Egyptians indeed were even able to enter the Roman senate.

But for the most part it was naturally the lower offices in the bureaucratic and military hierarchy which were open to smaller fry who could exploit useful connections. In about 337 or 338 a military officer named Flavius Abinnaeus was responsible for conducting refugees of the Blemmyes to the imperial court at Constantinople and some two or three years later he reminded the emperors of this when petitioning (successfully, in the event) for promotion to the command of a cavalry unit at the village of Dionysias in the Fayum. In 345 Abinnaeus himself was asked by the president of the council of Arsinoe to procure for him from the

49 The approach to Qasr Ibrim, Nubia. From David Roberts' *Sketches in Egypt and Nubia* (1846). In the 20s BC the emperor Augustus attempted, but eventually abandoned, a southward extension of the boundary of the province. A Roman garrison occupied the town of Primis (Qasr Ibrim) for some years and recent excavations have revealed substantial relics of the Roman presence.

emperors a letter of appointment to the post (perhaps purely honorary) of exactor of taxes – evidently the military officer was perceived as a figure with influence and this reflects one aspect of the very important changes in the role of the army and military personnel in Egypt from the beginning of the fourth century.

The army presence was certainly more noticeable than earlier. Split into a larger number of smaller units, its posts were consequently more numerous and more evenly distributed. No doubt, in principle, its primary function was to defend Egypt against invasion, from the north-east via Pelusium into the delta, from Berber attack through the western oases, from the Blemmyes and Nubades in the south. In fact, for much of the time defence was not needed and it played a prime role in the administration, transport and collection of taxes in kind, of which a large proportion was destined to supply the army units themselves. Hence, inevitably, a closer link with the civil bureaucrats involved and also with the producers themselves.

The papers of Flavius Abinnaeus, from the mid-fourth century, reveal very clearly indeed what an important role the military unit and its commander played in the whole canvas of village life.[41] Often it was not beneficent and townspeople complained violently of the excesses of the soldiery, as in this forceful note from the president of the council of Arsinoe:

'You are not justified in acting as you do but are running the risk of being convicted of criminal conduct. You sent to Theoxenis the soldiers under your command and amongst the many outrages that have been committed in the village you press-ganged them. For you know that the house of Hatres was looted, and that too when he had so many goods of other people deposited with him. And cattle have been driven off and you did not permit enquiry to be made for them but you carried them off as if there were no laws. For by god either you will send these men so that we may learn by them what happened or all we of the council will report to my master the Duke of the Thebaid.'[42]

This compares with the almost contemporary violence against the Meletians and points forward two hundred years to the complaints against the pagarch Menas by the villagers of Aphrodite, that he terrorised them with an army of brigands, country-folk and soldiers.[43] And by that time the phenomenon was given an interesting new twist in the shape of *bucellarii*, soldiers technically under the command of the imperial authorities who could hire themselves out as virtually private armies to powerful landowners.

On the other hand, civilians might try to use the power and influence of the military personnel to protect themselves and because, as we have seen, justice could be dispensed with varying degrees of formality, military officers of quite modest rank were able to develop and exercise a sort of jurisdictional power which did eventually become more formalised; this was in effect recognised at the highest level when Justinian's reform, amongst other things, conferred additional, over-riding civil power also on the military Duke of the Thebaid, an officer who had had some formal jurisdictional powers from the early fourth century. At the lower level the activities of Abinnaeus are again revealing. A handful of petitions from the 340s ask him to deal with misdemeanours and thefts, not only as a police-officer, but to liaise with civil authorities, arbitrate and enforce penalties.[44]

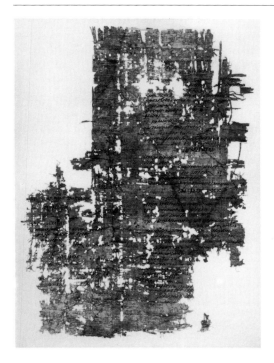

50 Military document. A Latin papyrus of AD 105 containing an official record of soldiers detached for various duties from their military unit which was serving in the Danubian province of Moesia. Its paradoxical discovery in Egypt is perhaps due to the fact that it was brought home by a soldier of Egyptian origin, after his discharge.

This brings out another important dimension in the enforcement of justice. Policing and imprisonment are much more frequently referred to in papyri of the Byzantine period than those of the Roman or Ptolemaic. The activities of police-officers (*riparii*), who were public functionaries, and the existence of prisons in the smaller context of private estates suggests that this is a crucial factor in making policing more effective, not necessarily that the society was more crime-ridden and oppressive. Again we are adumbrating the arrogation of essentially public civil functions to bodies other than the imperial civil authority. A final and very telling manifestation of this is the tremendous importance of the role of the ecclesiastical authorities, from the Patriarch of Alexandria all the way down the hierarchy. It is not difficult to understand how this will have developed from the right of bishops to arbitrate in ecclesiastical matters, or in disputes involving individual Christians – or a Christian and a non-Christian if both parties so chose – into areas which might impinge on the secular, such as the status of church property or taxation, the statutory right to receive monetary contributions for the upkeep of the poor; finally to become a natural focus for the protection of individuals in their communities, whether townspeople or monastics. Such activity is vividly illustrated in the letters of Bishop Pisentius of Coptos in the early seventh century. His patronage and defence of the poor and needy extended far beyond his diocese and he was compared to the civil legal officer, arbitrating with the municipal authorities and sorting out disputes over property amongst his flock.[45]

A recurrent theme in many of the developments described is the pervasive importance of the taxation system. Here too, momentous changes occurred from the reign of Diocletian onwards, particularly designed to bring the level of taxation and the mechanics of collection and transportation into a direct relationship with the need to supply the army, in effect to systematise the irregular levies made so frequently in the later third century. In 297 began the process of putting the method of assessment on a new basis whereby taxability was determined by reckoning in taxable units (human and property), used to calculate liability by multiplication against a rate which could, in theory, be varied from year to year. A new census followed a couple of years later and in 312 began the first of the fifteen-year tax-cycles (indictions), giving the system the basic shape which it retained throughout the Byzantine period. Although the monetary reform introduced by Diocletian in 300 was crucial in many ways to the fiscal policy of the period, many taxes were now paid in a large range of commodities, from chaff to clothing to gold.

Complaints from taxpayers, of course, abound. The collectors are over-zealous because they are liable for any deficit; unjust exactions are made; the taxpayer simply cannot afford it:

'Owing to the unfruitfulness of our lands, which are of poor quality, we were formerly assessed along with all the landowners of the unhappy pagarchy of Antaeopolis, at only two *keratia* per aroura of arable land and eight *keratia* for vineyards ... in the winter we live on vegetables instead of cereal food and nothing is left over to us and our children for our maintenance'.[46]

The case of the village of Aphrodite, from which this complaint comes in the late 560s, is instructive. Under the emperor Leo (457–74) the village had been given the privilege of paying its taxes direct to the imperial government rather than through the pagarch, but its rights were being ignored and the villagers finally were driven to placing themselves under the direct protection of the imperial house, which might mean abandoning some legal rights to their property. Again the official level of taxation was probably not excessive; surviving tax-registers suggest that it was surprisingly low and, after all, it is hard to see what could be gained by taxing people beyond their ability to retain a living surplus after payment, but it is perhaps more likely that, at any rate in the mid-sixth century, the government was having to struggle, as Justinian's edict shows, to make the administrative machinery work properly and produce the revenue required.[47]

The tensions and overlaps between the various branches of the governmental machinery which have been outlined give us a partial explanation for this. What needs to be added is something about the way in which counteractive institutions and practices developed – alternative authorities strong enough to force the government to encourage co-operation rather than coerce. Such strength, of course, needed an economic base; it has already been hinted that the church had such a base, both in totality and in its constituent parts, particularly the monasteries which are excellent examples of such institutions offering protection to their inmates.[48]

The other major phenomenon is the great importance of the wealthy landowners of the Byzantine period. This has to be explained to a large extent by the fact that from the beginning of the fourth century the imperial government yielded most

51   Aswan, Monastery of St Simeon. This is a seventh-
century foundation which was substantially rebuilt in the tenth
century and was dedicated to an eremite saint who became
Bishop of Aswan during the Patriarchate of Theophilus
(389–412). Facilities included this milling yard, with its massive
grinding-stone, decorated with Coptic crosses.

state-owned land into private ownership, perhaps on the calculation that more
revenue could be collected from private land with low tax-rates than from public
land with high rents. No doubt the people who owned or acquired such land were
already wealthy and will have become wealthier. The old royal or public tenants
who worked this land will not have moved – they simply changed status and
became tenants of a private landlord. The scale of their dominance in the Hermopolite
Nome in about 350 can be gauged from the fact that a list of 441 town-resident
landholders shows 274 holding amounts between 1 and 20 arourae (comprising
about 8 per cent of the total land in the list) and 16 holding amounts over 200
arourae (comprising about 51 per cent of the total).[49] But it also shows that many
independent smallholders survived – and this pattern will have been still more
dominant in the villages – and sought to safeguard themselves against government
oppression by placing themselves under the protection of their wealthier neighbours.
The legal validity of such patronage, by the church as well as by private individuals,
was officially recognised in an imperial constitution of 415.[50] This implicit acceptance
of the power of the wealthy perhaps foreshadowed a further development which
allowed certain privileged communities like Aphrodite (and, in effect, the church as
an institution possessed it too) and individuals the right to collect and deliver their
own taxes to the imperial authority, thus in theory releasing them from the potential

depradations of a corrupt pagarch, though the case of Aphrodite shows that it did not always work.

The fragmentation of authority, the polarisation of institutions which developed their own internal strength and coherence in a situation where lines of demarcation either did not exist or were in practice frequently ignored, is accompanied by the adaptation of the imperial authority to circumstance and goes along with the gradual reduction of the area under administration to smaller and smaller units whose boundaries, geographical or administrative, were not impermeable. Ultimately the hold of the imperial authority over Egypt was weakened and Byzantium forfeited it. But the failure was not the fundamental breakdown of the administration, which, it seems, the Arab conquerors were able to maintain with relatively little change, or even the economy – the root causes were military and political.

Indeed, much of the daily life of the inhabitants continued unaffected by political and administrative changes, through the turbulent years of the early seventh century. Nothing demonstrates this better than the following vivid account, by a distinguished legal historian of the period, of the content of a long and fascinating dossier of Greek and Coptic documents:

'Far south, in Apollinopolis Magna, during the epoch of the Persian invasion, seemingly in AD 622, a house-portion was mortgaged for a loan. Thereafter, the mortgagor travelled north, probably as far as Heracleopolis Magna. For a quarter of a century while Egypt passed from Persian hands back to Byzantine control and then succumbed to Arab rule, the house-portion remained in possession of the mortgagee. A dispute then arose, and in the midst of arbitral hearings at Apollinopolis Magna two of the parties thereto (a husband and wife) travelled north to Oxyrhynchus. There in AD 644/5, a deed of conveyance to that property far in the south was executed. The spouses journeyed back up the river, the hearings were concluded, and a deed renouncing all claim was drawn up in their favour in AD 647. Private strife had gone on while the fate of Egypt was being determined, and apparently with no intervention by public authorities, Persian, Byzantine or Arab. All the persons were Copts, strangers to the ruling class.'[51]

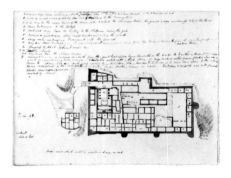

52 Plan of a military building. Gardner Wilkinson's sketched plan of a military complex at Gebel Dochan in the Eastern Desert. The military presence in the eastern desert became more marked in the Roman period, owing to the exploitation of the quarries and the need to protect the trade routes from the Red Sea coast to the Nile. This fortified building had two stories; the structure at the left (marked P) may be a furnace or bath-house.

53 Pen and ink sketch. Gardner Wilkinson's sketch of Egyptians operating shadoofs on the banks of the river.

4

Poverty and Prosperity

The shadoof or a'ood.

The foundation of the economy of this society lies in the human response to the natural environment; its economic institutions are the created means by which the government controlled and exploited that response. During the periods of Greek and Roman domination in Egypt the natural resources of the land were more efficiently and systematically exploited than ever before and, as a consequence, its population probably reached a level which was not matched again until the late nineteenth century.[1] Egypt's economic structure cannot be described simply in terms of a peasant society based on subsistence farming, free from complex market controls and exchanging goods largely through the medium of barter. Agriculture, commerce, trade and manufacture all had an important and interrelated role to play in a complex, highly monetised economy, where individuals and groups were frequently engaged in more than one of these types of activity. But it was the agricultural economy which determined, to a large extent, the character and operation of the other economic structures.

A brief general description of the economy of Egypt has to begin with the nature of the market. In a simplified form, it can be portrayed as a hierarchical structure: the simplest market facilities existed in the villages, more complex versions in the nome-capitals, the most sophisticated in Alexandria which played a very important role in international trade and commerce.[2] The existence of mechanisms for exchange of goods at the village level shows quite clearly first, that there was specialisation of

54 The Wardian tomb. This Alexandrian tomb decoration, which dates to the Roman period, contains naturalistic paintings of garden scenes of exceptional quality. The main scene represents an ox-drawn sakkiyeh, with a boy guarding the oxen and playing a set of pipes. Below it is a pond or canal, from which the sakkiyeh draws water, with plants and fowl. Apart from the sakkiyeh, there is little in the picture that is specifically Egyptian.

economic function in the rural population centres and second, that subsistence agriculture was not a simple matter of peasant families growing or producing everything they needed. Such a family would produce no overall profit in a year, but it would constantly have to engage in market exchange, trading off a surplus of one commodity to make good a deficiency in another.

Exchange of goods in this way was universal. Some proportion of such transactions took place in kind. In addition, a considerable quantity of tax was paid directly in commodities; loans were made in kind, at rates of interest as high as 50 per cent; often labourers' wages were paid wholly or partly in food rations. But, whilst barter of this kind does have a role in the market economy, exchange through the medium of coined money was very significant and widespread, even at the village level and much more so in the towns. People used and carried small coin for market transactions in much the same way as in modern society. By the standards of the ancient world, the economy of Ptolemaic, Roman and Byzantine Egypt was monetised to a high degree at the upper socio-economic levels and to a significant extent at the lower.

This could not have happened without the influence of market forces which regulated the relations of value not only between one commodity or service and another, but also between commodities and services on the one hand and cash on the other. Given the vast size of the country, the lack of effective media of communication and the absence of any consistent or coherent economic theory emanating from the government, the level of supply and demand in both goods and coin varied greatly from time to time and region to region and this sometimes caused quite dramatic variations in commodity prices.[3] Such few attempts as there were to regulate all prices officially on a country-wide basis seem to have had little success.

But even with this high degree of dislocation, successive governments at all times in the Ptolemaic, Roman and Byzantine periods exercised general economic control by various means, mainly with a view to maximising revenue from taxation. Thus, to oversimplify, we might suppose that in the first instance the government deliberately took, let us say, 30 per cent of the gross national product in tax. The remainder was at the disposal of the producers and subject to the local forces and variations mentioned. But the ways in which governmental control was organised and exercised obviously also determined, to a large extent, the degree of economic freedom enjoyed by the subjects in their use and disposal of the after-tax surplus. So the economic behaviour of the individual cannot be understood without some preliminary analysis of the economic role of the state.

In twentieth-century economic life a transaction between a vendor and a purchaser always involves a third party, normally indentified on the currency which changes hands – 'I promise to pay the bearer on demand the sum of one pound,' or the like. Similarly, in ancient Egypt, the state exercised ultimate fiscal control by determining the nature and behaviour of the currency and its relationship to goods and services. Throughout this period the volume, purity and value of the coinage was carefully regulated by the government. During much of the Ptolemaic period and the Byzantine period it involved an important non-fiduciary element. That is, the value of gold and silver coinage was directly related to the amount of precious metal each coin contained and the public knowledge of that fact. The smaller bronze denominations always tended to behave more like modern token coinage and during the Roman period this was the dominant feature of the currency. At other times the volume and purity of gold and silver coinage was directly related to the amount of precious metal available, with a premium to cover costs of production, circulation and exchange. Egypt's mines produced some gold but silver had to be imported from other areas.

From the beginning of the Ptolemaic period until the end of the Roman (AD 296), the Egyptian currency was 'closed', its export being forbidden and exchange of imported external coin mandatory. The general situation is well illustrated by a letter of 258 BC:

'The foreigners who come here by sea, the merchants, the forwarding agents and others bring their own fine local coins . . . to get them back as new coins, in accordance with the ordinance which instructs us to take and mint them, but as Philaretus (?) does not allow us to accept them we have no-one to refer to on this matter and we are compelled not to accept them. The men are furious since we refuse (the coins) at the banks . . . and they cannot send (their agents) into the country to purchase merchandise, but they say their gold lies idle and that they are suffering a great loss, since they brought it from abroad and cannot easily dispose of it to others even at a low price . . . For I believe it is advantageous that as much gold as possible should be imported from abroad and that the royal coinage should always be fine and new, at no expense to the king.'[4]

If gold and silver ran short, the coins could be debased or reduced in weight but this could not be concealed and it undermined public confidence. The effects of a gradual series of devaluations in the Roman coinage can be seen in Egypt in an official letter of 260:

'Since the public officials have assembled and have accused the bankers of the exchange banks of having closed them because of their unwillingness to accept the divine coin of the emperors, it has become necessary to issue an order to all the owners of the banks to open them and to accept and exchange all coin except the absolutely spurious and counterfeit – and not alone to them but to those who engage in business transactions of any kind whatever'.[5]

The last clause carries the important implication that sellers of goods might refuse to accept bad coin and insist on payment in kind. Alternatively, they might raise the cash price of their goods in order to compensate for the reduced value of the coin. And when, as sometimes happened in this period, the government itself demanded a greater proportion of its tax income in kind it further undermined the value of its own coinage.

Some attempt was made on an empire-wide basis to combat the effects of this spiral by the emperor Diocletian in 300/1, shortly after Egypt's coinage was integrated into that of the rest of the empire. First, there was an official revaluation of the coinage and then an attempt to fix maximum prices for all goods and services. As for the reasons, the preface to the imperial edict on prices is specific:

'Who does not know that insolence which insidiously undermines the public good and emboldens the profiteers to charge extortionate prices for merchandise, not just fourfold or eightfold, but on such a scale that human speech cannot find words to describe their profit and their practices? Indeed, sometimes in a single purchase a soldier is stripped of his donative and pay and the contributions of the whole world for the support of the armies fall as profits into the hands of these predators so that our soldiers appear to bestow with their own hands the rewards of their military service and their veterans' bonuses upon the profiteers.'[6]

The phenomenon of inflation evidently worried ancient governments and it is doubly interesting that the edict singles out as the main victim a group in which the state had a special and obvious interest, which might be officially represented, somewhat disingenuously as a matter of fact in view of the frequent extra donatives which they received, as living on a fixed salary. It is generally thought that, in the event, this attempt at price control failed. Certainly, successive waves of quite dramatic price increases continued through the first half of the fourth century. In a matter of a decade the price of glass, for instance, increased by 550 per cent.[7] But these increases seem always to have followed occasions on which the coin was deliberately depreciated and they did not necessarily affect people as adversely as the bare figures suggest since first, the prices of commodities and services were adjusted to meet the changed value of the coins and second, most assets were held in land, livestock, produce and bullion. Since the relative value of gold tends to increase somewhat in such circumstances, the wealthier people who did hold assets in gold coin and bullion would, in fact, be rather better off. What prevented general disaster and allowed the currency system to continue to work was the fact that the economy of the Roman/Byzantine empire, of which Egypt was an integral part, was not tied in to a network of international finance and did not have to maintain a strong currency in relation to the currencies of competing economies, as is the case in the modern capitalist world.

As for its role inside the context of this Mediterranean economy, Egypt in fact always maintained a very favourable balance of export over import and this brought in large revenues in cash. In the period when there was economic competition with other Hellenistic kingdoms, the cash revenues which enriched the Ptolemies are said to have amounted to 14,800 talents a year under Ptolemy II Philadelphus and 12,500 under Ptolemy XII Auletes[8] and the produce which they took in the form of rents could readily be turned into money in foreign markets. Even with the Ptolemies' penchant for extravagant luxuries from exotic places, there was still a huge surplus in the first century BC which attracted the attention of ambitious and avaricious Romans.

During the Roman and Byzantine periods, when the competitive element had disappeared, a good deal of this surplus was hived off in the form of taxes, in cash and in kind. It is very difficult to estimate how much of the gross product was taken in tax, the proportion of tax paid in money to tax paid in kind, or the general shape of the 'Egyptian budget'. In the first century AD Egypt is said to have brought to the Romans revenue equal to that from Caesar's Gallic conquests and more than twelve times that from the province of Judaea.[9] In the sixth century AD the annual wheat assessment, a proportion of which was shipped to Constantinople, was eight million artabs of wheat, perhaps very roughly the equivalent of 8–12 per cent of its total produce; it would be reasonable to believe that the tribute was not less than about six million artabs during the Roman period.[10] But this was supplemented by a large variety of taxes in other products and in cash as well as revenues from trade. Their total yield defies any plausible estimate but it must have far outweighed the value of the wheat. The longevity of Egypt's general prosperity suggests the obvious conclusion that, despite the endemic complaints from taxpayers, government control assured a revenue yield which was, in general, not so extortionate as to drive the producers to the wall.

There were, of course, periods of difficulty and changes in balance and method. The Ptolemies at first favoured royal ownership of land with rental, the production and marketing of major products such as oil and papyrus was stringently controlled in the private sector which co-existed with royal ownership and a variety of small taxes was collected in cash. Under the Romans state ownership of land was considerably reduced, government supervision of private enterprise was relaxed and the amount of tax collected in cash greatly increased. Three interrelated aspects of these developments need emphasis: first, the overall level of taxation appears to have been fairly low; second, the system of administration and collection which devolved largely upon the local communities was cheap; third, there were greatly increased opportunities for private enrichment. In fact, this system was extremely cost-effective for the Roman government, despite the occasionally acute difficulties. In the Byzantine period, the major new developments lay in the increase of the bureaucracy and the consequently higher cost of administration, offset to some extent by the right of some individuals and communities to collect and deliver their own taxes directly; growth of individual wealth was probably greater in scale, but restricted to a smaller elite; and although tax levels probably remained low, there was a more rational budgeting system which was intended to relate income from taxation more directly to the immediate needs of its major consumers, the city of

55 Glassware from Karanis. Much fine quality domestic glassware was discovered during the excavations at Karanis in the Fayum. This yellow flask has a dark green collar with pinched flaps and a palm-leaf wad acting as a stopper in the neck. When found it still contained the residue of brown liquid.

56 Aswan, Monastery of St Simeon. A baking oven and a section of the compound wall.

Constantinople, the personnel of the army and the civil bureaucracy in Egypt.

Direct and indirect taxation was the major means of fiscal exploitation in the Roman and Byzantine periods, but not the only one. The Ptolemies had operated to a much greater extent through direct ownership of land and this did not entirely disappear after the downfall of the dynasty. The Romans retained considerable areas as state land, under various titles, and the imperial house also acquired much property. At first quasi-private, this was granted to relatives and friends of the emperor but eventually, for all practical purposes, assumed public status. All agricultural land in these categories was leased out at fairly high rents; other kinds of property, such as government-owned mines and quarries, were often exploited through contractors working for a share of the proceeds. State-owned land virtually disappeared during the early Byzantine period, sold off to private individuals, some of whom thus became very wealthy and powerful magnates. Ownership by the imperial house continued, but probably on a reduced scale.

A certain amount of wealth and property was also allowed to accumulate in the hands of public or quasi-public corporations. Principal among these, during the Ptolemaic period, were the temples of the native Egyptian gods which enjoyed considerable income from the rental of sacred land, market facilities, the ownership of small industrial enterprises such as breweries, weaving-mills or dyeing establishments. Many temples probably enjoyed a substantial surplus, but their economic power was reduced by the Romans who substituted direct state subventions or grants of land at fixed rentals. The temples retained ownership of some other enterprises although they had to pay substantial taxes on them.

A more conspicuous and characteristic development of the Roman period was the ownership of land and other property by individual towns and villages. This is of a piece with the increase of autonomy in local government and provided a certain amount of revenue to finance public works and facilities, although the towns still had to rely very heavily upon private benefaction and munificence as well as compulsory public service.

The decline in the influence and wealth of pagan religious institutions during the Roman period was counterbalanced at its end by the rising power of the Christian church. From the reign of Constantine onwards it was able to acquire wealth and property on a very large scale indeed. This was not immune from taxation but the surplus was enough to provide a firm foundation for the Church's political power. The economic and social consequences of its importance as an employer are obvious and the economic self-sufficiency of the Egyptian temples in the Ptolemaic period is paralleled and outmatched by that of the large and numerous monasteries in the Christian era:

'In the district of Arsinoe we also visited a priest named Sarapion, the father of many hermitages and the superior of an enormous community numbering about 10,000 monks. Thanks to the labours of the community he successfully administered a considerable rural economy, for at harvest time all of them came as a body and brought him their own produce which each had obtained as his harvest wage, filling each year twelve artabs or about forty *modii*, as we would say. Through this they provided grain for the relief of the poor.'[11]

Finally, we must consider the ways in which the individual could exercise economic freedom and control of his affairs within this framework, after the state and the other public institutions had taken their slice of the cake. There was at all times considerable scope for private enterprise, even under the relatively restrictive legal conditions of property ownership imposed by the Ptolemies. Individuals could acquire and dispose of land which they held even if this were couched in the technical terms of the transfer of a grant. When full private ownership of property became more common such fictions were correspondingly rarer and less important. Land and residential or commercial property could be exploited in different ways. Even a person of quite modest means might (a) own a house or part of house and a few scattered plots of land, (b) lease out some of his private land to others or rent out part of his house-property (c) take parcels of private land on lease from others, (d) farm state or imperial land as a tenant-farmer and (e) hire out his labour on a casual basis. The precise configuration and use of his property could be determined by several factors. He might need, for instance, to offset the high rents payable on state land. Or the impracticality of farming scattered plots in person might induce him to lease out a distant parcel on a fifty-fifty division of the yield and take on lease, under similar terms, a plot nearer to his own centre of operations.

This degree of flexibility existed to some degree at all times but was probably at its most prevalent in the Roman period. It may not surprise the twentieth-century reader that under the Ptolemies state ownership created a relatively even spread of smallholding tenants. In the Byzantine period, increase in private ownership accentuated the gap between rich and poor. Wealthy magnates leased out their private estates to small tenants, ultimately developing a relationship of obligation and protection which legally curtailed the mobility and economic freedom of the peasantry. But even before this time there are signs that prosperous landowners provided some degree of fiscal patronage for their employees – by allowing the formation of tax-paying collectivities amongst estate-workers, for example – and it is questionable whether the growth of this practice radically changed the life of the average peasant.

Whilst the strict legal title of ownership of property may not have exactly corresponded to the physical space in which an individual, in a practical sense, worked to make his living, it was nevertheless very important. Since property was always the

57 Aswan, Monastery of St Simeon. A series of rooms which perhaps functioned as magazines or storage chambers. In the foreground is a courtyard which may have provided feeding facilities for livestock kept in the compound.

97

basis of privilege and obligation in the classical world, it defined the relationship between the state and its institutions, on the one hand, and each individual subject, on the other, in the most concrete fashion: for the Ptolemaic soldier-cleruch, earning his preferential treatment by his utility to the state as a fighting man; for the small-holder of the Roman period, the extent and location of his property and his tax liability carefully defined in the provincial census-records, maintaining the link with his place of origin and residence; for the Byzantine landlord, paying his dues to the state but powerful enough to resist government oppression and to protect his tenants against it as well.

In a purely economic sense, the importance of property is even greater for it underpinned the whole complex of commercial transaction in this society, buying and selling, speculation and investment, credit, loan and mortgage – all except the smallest daily transactions were founded ultimately on the security of property. And although the small cash transactions are the dominant and most visible part of the economic behaviour of the masses, it was the more complex transactions which enabled the smaller and lubricated the economy as a whole. Property could be mortgaged in various ways to raise cash, loans in money or kind were frequently made on the security of the borrower's property, even in the small villages. Lessees as well as owners needed capital to farm their land. One such, Soterichos from Theadelphia, is probably typical of many smallholders of the first and second centuries AD. Farming some land on his own, some in partnership, he operated on a system of credit based on the prospective earnings from his harvests and he died leaving debts which it took his heirs years to pay off.[12] In a society where life expectancy was short, the loss of the working capacity of the adult male might be catastrophic if it could not easily be compensated for by grown sons.

This example also underlines the importance of devolution of property by inheritance, another area in which the individual could exercise a fair degree of freedom within the general framework of rules imposed by the state and its laws. Eldest sons might normally expect a larger share than other heirs, but property, in the form of land, houses, livestock, movable goods and small amounts of cash, was generally divided fairly evenly. Egypt shows, for the ancient world, a relatively large proportion of property (perhaps as much as a third) in the hands of women who will have acquired it by inheritance and in the form of dowry. It is difficult to trace the way in which this affected the ebb and flow of family fortunes. Some practices will have developed to counteract fragmentation and many families will have continued to exploit their property in partnership, ignoring the potentially disruptive effects of a legal division.

The means by which people made their living in this society varied as much as the standard of living itself. An immense range of goods was traded and manufactured, creating the need for a great diversity of supporting services. The fact that very many of these trades, crafts and services were intimately linked into the agricultural hub of Egypt's economy meant not only that the reciprocal economic relationship between town and country, commerce and agriculture, was a very close one but also that many individuals did not obtain their livelihood exclusively from activity in one of these categories.

It is agriculture, however, which has the first claim on our attention. Exploitation of the land, which in many ways hardly changed until the twentieth century, supported far more of the inhabitants of Egypt than any other single activity. The wealth which it provided was always unevenly divided, most markedly perhaps in the last three centuries of our period. A list of town residents who owned land in the Hermopolite Nome in about 350, for instance, reveals that about 36 per cent of the total land recorded was owned by only 0.2 per cent of the landlords.[13] On the other hand, as the modern visitor may still observe, Egypt is very far from being short of manpower and in ancient times the land supported vast hordes of small producers at a level which ensured their subsistence and enabled them to contribute to the enrichment of the few. There were, at all times during our period and in all areas, both large and small agricultural concerns and a mixture of direct exploitation and tenancy, the latter much more common on large estates. Examples are not difficult to find. Apollonius, the finance minister of Ptolemy II Philadelphus, was given a grant (*dōrea*) consisting of an estate of 10,000 arourae at Philadelphia in the Fayum. This was agriculture on a truly massive scale, with the land leased partly in large tracts to groups of mainly Egyptian peasants, partly in small parcels to individual farmers who were mainly Greek.

In the early second century AD the family of a wealthy Alexandrian named Tiberius

58 Anubis stela. An Egyptian 'feeder of the jackals' named Pasos, from the estate of Apollonius, makes a dedication to Anubis in Greek on behalf of the owner of the estate.

Julius Theon owned property which included estates in the Oxyrhynchite and Hermopolite Nomes and the Fayum. This pattern of split holdings was probably the rule rather than the exception amongst the wealthy, but the Theon estates appear to have been unusual for the period in that they were organised through a centralised system of management rather than individually. A letter to two of his estate managers from one Aurelius Appianus, another high-ranking Alexandrian of the third century AD who owned a large amount of land in the Fayum, illustrates the extent to which absentee landlords might be involved in the detailed administration of their estates: 'Immediately on receipt of my letter send five donkeys to Philoteris for the transport of the lentils. And you, Heroninus, send up six artabas of those at your place, which are without fail to be handed over today to Eudaemon the receiver, for you have neglected this though you heard it here so many days ago.'[14]

Centralised management of split holdings is certainly operative much later on the sixth/seventh century estate of the Apion family of Oxyrhynchus. Although it is unclear precisely how much land the family owned at any one time, it was evidently extensive, consisting of many separate holdings in the Oxyrhynchite, Cynopolite and Heracleopolite Nomes and the Fayum, cultivated in small parcels by tenant-farmers under the supervision of area managers who were themselves responsible to a local head office; in the case of the Oxyrhynchus/Cynopolis holdings this was located at the nominal residence of the head of the family in the town of Oxyrhynchus itself. Two features of this, the best-known of the Byzantine large estates, need emphasis: first, these were not massive and consolidated 'baronial domains'; second, the terms of lease for the tenants, who enjoyed the fiscal protection and patronage of their powerful landlords, appear to have been rather generous, so that, whatever their legal position may have been, they cannot simply be described as downtrodden serfs.

At the other end of the scale, comprising the great majority at all periods, were the independent smallholders and the tenants. The latter owned no land of their own, merely a few agricultural implements, a handful of animals, the surplus of their produce, a modest residence and a few sticks of furniture. In the first category we have the recipients of small grants of five arourae of land found at Ptolemaic Kerkeosiris in the Fayum; the 188 (44 per cent of the total) landowners in the Hermopolite landlists of the mid-fourth century AD who held amounts under ten arourae, comprising only about 4 per cent of the total land; the villagers of sixth-century Aphrodite who described themselves as 'pitiable slaves' and 'wretched small owners'.[15] For these people there was the constant struggle to make ends meet, the ever-present threat of being engulfed by wealthier neighbours because they could not survive economically or were unable to pay back debts contracted on the security of their precious land; or the possibility of unforeseen disaster like that which compelled a certain Petesouchos of Kerkesephis to write to his brother at Kerkeosiris in the late second century BC:

'Know that our lands have been flooded over; we have not so much as food for our animals. It would be much appreciated if you would first give thanks to the gods and then save many lives by searching out five arourae of land at your village to feed and maintain us. If you can do this you will earn my eternal gratitude.'[16]

The survival of these smallholders depended upon the labour of the family, perhaps occasionally supplemented by the luxury of hired help at harvest-time. They naturally generate less detailed documentary evidence than their wealthier neighbours but, despite the tenuous financial position of the individual, the numerical predominance of the mass is a very important element of the economic picture of Egyptian society.

Between these extremes, there were always the modestly well-off, the wealthier peasants and the town-resident burghers, owning perhaps fifteen or thirty arourae of land in their local area. Their heyday was certainly the Roman period, when their well-being was essential to the prosperity of their towns and they were probably somewhat squeezed out of the picture in Byzantine Egypt; as the gap between rich and poor became more marked they tended to gravitate to one extreme or the other. But even in sixth-century Aphrodite we can find an industrious small-scale entrepreneur named Phoibammon, son of Triadelphos, enriching himself by the gradual takeover of about thirty arourae of land which originally belonged to one of his creditors, an ex-soldier named Flavius Samuel.[17]

The yield of the agricultural land of Egypt was immensely diverse and varied; most markedly so on the large estates of the rich but also on the smaller holdings of the peasantry. As it does today, the delta showed the fairest face of Egypt's abundant fertility. A female pilgrim of the fourth century enthused:

'Our whole journey (through the delta) led . . . past vineyards of grapes as well as balsam, orchards, well-kept fields and many gardens. All the way the road followed the bank of the Nile, past the extremely fertile farms which had once been the estates of the children of Israel and I really do not think I have ever seen a landscape better kept.'[18]

The impact of the arrival of the Greeks on the farming patterns was very marked. In the Ptolemaic period the Fayum in particular was a centre of lively agricultural experimentation and innovation. There, not only was the amount of land under cultivation tripled but new crops were introduced; most importantly the naked tetraploid wheat *durum triticum* supplanted the traditional husked *triticum dicoccum*. Viticulture was vastly increased and experiments were made with new oil-bearing and fruit crops. The cereals, principally wheat and barley, and vines were always the ubiquitous major crops but there was a great variety of other produce too. Flax, olives, dates, figs and walnuts, beans, lentils and other pulses, cabbage, garlic, onion and radish, cumin and mustard are all commonly found; also vetch, fenugreek and various grasses as fodder crops, sesame and croton, safflower and linseed for their oils.

The cultivation pattern for just over 1800 arourae of land around the Fayum village of Kerkeosiris in the late second century BC was as follows: wheat, 55 per cent, barley, 3 per cent, lentils, 11 per cent, beans, 11 per cent, fenugreek, 2 per cent, vetch, 10 per cent, cummin, 0.1 per cent, grass, 0.9 per cent, fodder crops, 4 per cent, pasturage, 3 per cent. A large estate at Hermonthis in the mid-fourth century yielded wheat, barley, beans, aracus, lachanus, croton, fenugreek, mustard, lupine, clover and pulse. Archaeological evidence from the village of Karanis in the Roman period shows the presence of wheat and barley, dates, figs, filberts, walnuts, pine-kernels, pistachios, olives, peaches, quinces, lentils, radish and lotus. But agriculture was not confined to farmers – even an artisan in a village of the Fayum or Oxyrhynchus might own a small plot of garden-land where he could grow vegetables and cultivate a handful of vines.

The fruits of the earth by no means exhaust the catalogue. Bee-keeping provided honey, the denizens of the ubiquitous village dovecotes yielded both fertiliser and food. Chickens and pigs were reared for food in the courtyards of town and village houses; wool, milk and cheeses were obtained from the flocks of sheep and herds of goats which ranged the pasturelands, not infrequently giving rise to complaints against careless shepherds from the indignant owners of trampled or half-eaten crops:

'Ever since Pharmouthi of the present year Seras son of Paes, herdsman, has let his flocks loose upon the public lands which I farm . . . and has grazed down two arourae of young vetch from which damage has resulted to the amount of twenty artabae. Wherefore I request you to write that the accused man be brought before you for fitting punishment.'[19]

Draught animals too were essential; the valuable oxen for driving the water-wheel and ploughing where necessary, certainly too expensive for a poor peasant to own outright. Then there were the numerous donkeys and, more rarely, a handful of camels which would serve their owners in teams as beasts of burden on a large and scattered estate. Sometimes they too were a source of trouble:

59 The tomb of Petosiris. This remarkable tomb belongs to a member of the local nobility of Hermopolis, a priest of the god Thoth, and graffiti on its walls show that it later became a place of pilgrimage for Greek visitors. The many vivid scenes which adorn its interior walls are striking for their predominantly Greek style because they date to the pre-Ptolemaic or very early Ptolemaic period. The watercolour sketches of the east wall, upper register, by H. Carr, depict the grain harvest in three scenes, of which this one shows the harvester drinking and the threshing of the grain.

'Yes, for if (you want to?) know my opinion just now, you ought not to be accounted a human being. On other occasions too I have written to you that I did not detain Hermias' camel nor anyone else's. If this is what you want me to write I'll write (it) to you. For perhaps you don't read what I write to you. All that Ammonas and the automata-maker, Anthropas, and all the rest suffered here on account of the camels from Coptos, you can hear from your brother. Those bloody bulls of yours are running wild and because of them I have appeared in court several times thanks to you.'[20]

But the poorer landowner would have to hire such animal-power as and when he needed it; as for the tenant-farmer, his lease sometimes explicitly stated that it was the responsibility of the landlord to provide draught animals.

For rich and poor farmers alike the agricultural years ran their appointed round, to the dictate of the river and its inundation. In the far south the river began its rise in June and the floodwaters receded in September (in Middle and Lower Egypt the stages were correspondingly up to four or five weeks later). Before the flood began the canals and dykes which carried the silt-bearing water and kept the right areas under water would need to be cleared and repaired; much of this work was imposed on peasants as compulsory public labour but private owners had to provide their own maintenance. Nilometers along the length of the river measured the height of the flooding and the consequent level of fertility to be expected in the coming year. A low flood, or a series of them, could spell economic disaster for smallholders and in such circumstances tax remissions were often granted by the government. Pliny the Elder is explicit about the fineness of the balance:

'An average rise is one of seven metres. A smaller volume of water does not irrigate all localities and a larger one, by retiring too slowly, retards agriculture; and the latter uses up the time for sowing because of the moisture of the soil while the former gives no time for sowing because the soil is parched. The province takes careful note of both extremes: in a rise of five-and-a-half metres it senses famine and even at one of six metres it begins to feel hungry, but six-and-a-half metres brings cheerfulness, six-and-three-quarters complete confidence and seven metres delight. The largest rise up to date was one of eight metres in the principate of Claudius and the smallest a little over two metres in the year of Pharsalus as if the river were attempting to avert the murder of Pompey by a sort of portent.'[21]

Some areas and types of land, especially vineyards, required constant artificial irrigation which was not dependent on the inundation in the same way. Here, the irrigation machinery, the shadufs, water-wheels and occasionally the Archimedean screw were an equally vital part of good land management.

When the flood-waters had receded, the sowing of cereal and leguminous crops began, in the rich layer of deposited silt. This would not need deep ploughing – indeed it would be counterproductive – but the ox-drawn plough would have seen some use on newly cultivated land. The seed had been stored from the previous harvest or, in some cases, distributed as a government grant. One cereal crop per year was the almost universal practice, though there were exceptions, as a letter of 256 BC from Apollonius to his estate-manager Zenon shows:

'The king has ordered us to sow the land twice. Therefore as soon as you have harvested the early grain, immediately water the land by hand. And if this is not possible set up a series of shadufs and irrigate in this way. Do not keep the water on the land more than five days and as soon as it dries out sow the three-month wheat.'[22]

But normally the annual crops were rotated on a two- or three-field system, with leguminous, oil or fodder crops grown on cereal-bearing land every other year or every third year.

The sowing will have been completed in the late autumn and the harvesting of the cereal crops took place from April to June. In the intervening months, there was plenty to be done apart from the cultivation of the growing crop – the care of the vines, olive-trees and date-palms which would yield their fruit in the following late summer and autumn. From harvest the cereals were taken to the threshing-floors – the wealthy had their own, the others used the public facilities in their villages. This was the busiest time of year and the work might sometimes be given added urgency by external circumstances:

'Eudaemon to Zoilos steward, greeting. I sent the letter by the hand of Eleutheros to the official in charge of the loading. Learn that the Goniotae have had soldiers from the prefect to search out the Mastitae. So, then, collect either barley or lentils or grass, and thrash it, before trouble starts. Farewell.'[23]

After harvest, perhaps a brief celebration and then rents and debts would be paid and the surpluses of these and other crops would be transported in an endless

60   **Karanis, granary courtyard**. The courtyard of a building which may have provided granary facilities for a complex; there are twenty storage bins accessible to three adjoining houses. The courtyard also contains a baking oven, a mill base and a lower mill-stone.

procession of donkey-loads to the villages or towns. Some would be sold in the market, some stored in granaries for later sale, some delivered to public granaries as tax and transported down-river by shipping contractors in government service, thence to the further parts of the Mediterranean world.

The efficiency of this agricultural economy depended on a complex network of interdependent activities. The larger estates were naturally the more sophisticated and diversified. Apollonius' estate at Philadelphia in the Ptolemaic period produced plenty of cereals but it also contained more than a dozen large vineyards, grew olives, fruit and vegetables in abundance, maintained beehives, raised cattle, kept donkeys, camels and horses for draught and transportation, sheep, goats, pigs and geese for wool and food. Apollonius' considerable local interests in the manufacture of woollen stuffs and of beer brewed from barley were obviously directly dependent on the produce of his estate.

Five hundred years later, the estates of the Alexandrian Appianus, also in the Fayum, provide, through the accounts and records of one of the estate-managers, an equally interesting picture of an agricultural complex devoted mainly to vine-growing. On each of the constituent parcels some land was leased out, the rest was worked by its own permanent staff of paid employees under a manager, which needed at times to be supplemented by the casual labour of local landholding peasants. The complex system of transportation between the various parcels and from them to the market-centres was centrally organised and directed from the nome-capital, Arsinoe. The large parcels at the villages of Theadelphia and Euhemeria undoubtedly dominated their regions, but it is important to note that they dovetail into an agricultural economy otherwise dominated by a small peasantry, which was there long before the estate came into existence and survived long after its dispersal.

This, too, was a determinant of the nature and organisation of a labour force, which might be quite sophisticated, even on modest holdings. Specialised activities, like vine-dressing, might be contracted in as and when needed. Extra labour for carrying olives or treading grapes could readily be recruited, perhaps especially among the women and children of local peasant families. Sometimes musicians were hired to give grape-treaders psychological and rhythmical help. An account of the late first century from Hermopolis shows the operation of a medium-sized estate of about sixty arourae, producing for sale wine, wheat, vegetable seed and reeds. The facilities included a house and bath, a dovecote, poultry sheds, wells, storage-cisterns, shadufs and water-wheels. Wage-labour was used for a great variety of jobs: chopping rushes, breaking clods, weeding, fertilising, irrigating, seeding, harvesting and threshing, pumping water, guarding embankments, transporting sheaves, building walls, repairing shadufs and water-wheels, shearing sheep, pruning vines and so on.[24] Difficulties in labour relations were not unknown: 'Horus to Pemenes, greeting. Herienouphis the swineherd has taken refuge at the altar of the king saying, "I shall not pasture the swine unless you pay my wages for the past four months," saying also, "I am a sailor, no-one can touch me or compel me to pasture your swine."'[25]

Even these few examples suggest that the social and economic interaction between the town or village and the agricultural land around it was very close indeed.

61 Karanis, dovecote tower. The larger dovecotes at Karanis were presumably run as commercial ventures or were connected with large estates. This example is a single nesting tower surrounded by single-storey rooms and courtyards on all sides, covering an area of 12.5 × 10.8 m. The actual nests are wheel-made earthenware pots with rounded bases which were embedded in the dovecote walls.

Neither was self-contained and neither could exist without the other. The wealth of the land enabled the growth of towns, but that wealth could not be extracted and used without the application of the technology, the manpower, the specialised trades, industries and commercial services which were able to flourish and develop only in the nuclei of the towns and villages. Every house courtyard with its animal-pens, storage bins and ovens, every village dovecote, granary and market, every estate pottery-kiln, brewery and weaving-shop, every transaction by a town resident which took money or other resources back into the rural milieu emphasises the essential integrity of an economic structure to which the simple model of agriculture occupying the primary role and trade, industry and commerce taking second place to it cannot be applied.

The impact of the Greeks on Egypt's trade, industry and commerce was even more marked than in agriculture. The Greek historian Herodotus described active merchandising in the towns of Egypt in the fifth century BC but there is no doubt that from the Ptolemaic period onwards the level and complexity of commercial activity greatly increased.[26] The urban Greeks of the Aegean and Asia Minor had a strong tradition of trade and entrepreneurial enterprise and they brought it to

Egypt with them. Furthermore, the volume of currency in the economy of Egypt in the late Pharaonic period was very small – in fact, most of the coins in circulation appear to have been Greek or Persian. Rapid and thorough monetisation took place early in the Ptolemaic period and this profoundly affected not only the character of the local economies in particular areas but also inter-regional movement of goods and services as well as international trade in the Mediterranean and the east. Vitality and growth continued and probably reached a climax in the Roman period, encouraged by the peaceful conditions which obtained under Roman imperial rule. Under Byzantium, in the last three centuries of our period, there are still plenty of clear signs of lively, currency-based trade and commerce, despite the common belief that economic decline in the late Roman and Byzantine periods brought an increase in barter and a reversion to a 'natural' economy.

The range of goods and services available in the towns and villages of Egypt was very wide indeed, though it will obviously have varied somewhat according to size, population and location. The establishment and development of markets as commercial centres, often linked to temples or other public building complexes, so characteristic of the Greek urban milieu, was encouraged in Egypt. A document of the second century from the town of Oxyrhynchus records the market-taxes levied on the various groups of traders operating in a market connected with the Temple of Sarapis: sellers of rushes, wood, olives, vegetables, wool, yarn, bakers, fruit-growers, garland-plaiters, crop-buyers, grain-dealers, clothes-makers, leather embroiderers, tinsmiths, butchers and brothel-keepers; and import taxes on olives, dates, cucumbers, marrows, vegetables, spices and beans, nitre, rock-salt, pottery and green fodder, wood, dung and cowpats.[27] This indicates a high degree of organisation and centralisation in the commerce of the town, further illustrated by the fact that the Temple of Sarapis was also a centre for the town's notarial and financial offices.

The Egyptian towns have not yielded much archaeological evidence of commercial buildings but at Marea near Alexandria there is an arcade of the Byzantine period lined with shops which are divided into residential and business quarters and the undoubted existence of colonnaded main streets in the other larger towns certainly suggests the presence of shops there too. There are some isolated indications, such as the reference to an establishment in Hermopolis immediately recognisable as a basket-weaving shop.[28] An inhabitant of Oxyrhynchus registered, in 222, a vegetable-seller's shop in Broad Street which he held on lease from the government.[29] From the same town there is evidence of general stores in stock-lists and receipts, one containing jars of pickled fish, ropes, fish, mattresses, meal, wrought iron, mats, couch legs, purple, fishbaskets and wicks, another drugs, pitch, sauce, purple, papyrus, cedar-oil, boxes, a pole and a ball.[30] Sale of goods and services might also be conducted on something like a 'door-to-door' basis. The list of market-taxes from Oxyrhynchus, mentioned above, refers to a levy on 'those who sell throughout the city'. Itinerant trade is perhaps also suggested in a reference to the presence of a bookseller in a small village in the Fayum.[31]

There was a wide range of services available in the sizeable towns and villages – teachers, lawyers, scribes, and shorthand-writers, donkey-drivers, carpenters, builders, smiths and plumbers, wet-nurses, prostitutes, hairdressers, cooks, mouse-catchers and entertainers are all found. Many such people often travelled in order to sell their services. The Zenon papyri have frequent allusions to travelling construction workers of various kinds. Glazing for three sets of public baths in the town of Panopolis was provided, in 253, by three glass-workers from Coptos.[32] A letter from Oxyrhynchus of the late third or early fourth century asks a correspondent to send out a cobbler and a goldsmith; another indicates the possibility of getting a fuller to make a house-call.[33] Many of the services which were available in the towns and villages would not have kept their purveyors alive if they had not been willing to travel about in their local area.

But there is more to it than that, for the manufacture of all goods did not take place in the market. In some towns there is evidence for the traditional concentration of groups of artisans in particular quarters – at Oxyrhynchus there was the Goose-herds' Quarter, the Shepherds' Quarter, the Cobblers' Market Quarter and at Thebes a whole suburb was associated with the pottery industry – although it may have eventually become more diluted. Manufacture of most commodities for local consumption probably took place in small artisans' workshops, which will as often as not have also been their retail outlets and their places of residence, scattered through the towns, the labour supplied by a handful of paid workers, apprentices and slaves.

There are other kinds of manufacturing establishments, too. Bakehouses might be in or near a granary, as the piles of bread discovered in one of the Karanis granaries suggests. The brewery and wool-factory of Apollonius at Philadelphia have already been mentioned. Oxyrhynchus has yielded evidence of a copying-house and the fees paid for the production of books, which may have been retailed or sold through booksellers who are also found in the town.[34] Pottery manufacture on a large scale is found in one of the villages of the Oxyrhynchite Nome, Senepta,

62 Bread from Karanis.
Piles of flat loaves of bread found in a granary on the north side of the hill.

63 Brickmaking c. 1900.
A photograph taken by A.S.Hunt, an early pioneer of papyrology, illustrates a technique of making bricks from mud and straw which can hardly have changed at all since antiquity.

in the middle of the third century. Here, a potter named Paesis leased a pottery with its store-rooms, kiln, wheel and other equipment to make, with the labour of assistant potters, underlings and stokers provided by himself, a total of more than 15,000 wine-jars a year.[35] It is hardly surprising that manufacture on this scale should take place outside the nome-capital when the raw materials and the finished articles were so closely tied in with the agricultural economy.

The weaving industry also had a long and vital tradition in the villages, but master-weavers were found in the towns too. One such was Tryphon of Oxyrhynchus in the early first century, whose family practised the trade for five generations, and who had several apprentices and paid employees. One of the difficulties which might occasionally face such an employer is strikingly illustrated in a letter of the third century:

'I had a meeting with Skoru respecting the workshops and he said "Either give me twelve artabae or take twelve artabae", as I told you in a previous letter; but now he said to me "We have given the workmen one and a half times as much". I accordingly would not make an agreement with him about this before telling you. For he said that the workmen had not agreed even on these terms since the value of the corn is small.'[36]

Sometimes the conditions of work were unequivocally spelled out in a contract:

'Tesenouphis and Stotoetis . . . acknowledge to Tesenouphis son of Horus . . . that they have from him the price of 65,000 bricks and they agree of necessity to remain with Tesenouphis making brick in the brickyard of the aforementioned village from the present day, without lingering or being absent for a day from their work in making bricks for Tesenouphis.'[37]

The training of workers in the skilled crafts was largely hereditary, as one would expect in a society of this kind – Tryphon, the weaver of Oxyrhynchus, will have learned his trade with his father. Alternatively a boy or girl of thirteen, free or slave, might be bound by a contract in a traditional system of apprenticeship to a skilled craftsman outside the family in one of number of trades – weaving, building, smithing, embroidery, shorthand-writing, flute-playing and so on. The examples which best illustrate the stipulations of such contracts come from the Roman and Byzantine periods:

'Panechotes through his friend Gemellus to Apollonius, writer of shorthand, greeting. I have placed with you my slave Chaerammon to be taught the signs which your son Dionysius knows, for a period of two years dating from the present month at a salary agreed upon between us of one hundred and twenty silver drachmae, not including feast days; of which sum you have received the first instalment amounting to forty drachmae and you will receive the second instalment consisting of forty drachmae when the boy has learnt the whole system, and the third you will receive at the end of the period when the boy writes fluently in every respect and reads faultlessly, viz. the remaining forty drachmae. If you make him perfect within the period, I will not wait for the aforesaid limit; but it is not lawful for me to take the boy away before the end of the period, and he shall remain with you after the expiration of it for as many days or months as he may have done no work.'[38]

The most important feature of the way in which trade, industry and commerce were organised in Egypt was the existence of numerous guilds and associations.

64 Clothing. A selection of woven linen garments. These were discovered by Grenfell and Hunt during their excavations in the villages of the southern Fayum in 1895–6 and 1898–9 on behalf of the Egypt Exploration Fund.

The nature and origins of such bodies may have something to do with the religious associations attached to temples in Pharaonic Egypt, but the Greek influence in the Ptolemaic period infused the characteristics of the traditional Greek institutions. These associations were in no sense like modern trade unions. To begin with, in Marxist terminology, they were composed of the owners of the means of production, not of the workers and in this respect they bore rather more resemblance to medieval guilds. Secondly, although they were certainly concerned to define and protect the economic interests of their members, social activities and obligations played an equally important role. Thus, their annual subscriptions financed regular banquets, celebrations of special occasions and corporate funeral arrangements for deceased members. Both these characteristics are illustrated in an ordinance of the guild of salt-merchants of the village of Tebtunis in the Fayum:

'The undersigned men, salt merchants of Tebtunis, meeting together have decided by common consent to elect one of their number, a good man Apunchis, son of Orseus, both supervisor and collector of public taxes for the coming year . . . and that all alike shall sell salt in the aforesaid village of Tebtunis, and that Orseus alone has obtained by lot the sole right to sell gypsum in the aforesaid village of Tebtunis and in the adjacent villages, for which he shall pay, apart from the share of the public taxes which falls to him an additional sixty-six drachmae in silver. And that Harmiusis . . . has obtained by lot the sole right to sell salt and gypsum in the village of Tristomou also called Boukolou, for which he shall contribute, apart from the share of the public taxes which falls to him, five additional drachmae in silver; upon condition that they shall sell the good salt at the rate of two and a

65 Painted wooden tablet. From the Roman period cemetery at Hawara, discovered lying at the head of a female mummy covered with a cloth on which are laid out miniature versions of equipment used by women: mirrors, perfume flasks, jewellery boxes. The picture is of a draped man, perhaps a tailor, seated on a chair holding scissors; in the wall behind him is a cupboard containing rows of rolls. On the reverse of the board is a painting of a woman giving birth on a birthing stool, suggesting that the mummy is a young woman who died in childbirth.

half obols, the light salt at two obols, and the lighter salt at one and a half obols, by our measure or that of the warehouse. And if anyone shall sell at a lower price than these, let him be fined eight drachmae in silver for the common fund and the same for the public treasury ... And if anyone shall bring in gypsum and shall intend to sell it outside, it must be left on the premises of Orseus until he takes it outside and sells. It is a condition that they shall drink regularly on the 25th of each month each one a chous of beer ... But if anyone is in default and fails to satisfy any of the public obligations, or any of the claims that shall be made against him, it shall be permissible for the same Apunchis to arrest him in the main street or in his house or in the field, and to hand him over as aforesaid.'[39]

The last clause is undoubtedly connected with the fact that a guild could be held corporately liable for default in tax-payment by one of its members.

Trade guilds thus functioned, at least partially, somewhat like cartels and their continuing importance is evident right through to the end of the Byzantine period. It is probable the stimulus to their formation and growth came from the natural desire of people engaged in the same trade to associate themselves for mutual benefit, but, at the same time, the government had good reason to encourage and support them since they were very useful as instruments of economic and fiscal control. Thus, in the Ptolemaic period the concession to sell at fixed prices goods produced under royal ownership was contracted out to the guilds, and their dealings in goods which were not royal property could also be monitored:

66 Stela of a Cretan dream-interpreter. The Cretan was plying his trade on the avenue leading to the Serapeum at Memphis *c.* 200 BC. The stela portrays a Greek pediment, Egyptian pilasters and two caryatids. The horned altar in front of the Apis bull is of Syrian origin and is found in both Greek and Egyptian contexts.

'Take care also that goods offered for sale are not sold at a higher price than those prescribed. All those which do not have fixed prices and for which the dealers may fix any price they wish, you must also inspect carefully, and after fixing a reasonable profit for the goods that are being sold, you must compel the . . . to dispose of them',

wrote a Ptolemaic financial official to a subordinate in the late third century BC.[40]

In the Roman and Byzantine periods when the trade associations grew and multiplied they were still used in the few remaining government controlled manufactures but they also played an important role, under increasingly stringent government direction, in the movement and transport of goods, particularly the provision of supplies for the army, and as the means by which the central authority ensured supplies of vital foodstuffs and other commodities in their towns at reasonable prices. Thus, the fact that in the fourth century guilds of retailers were obliged to make sworn declarations to local officials of the value of goods in stock probably indicates a government mechanism for ascertaining local market prices.[41] Occasionally, if government impositions were inconvenient, the members of a guild might try to shift the burden on to someone else:

'To Aurelius Dioscorus, president of the council of the glorious and most glorious city of the Oxyrhynchites from Aurelius Timotheus. Since the donkey-sellers of the same city have harassed me without justification concerning delegation of the delivery of two donkeys to the most perfect master of the private account on the ground that I am engaging in their trade, I accordingly declare . . . that I have never practised their trade nor do I do so.'[42]

Such associations clearly found that privileges which they had jealously guarded in periods of prosperity might, in harder times, turn out to be burdensome obligations.

Similar features are present in the organisation of finance, which was also of considerable importance to successive governments. Much is obscure about the organisation of royal and private banks in the Ptolemaic period but even the right to engage in the private sphere was a concession controlled by the government and the same sort of general restrictions probably also prevailed in later periods. The three most important functions of banks were first, to assist in the collection of taxes and state revenues, second to take money on deposit from individuals and to pay it out on order, and third, to exchange currency at officially determined rates, to which was added a fixed service charge. Service charges were probably the main source of income for bankers and the fact that the supervision of banks, at least in the Roman period, was imposed as a compulsory public service may well indicate that the opportunities for enrichment were not very great.

One thing which banks did not regularly do was to make loans at interest. Money-lending was a prominent feature of the economy of Egypt at all periods but, apart from a small proportion of official government loans, it was conducted on private initiative and by private contract, which was, of course legally enforceable. But the formation of money-lending associations is known from the Roman period:

'Whereas Chaeremon, on the request of Artemidorus and Hermione had himself named with them in two loans from Artemidorus son of Heraclides, president of the club, so that

67 Mummy portrait. Unusually, there are two versions
of the portrait, one on either side of the board. On the right,
the subject is portrayed with Egyptian hairstyle, clothing
and jewellery. On the left, the added hairpiece and cloak
make her look more Roman. *c.* AD 100.

they might borrow up to x drachmae in bronze in accordance with the agreement made on the same day before the same tribunal, Artemidorus and Hermione acknowledge that Chaeremon received absolutely nothing of the above mentioned sum, but that they have used the whole amount for their own private needs, and that they shall pay it back to Artemidorus in the prescribed instalments according to the terms of the aforesaid agreement, and they shall release Chaeremon from his agreement and from this time on shall in every way protect him from arrest or exaction in regard to the loan. This they shall do without any dispute. If not, they shall be liable to arrest and detention until they pay whatever they owe on the two loans with a penalty of 50 per cent and the legal interest as well as damages. Chaeremon shall have the right of exaction from both, being mutually liable for payment, or from whichever one he chooses and from all their property as if legal judgement had been given, whatever bonds they may plead of any kind being invalid.'[43]

Predictably, it was this kind of arrangement, along with contracts of sale in very similar terms, which gave rise to most private disputes. Interest rates on cash loans were legally controlled – a maximum of 12 per cent in the Roman period – but were sometimes exceeded notwithstanding.

The volume of money which changed hands in such transactions was quite considerable even if individual amounts were small, because very large numbers of people at all levels of society were involved both as lenders and borrowers. A ledger from the public record-office of the small village of Tebtunis in the Fayum contains abstracts of 113 contracts of cash loans over a period of sixteen months in AD 45–7, in 97 of which the amount is recorded. In 33 cases the amount involved was between 100 and 120 drachmas and the remainder cover a range from 16 to 832 drachmas.[44]

68 **Shoes**. A variety of embroidered footwear from the Fayum.

Even if this period was, for some reason (such as a year or two of low fertility) untypical, it nevertheless shows that the cash was available for circulation in the village and that it was the prime lubricant in the small-scale local economy, flowing especially, but not exclusively, from metropolis to village. The formulaic phrase of the loan contract, 'from hand to hand from the house,' reveals the simplest kind of mechanism for ensuring liquidity – personal transaction in a domestic context – and whilst money might sometimes have been borrowed for speculation, there is no doubt that in most cases the loan served simply as a means to tide a family over a bad patch. The papers of Tryphon, the weaver of Oxyrhynchus, for instance, reveal that he was involved in money-lending on a small scale on five occasions, twice as a lender (in 37 and 57) and three times as a borrower (in 55 and 59); on all the latter occasions his debts were duly settled.[45] But if a debtor defaulted he could lose his property or even his freedom.

Straight cash loans were not the only way of raising capital. There was also a variety of types of mortgage agreements which could be made but these were naturally not available to anyone who was temporarily or permanently short of money, for a borrower needed property against which a loan or mortgage could be secured. Failing this, a farmer might sell a standing crop before harvest to a speculator, with crossed fingers; a skilled or unskilled worker might pledge his or her labour by contract for a capital sum which would be deducted from wages. People

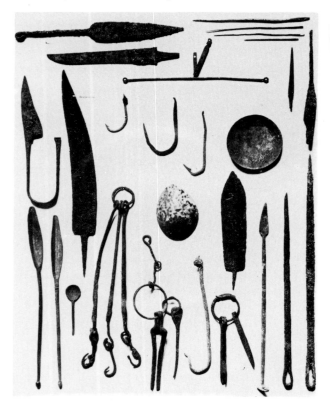

69 Metal objects from the Fayum. The assortment includes fish-hooks, knives, dishes, spoons and writing styli.

with more meagre resources could resort to the time-honoured device of pawning their goods. Pawnbrokers' accounts of the Roman period show that the customers were largely women who pawned their clothing, kitchen-ware or jewellery for small sums and redeemed them by repaying the capital with 12 per cent interest.[46]

For the poorer people, as always, life consisted largely of the effort to make ends meet. Not until the flowering of Christianity in the Byzantine period was there any attempt to establish charitable donations for the relief of the poor and then, inevitably, these donations were open to malversation for political ends. A benefaction by a wealthy citizen of Oxyrhynchus in about 200 was directed specifically at supporting the upper-class youths of the Greek citizenry and ensuring the ability of villagers in the region to perform their compulsory public services.[47] For those unfortunates who could not make ends meet, the options were limited. When all else had failed a man could only run away to try his luck elsewhere or resort to theft or brigandage, leaving his family or associates to enter his name officially on the register of 'those who had fled' (*anakechōrēkotes*), so that they would not be liable for his tax-payments. But the dependants he had abandoned might well face destitution, starvation or slavery.

At the other end of the scale, the wealthy men whose landholdings have already been discussed also played an important role in trade and commerce, both in the local economy and in a wider context. For the Ptolemaic period, Apollonius might again serve as an example, although the scale of his wealth was certainly quite untypical. His manufacturing concerns provided employment in Philadelphia for artisans, just as his land provided employment for agriculturalists and his other property for builders and technicians. There is a striking similarity to be found, eight centuries later, in the large estates of the Apiones of Oxyrhynchus which were by no means economically self-sufficient. They employed independent craftsmen – builders, brickmakers, carpenters, mechanics for irrigation machinery – on a casual basis, purchased pots from local potters and mats and ropes from a nearby monastery.

However great the clear profits of such men might be after overheads, they had inevitably put something back into the rural context which supplied their wealth. Even a fairly modest estate of perhaps sixty arourae in the early Roman period might require expenditure of the order of 2,500 drachmas per month on labour – a sum which would keep three hundred active working men alive at subsistence level for the month. At the highest level of the social ladder of the metropolis, a councillor of Oxyrhynchus in the third century was able to leave in his will property valued at 200,000 drachmas.[48] This was probably twice the qualification required for membership of the council, but all such members had to be able to pay, even if they borrowed to do so, an entrance-fee of 10,000 drachmas, a sum which would probably support a dozen families for a year.

On the negative side, it might be observed that a disproportionate amount of the wealth of such people was either drained off in a non-productive manner – erecting buildings to beautify their towns and give the benefactors prestige, financing social and professional mobility in the form of a public career in Alexandria, Rome or Constantinople; or worse, it was available for loans to the struggling villagers who became increasingly entangled in the toils of debts which they could only redeem

70   **Brushes manufactured from reeds and papyrus stalks.**

by sacrificing control of their property and ultimately their independence. Such a form of exploitation inevitably shocks modern sensibilities, but exploitation of the poor by the rich is not exclusive to Egypt in particular or the ancient world in general and it is questionable whether the day-to-day lives of the majority of the poor were radically affected by such developments. Perhaps more plausible is the notion that, in the long term, the rich became fewer and richer and the poor more numerous.

Certainly, the role played by the rich in Egypt's economy extended beyond their own regions and beyond the borders of Egypt itself. These were the people who had the means to move goods and money around on a significant scale; indeed they actually needed to do so in order to realise their profits for in many cases the local area would simply not be able to absorb what they could make available. Witness an agent of Apollonius, not very far from the home base in Philadelphia, using an opportunity to make money for his employer:

'Sosos to Zenon, greeting. I received your letter in which you asked me to put aside the hundred artabae of wheat which we have on board and to sell the rest at the highest price we can get . . . We sold the whole cargo of wheat in the harbour over against Aphroditopolis, a total of 241 artabae at seven artabae for each gold stater (=twenty drachmas). And we gave the purchasers three artabae extra on every hundred to balance the incidental expenses.'[49]

Alternatively, such men might merely transport produce or artefacts from one estate to another, they might buy speciality products like the distinctively woven textiles of a distant region and in doing so they ensured the livelihood of the owners and sailors who plied their numerous small craft up and down the river. Such facilities helped bring goods (especially artistic products and glassware) of Alexandrian manufacture to all parts of the valley and beyond Egypt's southern border and, in a more routine manner, they could be used by the more humble for a trip to Alexandria, sending purchases home and receiving parcels from their families:

'I received through Heraclas the boxes with the books, as you write, and the half-chous jar of oil which Nicanor writes that he has sent. You will receive through Origas two wristbands, one scarlet and one purple . . . write and acknowledge their receipt. If I can buy a cloak for you privately I will send it at once, if not I will have it made for you at home.'[50]

71 Palestrina mosaic (detail). The great variety of boats on the river includes skiffs, cargo boats, a warship and a hunting ship. The secular buildings include a tower-house with a dovecote (top right) and a crude rustic hut, with an agricultural labourer to the left. In the foreground is a group of picnickers under a trellis.

The enormous potential of the river as a natural artery of large-scale trade was exploited at all times but to its best advantage in the Roman period, with varying degrees of government control and private initiative. Much of this trade was in the hands of Alexandrian merchants who will certainly have worked both in their private capacity and under government contract as they did in shipping the grain tribute from Alexandria to Rome or Constantinople.[51] Thus the public and private sectors dovetailed and interlocked – individuals could take advantage of the facilities afforded and developed by the state to enrich themselves and in doing so they further augmented the state coffers with the taxes and duties which they paid. And the volume of trade was enormous – Pliny the Elder records fifty million sesterces' worth of trade with India and Arabia in the first century.[52] Asia Minor and the Aegean were traditional trading areas too. In the third century BC the agents of Apollonius were trading on his behalf in Southern Asia Minor, Cyprus and the Levant. One of his business documents records the duties on a wide variety of goods which he imported by sea in 259 BC: grape syrup, nuts, Chian and Thasian wine, Rhodian, Attic and Lycian honey, cheese, tuna fish, mullet, wild boar, venison and goat – all helped to provide a rich variety of delicacies at the table of man who could well afford to recreate the lifestyle of a Greek aristocrat in a small village in the middle of the Fayum.[53] Purchase of slaves on the island of Rhodes is recorded in the Roman period and Spanish copper, Gallic soap and Rhodian wine are still found in Egypt in the Byzantine period.[54]

It is perhaps inevitable that our documentation should bias the picture in favour of the wealthier and more influential, for it is their transactions which tend to find their way into the written record, whilst the struggles of the far greater numbers who lived on or near the breadline go unremarked. It is not difficult to see how, in general terms, the prosperity of the former depended upon their exploitation of the latter. A simple calculation to show that the resources of Egypt were sufficient to maintain its population at subsistence level may be misleading unless we emphasise the fact that the demographic and social patterns of that population were dictated, to a large extent, by the pattern of exploitation and determined in accordance with the distribution of the economic resources available to it.[55] But with that proviso duly made, the sophistication and complexity of the economic structure of Egyptian society in this millennium is still a striking fact. Even if its large-scale benefits were in general available only to the elite minority, it is still tempting to suggest that it compares very favourably with any historical period prior to the late nineteenth century.

72 Stela of Isidorus. One of a group of distinctive marble stelae from Terenuthis in the delta, but of Alexandrian manufacture, showing a mixture of Greek and Egyptian characteristics (a thyrsos staff and an *atef* crown). Isidorus, whose death at the age of 25 is recorded, was perhaps here identified with Osiris-Dionysus.

5

Greeks and Egyptians

Class and Status

The Egyptian social order before the coming of the Greeks appears to have been closely tied to function. Thus, the social identity of groups of administrators, priests and soldiers is clear; and further down the scale that of free artisans and traders, of serfs and slaves. But outside this functional classification there were also foreigners who were, of course, culturally and linguistically distinct from the native Egyptians. We can point to the existence of the Greek trading post at Naukratis, to Carian Greeks known in Memphis during the Persian occupation and, in the same period, to a Jewish military colony at Elephantine near the southern frontier, which has left records of its presence in the form of a number of Aramaic papyri. These documents reveal that the colonists firmly preserved their ancestral identity but at the same time were by no means isolated from contact with their Egyptian surroundings – some intermarried, Egyptian shrines are in evidence at Elephantine, they could swear oaths by the local native deity.[1]

The coming of the Greeks created, in effect, a social revolution, overlaying Egyptian society with a new dominant elite. Through the first century of Ptolemaic rule Greek immigration continued on a large scale – from mainland Greece, Macedonia, Thrace, the Aegean islands, the Greek cities of Asia Minor – a heavy concentration in Alexandria, but also penetrating all parts of the Nile valley. In their wake came others too, even the odd Roman, but most conspicuously, in the middle of the second century BC, great numbers of Jews. Numerically, of course, the Egyptians remained far superior to the aggregate of all these immigrants, but the political, economic and social dominance of the Greeks had far-reaching effects. It naturally tended to draw upwards the more ambitious Egyptians, and it did so without eradicating the Egyptian social and cultural patterns. It is sometimes difficult to catch more than a passing glimpse of these since our evidence is heavily skewed in favour of the Greek-speaking elite, but there can be no doubt of their importance amongst the native population. The truth of this for the whole of our period is guaranteed by their prominent re-emergence in Coptic Christianity at the end of it.

The clearest manifestations of the dominance of Hellenism – whose legacy stretched far beyond the Arab conquest, even into the nineteenth century – are cultural and linguistic. The impact of a more pervasive literacy was radical and profound. Access to privilege was provided through social and political institutions and economic distinctions were encouraged as well. But Egyptian society was not simply divided along economic lines between rich and poor – there were certainly some wealthy Egyptians and some poor Greeks. The Greek/Egyptian dichotomy might appear very stark in some spheres and some periods but in others boundaries are less rigid. We have seen that Dionysius son of Kephalas was an Egyptian who took a Greek name and could write both Greek and demotic; so could the Egyptian priest Hor of Sebennytos.[2] This was a society in which many people were bilingual, no less so seven hundred years later, when we find the poet and lawyer Dioscorus of Aphrodite writing amateurish poems in Greek, compiling a Greek/Coptic literary glossary and operating in his legal activities in both languages. Just as telling, in a different way and much earlier, is the example of a certain Dryton, son of Pamphilus, a Greek of Ptolemais in the second century BC, married to a woman whose ancestry for three generations back carried both Greek and Egyptian names.[3] In the Ptolemaic period Egyptians who wanted to infiltrate the higher echelons of the bureaucracy, as they were able to do from the second century BC onwards, had to hellenise.

The Jewish population was also an important element in society. The trickle of Jewish immigrants in the third century BC swelled significantly in the reign of Ptolemy VI Philometor both as a result of the 'philo-Semitism' of the king and of the efflux of various elements from Judaea after the revolt of Judas Maccabaeus. One of these exiles, Onias, was put in command of a Jewish military unit in the service of the king and given a grant of land in the Heliopolite Nome on which to settle the soldiers and build a temple. Other groups of Jewish immigrants settled in many of the towns and villages of the valley and the delta, from Elephantine to Alexandria, leaving evidence of their presence in the existence of synagogues, 'Jewish streets' and distinctive names. These are indications of the corporate identity and a letter from the first half of the first century BC carries a sinister recognition of the distinction in the phrase 'You know that they loathe the Jews'.[4] The coherence of the Jewish community will have been reinforced through the Ptolemaic and early Roman periods by the privilege which they enjoyed of practising their ancestral religion. This was considerably undermined after the Jewish revolt in Judaea (AD 66–73), when the emperor Vespasian diverted into the imperial coffers the half-shekel tax which every Jew had previously paid annually to the temple at Jerusalem.

The Jews in the towns of the valley appear in all walks of life, as soldiers, farmers, artisans, labourers, traders and were thus necessarily in close and constant contact with their Greek and Egyptian neighbours. One sign of the social and economic interaction is the fact that there are numerous examples of Jews choosing

73   The Antinoite charioteers. This illustration from a codex, which is probably to be dated after the middle of the fifth century AD, is in a hellenistic style which contrasts sharply with 'Coptic' art of the Christian period. It is a very early example of book-decoration, though the text which it accompanies is lost but for a few letters. It shows five charioteers (and parts of a sixth), perhaps standing under an arcade. They may represent the rival factions in the hippodrome.

to use Greek law and Greek courts, despite the availability of their own independent and protected Jewish legal institutions.[5] The degree of cultural assimilation of individuals will have varied, much as it does in modern Europe and North America, but Greek or hellenised names are very common and the use of the Greek language was practically universal until the Byzantine period, even amongst the survivors of the unsuccessful revolt of AD 115–7.

There is less evidence for the penetration of Greek or Jewish elements into Egyptian society. Time and time again we are struck by the way in which our documents emphasise the dominant few and time and time again we need to remind ourselves of the many who make little impression at the higher social levels. The corporate social identity of the Egyptians as such tends to be expressed institutionally in the native religious cults, whose political and economic power was severely curtailed by the Ptolemies (and even more by the Romans). The Greeks created their own identifications of Egyptian gods, but there is a little evidence in the Ptolemaic period for Greek-named priests in Egyptian cult.[6]

On the more strictly secular side, there are numerous Ptolemaic contracts (marriage, division or sale of property and the like) in demotic, or a mixture of Greek and demotic which suggest adaptation of Egyptians to the use of Greek rather than the reverse.[7] But there are some striking counter-examples. A relieved mother writes to her son in the second century BC: 'I was delighted for you and myself when I heard that you are learning Egyptian writing, since now, at least, when you return to the city you will go to the purge-doctor to teach the apprentices and will have a means of support until your old age.'[8] Or again, one Greek to another: 'I decided to describe the dream to you so that you may know how the gods have knowledge of you; and I have written it below in Egyptian so that you may know the exact details. When I was about to go to bed I wrote two letters, one about Taychis, the daughter of Thermouthis and the other about Teteimouthis, the daughter of Taues and Ptolemaeus.'[9] It is notable that both medicine and dream-interpretations are common subjects in demotic writings but the second text also gives us a clue to one feature of intermarriage. Taues was clearly an Egyptian woman, married to a Greek, Ptolemaeus, but the name of the daughter is Egyptian, not Greek. A dedicatory inscription from the late third century BC reveals two Greek ladies from Cyrene, Eirene and Theoxena, daughters of Demetrius and an Egyptian mother, taking Egyptian names as well, Nephersouchos and Thaues.[10] In fact, such patterns of nomenclature are amongst the clearest signs of Egyptian influence on Greeks in the ordinary social milieu and the same effects can be also observed in the Egyptian names taken by Jews of the Nile valley in the Ptolemaic period.

Distinctions of status depended on, or were reinforced by, a whole array of legal and social institutions and the evolution of Egyptian society can be analysed in terms of their modification or breakdown and replacement. As far as Greek institutions are concerned, the most emphatic examples, outside Alexandria, are to be found in the so-called Greek cities: Naukratis, originally a seventh-century trading colony founded from Ionian Miletus, Ptolemais in Upper Egypt, founded under Ptolemy I Soter and later Antinoopolis, created by the emperor Hadrian in 130, are all corporate expressions of the civic prestige, status and privilege of the

Greeks and contrast sharply, especially in the Ptolemaic period, with the other substantial towns of the valley (whose populations also contained, of course, a very important Greek element).

Citizenship of the Greek cities was carefully controlled and limited. The citizen body was divided along traditional Greek lines into tribes and local units (demes), with distinctively Greek names. They had citizen assemblies, councils, magistrates and other civic institutions such as gymnasia, although these did not betoken any real degree of democratic government. The general ambience in such places is well illustrated by a decree from Ptolemais in which the presidents of the council admit someone to citizenship, enroll him in a tribe and deme and grant him a crown and maintenance at the public expense, a fine example of the invariable practice of providing public welfare only for those who did not need it.[11] These Greek cities preserved their distinctiveness in the first two centuries of Roman rule. Citizens of Antinoopolis, amongst other privileges, were exempted from performing public services elsewhere but from the start they were allowed to intermarry with Egyptians, which citizens of Naukratis were not. The distinctions were gradually being eroded and by the beginning of the third century the nome-capitals too boasted their own versions of civic institutions of the Greek type.[12]

This process of change had accelerated under Augustus with a clearer definition of the Greeks in the nome-capitals, even though many will have been descendants of mixed Greek/Egyptian marriages in the Ptolemaic period. They were allowed magistracies and gymnasia (essentially private institutions, except in the Greek

74 Antinoopolis. Drawing of the triumphal arch by members of the Napoleonic expedition to Egypt.

cities in the Ptolemaic period, but now made public); initiation procedures for the young men (ephebes); lower rates of poll-tax, a privilege enjoyed to a lesser degree by other citizens of the nome-capitals in comparison to villagers; Elders' Clubs (*gerousiai*) providing free maintenance as a pension, and associations of various kinds. All in all, a system of civic privilege and obligation tied to birth and wealth – a genuine and far-reaching innovation of the Roman period. The right to enter this order depended on the ability to show Greek ancestry on both maternal and paternal sides, based on lists of original members of this gymnasial class drawn up in AD 4/5. The metropolite citizens were already a privileged group in comparison to villagers, the gymnasial class was a more exclusive and even more privileged sub-group.

All this points to a greater degree of social direction and control in the Roman period and it was reinforced in all sorts of ways. Thus, the emperor Caracalla in 215:

'All Egyptians in Alexandria, especially countryfolk who have fled from other parts and can easily be detected, are by all manner of means to be expelled, with the exception, however, of pig-dealers and riverboatmen and the men who bring down reeds for heating the baths. But expel all others, as by the numbers of their kind and their uselessness they are disturbing the city… For genuine Egyptians can easily be recognised among the linen-weavers by their speech, which proves them to have assumed the appearance and dress of another class; moreover in their mode of life, their far from civilised manners reveal them to be Egyptian countryfolk.'[13]

Such sentiments were shared by the more humble: 'Perhaps you will think, brother,' remarks a writer of the third century apologetically, 'that I am some kind of a barbarian or an inhuman Egyptian,'[14] Distinctions will have been reinforced by the fact that there certainly were many Egyptians who remained unable to speak Greek. In a long and fascinating legal wrangle between a daughter and father in 186

75 Statue from Karanis. The black basalt sculpture, dating to *c.* AD 50, was found in an area to the west of the southern temple. It is a good example of the Egyptian style of statuary of this period and may be intended to represent a local priest or dignitary. There are indications that the piece is unfinished.

a precedent was cited in which, fifty years earlier, an official settled a disputed claim of the rights of a father in Egyptian law over his daughter quite simply: '"In accordance with the decision of his highness Titianus (a prefect), they shall find out from the woman," and he ordered that she should be asked through an interpreter what was her choice.'[15] It is very interesting to observe that although the Romans continued to maintain and reinforce social distinctions between Greeks, Egyptians and Jews, for instance, what they called 'Egyptian law' in circumstances like those described comprised the heterogeneous mass of pre-existing Greek, Jewish and Egyptian law and custom – in fact everything that was not Roman law.

The advent of the latter, predicated upon the spread of Roman citizenship, also profoundly affected Egyptian society. Citizenship was granted to the privileged group of veteran soldiers on discharge (but to their children only if both parents had the status), and to other Egyptians, though far from open-handedly, as Pliny the Younger attests in a letter to the emperor Trajan about a grant of citizenship for a therapist named Harpocras:

'I was advised by people more experienced than I am that, since he is an Egyptian, I should first have obtained for him Alexandrian citizenship, then Roman. Not realising that there was any difference between Egyptians and other aliens, I contented myself with writing to you only that he was a freedman of an alien woman and that his patron had died some time ago.'[16]

Once obtained, the Roman citizenship carried very considerable legal and fiscal privileges, gave its holder the right and obligation to follow Roman legal practices in contracts, wills, marriages, rights over property and practices of guardianship of those not fully empowered to act in law (women, unless exempted, and men under twenty-five). It did not, however, extinguish the rights and obligations of the new Roman citizen to the local community from which he originated.

The social, legal and fiscal implications of all these distinctions between Romans, Alexandrians, gymnasials, metropolites and villagers are nowhere illustrated with more force than in parts of the Code of Regulations of the emperors' Special Account, as it existed in the middle of the second century – the clearest possible demonstration of the way in which law and practice shaped and controlled the social structure:

'If to a Roman will is added a clause saying "whatever bequests I make in Greek codicils shall be valid", it is not admissible, for a Roman is not permitted to make a Greek will.

The property of freed slaves of metropolites who die childless and intestate is inherited by their former owners or the owners' sons, if there are any and they make legal claim, but not by their daughters or anyone else; over them the Special Account takes precedence.

A metropolite cannot bequeath to his freed slaves more than five hundred drachmae or an allowance of five drachmae a month.

Inheritances left in trust by Greeks of the gymnasial class to Romans or by Romans to Greeks were confiscated by the deified Vespasian; nevertheless those acknowledging the trust have received half.

Romans are not permitted to marry their sisters or their aunts, but marriage with their brothers' daughters has been allowed. Pardalas, indeed, when a brother married a sister, confiscated the property.

Children of a metropolite mother and an Egyptian father remain Egyptian, but they can inherit from both parents.

Children of a Roman man or woman married to a metropolite or an Egyptian assume the lower status.

Children of Egyptians falsely claiming Roman citizenship in writing for their deceased father forfeit a quarter of their property.'[17]

As far as Roman citizenship was concerned such privileges were meaningful only until 212, when the emperor Caracalla granted this status to almost all the inhabitants of the empire. Individuals marked their newly acquired citizenship by adding the Roman element 'Aurelius', the imperial family name, to their nomenclature. The status distinctions already embedded in the social structure before the spread of Roman citizenship again became overtly prominent, along with another important phenomenon clearly implicit in principle in the Regulations of the Special Account and elsewhere. This was the rather vague notion of a division between upper and lower classes (*honestiores* and *humiliores*). They cannot be precisely and exhaustively catalogued, though it is obvious where one would put senators, equestrians or councillors on the one hand and peasants and artisans on the other. Philo noted the difference in treatment of Alexandrians and Egyptians when they were punished:

'There are differences between the scourges used in the city, and these differences are regulated by the social standing of the persons to be beaten. The Egyptians actually are scourged with a different kind of lash and by a different set of people, the Alexandrians with a flat blade, and the persons who wield them are also Alexandrians.'[18]

The prominence of the distinction throughout the later Roman and the Byzantine period makes explicit the fundamental principle of according greater social and legal privilege to those of higher status and, in general, defining that status in terms of birth and wealth.

However, the erosion of civic prestige in the later third century and the consequent decline of the local magisterial classes does have important effects on the

76 **Papyrus letter**. This papyrus of the first century AD from Oxyrhynchus contains an indecent proposal from two men named Apion and Epimas to a boy called Epaphroditus. A crude drawing in the margin makes their intentions explicit.

social structure in the Byzantine period. Social status is more overtly tied to functions of a rather different kind, sharpened by the more emphatic gulf between rich and poor. Administrators and bureaucrats, soldiers, clergy, great landowners and local magnates, tenant-farmers all seem more coherently defined as status groups. Tendencies towards enforced inheritance of function and status are more explicit. But this does not necessarily mean that the social structure was immobile and ossified; there is much evidence of movement which suggests that the restrictive measures in the law codes do not truly represent the reality on the ground.

Many of these elements can be traced in embryo in the earlier Roman period. But one influence which was emphatically new and important was the emergence of the Church and Christianity as a social force. Its effects can be seen in several interconnected developments. The increasing use of the Coptic language – basically demotic Egyptian written in Greek characters with a few additions – from about 300 can be ascribed to the Church's need to reach the non-hellenised Egyptian population and it had the effect of re-emphasising the cultural divide and the antipathy between Greek and Egyptian, giving a new medium of expression to a stratum which had always existed and always been numerically superior. Partially co-extensive with this process is the rift between pagan and Christian and, on the whole, paganism survived longer and more vigorously among the Greeks. It also re-emphasised the identity, by antithesis, of the reviving Jewish element which turned again to using Hebrew in everyday communication. Hellenism had attracted it to a greater cosmopolitanism, but that was fading and to the Christian Church there could be nothing but indifference or hostility. Another new element is the Church's paternalism which found an outlet in a concern for the welfare of the poor, strikingly absent in earlier times, and thus a new concept of social obligation. Witness a village dignitary describing his own virtues to the monk Paphnutius:

'I have not ceased to practice hospitality to this day. No one in the village can claim to be more prompt in offering shelter to a stranger. No poor man or stranger has gone away from my courtyard empty-handed without first having been supplied with suitable victuals. I have never come across anyone destitute without giving him ample relief.'[19]

Finally, the Christian Church gave rise to new social units – the monasteries, large numbers of communal settlements, sometimes alleged to hold as many as five hundred or a thousand monks, which dominated many parts of the countryside from about the middle of the fourth century onwards, offering not only spiritual sanctuary, but also physical security and economic self-sufficiency for those who heeded the call. They were self-contained, but not by any means isolated from the villages in their vicinity, as an episode in the life of the monk Apollo shows:

'Not long afterwards two villages came into armed conflict with each other in a dispute concerning the ownership of land. When Apollo was informed of this, he went down to them at once to restore peace among them.'

Dealing with the chief protagonist, a brigand,

'Apollo said to him, "If you obey me my friend, I shall ask my master to forgive you your sins." When the brigand heard this he did not hesitate. He threw down his arms and clasped the saint's knees. Then Apollo, having become a mediator of peace, restored to each person his property.'[20]

One of the fundamental principles of monastic life was the rejection of marriage and procreation and thus, however populous the monasteries were, they stood firmly outside what was and always remained the most important cellular unit in society, the family. It is hardly surprising that their growth failed to undermine it.

The extended family was at all times in Graeco-roman Egypt a cohesive entity. Census returns show heads of households often recording parents, children, brothers and sisters and their children as living in the same house, or part of a house. The archaeological evidence for housing in the villages suggests that the occupancy and ownership of blocks of houses of modest size would be shared by a number of households living in conditions of great proximity and intimacy, probably without strict correspondence between the house-unit and the individual household. It is probably misleading to suggest a typical size since households evidently varied from as many as fifteen or twenty down to a nuclear family of two or three. The average may be about seven or eight. A declaration of 117–8 may show a household of larger than average size, but it is certainly not unusual in the structure it reveals: declarant, his wife and one son, another son of the wife, perhaps from a previous marriage, two brothers of the declarant and their wives, their two daughters and three slaves.[21] Other examples show that it was not uncommon for adults to remain living with their parents at least until the birth of their own children. Supplementation of the workforce in the domestic situation by small

77 Stela of a family group. Once considered to be a representation of the family of the emperor Antoninus Pius, *c.* AD 150, this is now regarded as a private family group, the men in which seem to be priests of Sarapis.

numbers of slaves is common, especially where a husband is no longer present.

This kind of structure has an important bearing on the devolution of property and laws which affect the family are very much concerned with rules of inheritance and control of property in the relations between parents and children, husbands and wives. A characteristic feature of Egyptian practice was the custom of dividing property between all children with little regard to sex or age. One natural result of this was a large proportion (for the ancient world) of female property-owners, another was the astonishing degree of fragmentation, which probably bore little relation to the actual patterns of residence in blocks of houses shared by a number of households. A property declaration of the year 184 records paternal inheritances of $\frac{1}{12}$ of an empty lot, $\frac{1}{12}$ of another, $\frac{43}{240}$ of a house and courtyard, $\frac{1}{6}$ of a house and courtyard, $\frac{5}{12}$ of an aroura of land, another plot of $\frac{1}{4}$ aroura, and maternal inheritances of $\frac{1}{6}$ of a house and courtyard and $1\frac{3}{8}$ arourae of land, all owned by one person![22]

Innumerable letters testify to the strength of feeling within the family and the household in Egyptian society – the examples which follow require no elaborate comment.

A wife to her husband, involved in fighting the Jewish dissidents of 115–7:

'I am terribly anxious about you because of what they say about what is happening and because of your sudden departure. I take no pleasure in food or drink but stay awake continually night and day with one worry, your safety. Only my father's care revives me and, as I hope to see you safe, I would have lain without food on New Year's Day, had not my father come and forced me to eat.'[23]

A penitent son to his mother in Karanis:

'I was ashamed to come to Karanis because I go about in filth. I wrote to you that I am naked. I beg you, mother, be reconciled to me. Well, I know what I have brought on myself. I have received a fitting lesson. I know that I have sinned. I heard from . . . who found you in the Arsinoite Nome and he has told you everything correctly. Do you know that I would rather be maimed than feel that I still owe a man an obol?'[24]

A distraught husband to his wife:

'I would have you know that ever since you left me I have been in mourning, weeping by night and lamenting by day. Since I bathed with you I have not bathed or anointed myself. You have sent me letters that could move a stone, so much have your words stirred me . . . apart from what you say and write, that "Kolobos has made me a prostitute."'[25]

A reproachful student to his father:

'Look, this is my fifth letter to you and you have not written to me except once, not even a word about your welfare, nor come to see me, though you promised me, saying "I am coming," you have not come to find out whether the teacher is looking after me or not. He himself is inquiring about you almost every day, saying "Is he not coming yet?" And I just say "Yes." . . . Come to us quickly, then, before he goes up country . . . Remember our pigeons.'[26]

A respectable matron expresses disgust to her husband at the behaviour of their daughters:

'If you want to know . . . about the harlotries of your daughters ask the priests of the Church, not me, how they leaped out saying "We want men" and how Lucra was found with her lover, making a whore of herself.'[27]

Family loyalties, as we would expect, could be undermined. A certain Chaeremon tries to exercise control over his married daughter, Dionysia, in a dispute in 186:

'Since, my lord, she continues her outrageous behaviour and insulting conduct towards me, I claim to exercise the right given to me by the law . . . of taking her away against her will from her husband's house.'[28]

A maltreated Christian wife of the fourth century complains about her husband:

'He shut up his own slaves and mine with my foster-daughters and his agent and son for seven whole days in his cellars, having insulted his slaves and my slave Zoe and half-killed them with blows, and he applied fire to my foster-daughters, having stripped them quite naked, which is contrary to the laws . . . He swore in the presence of the bishops and his own brothers, "Henceforward I will not hide all my keys from her" (he trusted his slaves but would not trust me): "I will stop and not insult her." Whereupon a marriage deed was made and after this agreement and his oaths, he again hid the keys from me . . . he kept saying, "A month hence I will take a mistress." God knows this is true.'[29]

A father disowns his children in an extraordinary virulent declaration of 569:

'Proclamation of disownment and rejection, having my mind and understanding unaffected, with true and unerring judgement, without any guile or fear or violence or compulsion or deceit, in a public place of business. And this I transmit to my parricidal children, though children in name only . . . thinking to find you helpful in all things, a comfort to my old age, submissive and obedient, and on the contrary you in your prime have set yourselves against me like rancorous things, as I learned through experience of your heartless parricidal conduct and lawless disposition, seeing that I fell grievously ill through you . . . and it is no longer lawful for you in future to call me father, inasmuch as I reject and abhor you from now to the utter end of all succeeding time as outcasts and bastards and lower than slaves . . . for ravens to devour the flesh and peck out the eyes, in this manner I debar you from receiving or giving anything on my behalf whether I am alive or dead because I have rightly and justly thus resolved.'[30]

But the inexorable litany of birth, marriage and death was, if relatively brief in span and straitened in circumstance, usually more tranquil. This is a population in which the rate of infant mortality was enormous, through disease or the dangers of childbirth (half of thirty-four infant skeletons found in a recent necropolis excavation were less than one year old);[31] in which females would normally marry at thirteen

78 Mummies. These mummies of the Roman period, complete with gilded masks, were discovered in 1911 in the cemetery at Aphroditopolis (Atfih), about 40 km south of Memphis.

or fourteen and males well before twenty; in which half the males and probably less than half the females who survived to adulthood (which can arbitrarily be set at fourteen, the age at which they became liable to pay taxes) could not expect to live beyond the age of thirty.

Contraception was unknown except for primitive and presumably ineffective prophylactics:

'Take some vetches, one for each year you wish to remain infertile, rub them in the menses when the woman is menstruating. Let her rub them in her own genitals. Take a frog and throw the vetches into its mouth that it may swallow them down, let the frog loose and let it go back to where you took it from. Take the seed of henbane, wet it in horse's milk, take the mucus of a frog and its excrements and throw them into the skin of a stag and tie it together outside with skin from a mule and bind it round you as an amulet when the moon is waning, is in a female sign of the zodiac, on the day of Saturn or Mercury.'[32]

Serial and multiple births were normal, stillbirth endemic and live birth often accounted for the mother:

'This is the grave of Arsinoe, wayfarer. Stand by and weep for her, unfortunate in all things, whose lot was hard and terrible. For I was bereaved of my mother when I was a little girl, and when the favour of my youth made me ready for a bridegroom my father married me to Phabeis and fate brought me to the end of my life in bearing my firstborn child. I had a small span of years, but great grace flowered in the beauty of my spirit. This grave hides in its bosom my chaste body but my soul has flown to the holy ones. Lament for Arsinoe.'[33]

Even live birth was no guarantee of survival for not infrequently, circumstances might dictate contraception after the event, so to speak:

'Hilarion to Alis, very many greetings . . . Know that we are still in Alexandria. Do not be anxious; if they really go home I will remain in Alexandria. I beg and entreat you, take care of the little one, and as soon as we receive our pay I will send it up to you. If by good fortune you bear a child, if it is a male, let it be, if it is a female, throw it out.'[34]

In a world in which such apparently harsh realities enforced more modest expectations than the modern reader can easily appreciate, the humdrum and the routine will have dominated personal relationships. Romance, love, sex are infrequently mentioned. The love-spell is not uncommon, but rather impersonal: exotic potions and obscure incantations are followed by the explicit request: 'make her to be sleepless to fly through the air, to love me with a most vehement love, hungry, thirsty and without sleep until she comes and joins her female member with my male member.'[35] The occasional indecent proposal in a letter is practical, not romantic. In the later period sex is conspicuous only in the Christian literature, where self-denial is proper to the chaste or celibate: a monk named Amoun 'was of noble birth and rich parents, who forced him to marry against his will . . . he persuaded the girl in the bridal chamber that they should both preserve their virginity in secret.'[36] Its temptations were an ever-present element in the battleground of the spiritual and the corporeal. A monk who had too much confidence in his own virtue is presented with an image of a beautiful woman lost in the desert, asking for shelter in his cave:

79 Incantation. From Hawara, second or third century AD. The spell, designed to attract a loved one, is rolled and tied to a crude figurine of a human. The author of the spell is Serapiacus, the son of a slave woman; the object of his love is one Ammonius.

80 Coffin of Soter. The Roman period coffin belongs to a man with Roman and Greek names. The lid of the coffin which the corpse would face is supposed to represent the vault of the sky and contains a picture of the goddess Nut in Graeco-egyptian style surrounded by the zodiacal signs.

'With so much talking she led him astray. Then she began to touch his hand and beard and neck . . . his mind seethed with evil thoughts as he calculated that the matter was already within his grasp, and that he had the opportunity and the freedom to fulfil his pleasure. He then consented inwardly and tried to unite himself with her sexually. He was frantic by now, like an excited stallion, eager to mount a mare. But suddenly she gave a loud cry and vanished from his clutches, slipping away like a shadow. And the air resounded with a great peal of laughter.'[37]

'Theon son of Origenes invites you to the wedding of his sister tomorrow, Tybi 9, at the eighth hour.'[38] The invitation is brief and formal but the feast provided for friends and relatives might be lavish and trouble might be taken to make the occasion a colourful one:

'You filled us with joy by announcing the wedding of the excellent Sarapion . . . There are not many roses here yet; on the contrary, they are in short supply, and from all the estates and from all the garland-weavers we could hardly get together the thousand that we sent you with Sarapas, even by picking the ones that ought to have been picked tomorrow. We had as much narcissus as you wanted, so instead of the 2,000 you wrote we sent 4,000.'[39]

As for the forms of matrimony, the range runs from full marriage with contractual agreement down to simple cohabitation, and illegitimacy of any offspring carried no special stigma. Marriages were certainly often arranged; the religious element is of little significance and practical considerations of wealth and property are much more important. The need to counteract fragmentation of family property through inheritance might explain the commonness of marriage between full brother and sister, though the example set in this respect by the Ptolemies must have played a part too. The general acceptability of this practice was presumably due to the fact that it did more to preserve important social and economic structures than to destroy them and this must have been a strong enough factor to overcome any revulsion against it.

Women brought to marriage dowries in the form of land or other property and a bottom drawer of personal possessions over which they, or their fathers or legal guardians, exerted control in the event of divorce. One contract specifies a dowry consisting of one hundred drachmas in silver, a pair of gold earrings, a gold crescent, two gold rings, a pair of silver armlets, two bracelets, two robes, five mantles, copper vessels and a basin, two minae of tin and ten-and-three-quarter arourae of land as a gift from the wife's father.[40] In the event of divorce, the land would revert to the father (or the wife if he were dead), the rest to the wife.

Divorce was a procedure as relatively straightforward as marriage:

'Zois and Antipater agree that they have separated from each other . . . and Zois acknowledges that she has received from Antipater by hand from his house the material which he received for dowry, clothes to the value of 120 drachmae and a pair of gold earrings. The agreement of marriage shall henceforth be null, and neither Zois nor other person acting for her shall take proceedings against Antipater for restitution of dowry, nor shall either party take proceedings against the other about cohabitation or any other matter whatsoever up to the present day, and hereafter it shall be lawful for Zois to marry another man and for

Antipater to marry another woman without either of them being answerable.'[41]

Finally, at the end of the road, death, often accepted by the bereaved with a calm and philosophical practicality: 'I was very distressed when I heard about his death. Well, that is mortality. We too are going the same way. I spoke a lot to Marcus also, to console him, since he is much grieved, whether because of his death or because you yourself are grieved,' or more starkly: 'Do not grieve over the departed. They were expecting to be killed.'[42] Christianity, of course, brings a different spiritual framework:

'But let us glorify God because it was He who gave and He who took away; but pray that the Lord may give them rest and may vouchsafe to behold you among them in Paradise when the souls of men are judged; for they are gone to the bosom of Abraham and of Isaac and of Jacob. But I exhort you, my lord, not to put grief into your soul and ruin your fortunes, but pray that the Lord may send you his blessing.'[43]

There were also more practical concerns and responsibilities, which some tried to avoid:

'Melas . . . to Sarapion and Silvanus . . . greetings. I have sent you by the grave-digger the body of your brother Phibion and have paid him the fee for transporting the body, being 340 drachmae of the old coinage. And I am much surprised that you departed for no good reason without taking the body of your brother, but collected all that he possessed and so departed. And from this I see that you did not come up for the sake of the dead, but for the sake of his effects. Now take care to have ready the sum spent. The expenses are: cost of preservatives 60 old drachmae; cost of wine on the first day, two choes 32 old drachmae; for expenditure on loaves and relishes 16 drachmae; to the grave-digger for the desert journey, besides the above-mentioned fee, one chous of wine 20 drachmae, two choes of oil 12 drachmae, one artaba of barley 20 drachmae; cost of linen 20 drachmae; and fee as aforesaid of 340 drachmae . . . You will therefore make every effort to serve the person who will bring the body by providing loaves and wine and oil and whatever you can, which he may testify to me.'[44]

Alternatively, for some, both Greeks and Egyptians, arrangements and expenses of burial might be met by the funds of a guild or religious association to which they belonged.

The archaeological remains of burials give us a vivid picture of the ways in which the identity of the individual was reflected in death.[45] How was it claimed in life? Did people show that they regarded themselves as more than mere cogs in the wheels of the social machinery which we have described?

The patterns of personal and social identification in a literate society emerge from the ways in which people responded to the need to designate themselves in official documents, most commonly with reference to status groups of various kinds: the ethnic (Macedonian), rank (Of the First Friends, or later 'illustrious', 'excellency'), bureaucratic or magisterial position (royal scribe, village elder, gymnasiarch, councillor), membership of a social or religious organisation (President of the Guild of Glass-workers, Priest of the first tribe of the twice-great god Socnopaios), place of origin (of the glorious and most glorious city of the Oxyrhynchites) or occupation (linen-weaver, egg-seller). One or more of these might occur depending on what was appropriate to the context. Many documents include a physical description which would enable a person to be certified visually as party to a transaction: 'Achilleus, aged about twenty years, of medium height, with fair complexion, long face and a scar in the middle of his forehead'.[46] It is difficult to believe that he could be so vague about his age but there are examples which show that, although many people might very well know when to celebrate their birthday, they did not know how old they were. A classic case is that of Aurelius Isidorus, an illiterate farmer of Karanis, who recorded his age in various dated documents as follows: thirty-five in 297; thirty-seven in 308; forty in 308; forty-five in 309; forty in 309![47] Evidently, it did not much matter to him and he follows a common tendency to round off to fives or tens.

All this perhaps rightly suggests a society in which the identity of the individual was not, for most people of low status, as psychologically important in life as in death. Some could not even choose to identify themselves by association with institutions of the kind listed above. Slaves, of course, are the most obvious case in point. They were never very numerous in Egypt, but were certainly there at all times in our period, employed far more (generally in small numbers) in the domestic setting than in agriculture where they hardly appear at all. Slavery bore no respect for race, creed or origin: we hear of the elders of a Jewish community at Oxyrhynchus in 291 buying the freedom of a female Jewish slave and her two children, of a fifteen year-old Christian girl who had been sold into slavery when her father fell upon hard times.[48]

Slaves could not claim legal standing as persons and were sold simply as goods, but there were alleviations. Frequently, exposed infants were picked up and reared as foundling slaves, put out to wet-nurses and then taught a respectable skill, weaving or shorthand. Again, slaves might be freed, on the death of their owner by will, or by purchase of their freedom in their own person or by another (e.g. an ex-slave 'spouse'). This was advantageous to the owner in that it relieved him of the cost of upkeep and went some way towards paying for a replacement for an elderly slave. Slave marriages, although entirely without legal standing, were unofficially countenanced and in periods of peace provided the only effective means of keeping up the slave population. Under the most humane conditions, slaves might well be treated as a real part of the family, the only identity, apart from their economic function, available to them and those slaves who bought their freedom often entered a contractual obligation to remain in employment with their former owner.

For the free man who was oppressed or constrained by his social or economic circumstances there were alternatives, apart from simply moving to another set of institutions, a similar place or means of livelihood. For those who embraced complete rejection of social values, one means of expression lay in running away (*anachōrēsis*) to become a brigand, living in desert caves and plundering the nearby settlements. Sometimes they rejoined society, as did the brigand chief bested by Saint Apollo, who finally joined a monastery, or another, sought out by the monk Paphnutius, who was on his own confession 'a sinner, a drunkard and a fornicator, who not long ago had abandoned the life of a brigand for that of a flute-player.'[49]

81 Mummy portrait. A painting in tempera on canvas, from
Hawara. The subject wears earrings, bracelet and tunic
fashionable in the first century AD and the hairstyle is Neronian.
She holds a garland of roses in her right hand (see also Plate 9).

Or, more respectably, in these Christian centuries, a man might turn to the ascetic purity of life of the anchorite, the austerity of which is the subject of much vivid and exaggerated detail in our homiletic sources:

'In this desert . . . there is a brother of ours called John. It is not easy for anyone to find him because he is always moving from place to place in the desert. He began by standing under a rock for three years in uninterrupted prayer, not sitting at all or lying down to sleep, but simply snatching some sleep while standing. His only food was the Communion which the priest brought him on Sundays.'[50]

Often, after long periods of such privation, these hermits came back to civilisation and the protection of a monastic community.

For the more worldly and ambitious the way up might be the way out. Preferment might be sought in official employment, leading to the great offices at the imperial court, as it was by members of the Apion family of Oxyrhynchus.[51] Intellectual achievement might lead men like the Neo-platonist philosopher Plotinus away from his native town of Lycopolis, first to study in Alexandria and then to Antioch and Rome, where 'he would never talk about his race or his parents or his native place.'[52] Or Olympiodorus of Thebes, poet, historian and diplomat, who went on an imperial embassy to the Huns in about 412, was in Athens in about 415 helping a friend to obtain the Chair of Rhetoric, and in Rome about 425. He did maintain links with his native land, journeying up to Syene and the territory of the Blemmyes in the company of his pet parrot, a constant companion for twenty years, which could dance and sing and call its owner by name.

These intellectual superstars, as in more modern times, were perhaps outdone by the great athletes and artists who are the only real counterparts in the ancient world of an 'international jet-set', earning fame and wealth for themselves and reflected glory for their home town. The membership certificate of a guild of artists, from the year 289, speaks for itself:

'Know that there has been appointed as high priest of the holy, artistic, travelling world-wide, grand society, under the patronage of Diocletian and Maximian, Aurelius Hatres . . . of Oxyrhynchus and that he has paid the entrance-fee prescribed by imperial law . . . We wrote so that you might know. Farewell. Executed in the noble and most renowned and most reverend city of the Panopolites in the seventh Pythiad, during the presentation of the sacred, triumphal, international, Pythian, scenic and athletic games of Perseus of the Sky, at the great festival of Pan in the presence of the following officers of the society. First officer: the astounding Marcus Aurelius Heracleius Comodus, citizen of Antinoopolis and Panopolis, victor in the Olympic, Pythian and Capitoline games, victor of many games. Second officer and secretary: the astounding Agathocles, called Asterius, singer and lyre-player, citizen of Alexandria, Antinoopolis and Lycopolis, victor in the Pythian games, victor of many games. Officer in charge of the constitution: the astounding Aurelius Casyllus, citizen of Panopolis and Antinoopolis, trumpeter, victor in the Olympic and Pythian games, victor of many games.'[53]

The Physical Setting

The population of Egypt in the Nile delta and valley was concentrated in a small number of largish towns and a very large number of small villages. A general picture of the physical characteristics of these settlements which is broadly plausible can be sketched, with the proviso that a great deal of what is known applies particularly to the Roman period, during which they reached their highest point of urban development. The stages which preceded and followed it, steady growth in the Ptolemaic period and steady decline, at least in some areas, in the Byzantine period are largely matters of speculation.

There were, then, between thirty and forty towns of considerable size which developed as nome-capitals, and some few besides. The best-known of these, Oxyrhynchus and Hermopolis may have had, at their height, populations in the region of 30,000 or more. A fourth-century Christian source claims that there were 5,000 monks within the city walls of Oxyrhynchus;[54] this must surely be a gross exaggeration but it suggests that the population at large should be numbered in tens of thousands. A better guide is the fact that in the later third century 4,000 adult male citizens at Oxyrhynchus, a figure which is unlikely to represent much less than one sixth of the total population, were eligible for free grain distributions. At Hermopolis, an estimated number of about 4,300 houses in the southern part of the town might suggest a larger total population, but the topography shows that the northern part was less densely residential. If the estimate of an average of 30,000 per nome-capital were multiplied by a factor of forty it would still account for only 1.2 million of Egypt's people.

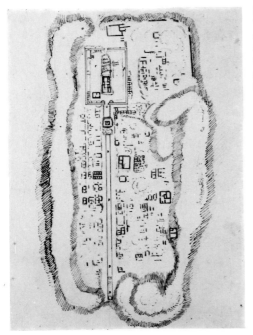

82 Plan of Socnopaiou Nesos. Gardner Wilkinson's sketch of the ruins of the village in the north Fayum. A notable feature of the layout is the enormous causeway leading up to the temple. Housing is modest; the ground plans generally reveal three small rooms on each storey.

The remainder lived in villages. Guesses at their size are rather less useful because there was evidently great variation. Karanis, one of the larger villages in the Fayum might have held 4,000 or more in about 150, when it occupied a maximum area of approximately 750 by 1050 metres; Kerkeosiris in the second century BC has been estimated at about 1,500. The smaller villages perhaps numbered only a few hundred and there are other settlements which may not be much more than tiny hamlets or the Egyptian equivalent of rustic villas. Fluctuations of population in individual villages can also be traced. By 200 the population of Karanis was down by about 40 per cent, probably an effect of the devastating and widespread plague in the 160s. By the fourth century it was perhaps as low as about 420. The once populous village of Theadelphia was reduced from perhaps 2,600 in the early second century to only about 100 by 312. The village of Socnopaiou Nesos disappears completely from our records after the second decade of the third century and must have been abandoned.

These Fayum villages might have been special cases, and excepting catastrophes like a plague, the cause is just as likely to be population movement as overall decline. Elsewhere, the bare record of names which survive through the Byzantine period indicates a great degree of continuity. A recent compilation of about 280 place-names in the Hermopolite Nome shows the very high proportion of eighty-nine attested over a chronological span of 400 years or more.[55] The nome-capitals, or metropoleis, were, as we would expect, the administrative, economic and social nuclei of their regions. The many villages in the nome, well over one hundred in the

83 Bacchias. The sand-blown remains of mud-brick houses of the Roman period in one of the smaller villages in the north-east Fayum.

Arsinoite and the Oxyrhynchite, for example, were all dependent in some way (if only for tax purposes) on the metropolis, but the model of a primate town with a number of directly dependent villages is too simple. The villages varied in size and importance and established interlocking central-place hierarchies of their own, the larger, with more facilities, serving as centres for the smaller in a microcosm of the relationship between the metropolis and the nome as a whole.

Life for the townspeople and villagers of Egypt, with its hot Mediterranean climate, revolved as much around public facilities as private, so the physical aspects of these places are of considerable importance. A guided tour of one of the populous metropoleis or the larger villages is hardly feasible since there is none which can be completely reconstructed, but a combination of archaeological remains and documentary evidence from a number of sites yields a composite picture which is reasonably representative.

The large town of Oxyrhynchus, lying on a branch of the Nile some 200 kilometres south of the apex of the delta, occupied a site about 2 kilometres long and 0.8 kilometres in breadth. It was enclosed by a substantial wall, with five gates which gave access to the town. The layout within the walls was not systematically planned around a central market and temple complex as in many foundations of the Hellenistic or Roman period such as Alexandria and Antinoopolis, but the public buildings, constructed of stone blocks and connected by the axes of colonnaded main streets, nevertheless dominated the townscape. Temples were numerous, the oldest those of the native Egyptian gods, followed by the Ptolemaic then the Roman foundations. First in size and importance was the Temple of Sarapis, not merely a shrine but a complex of great social and economic importance, including, as most temples did, a cluster of smaller buildings – workshops or ranges of small living units – connected with the cult, the centre of banking activity and the site of a public market for traders in a great range of commodities, who paid a tax for the privilege of selling there. The cult of Sarapis was common to all major towns, as were some of the widely popular Egyptian deities, cult of the Ptolemaic monarchs and, later, Roman cult of living and dead emperors and also perhaps of Jupiter Capitolinus. But over and above this there was a great deal of individual local variation. At Hermopolis, for instance, the great Temple of Hermes-Thoth, from whom the town took its Greek name, dominated the northern half of the town. In time, the pattern changed. By the late third century Oxyrhynchus had two churches. By the early fourth century, a Temple of Hadrian was being used as a prison. An evangelistic Christian source claims that in this period there were twelve churches and 'the temples and shrines of the Capitoline deities were bursting with monks.'[56] At Hermopolis a church was built over the earlier Temple of the Deified Ptolemies; elsewhere, pagan temples were simply converted to Christian use.

Public buildings of other kinds are ubiquitous in the towns. The gymnasium, the public baths, the record-office, the civic treasury, the council-chamber, the theatre, sometimes a hippodrome as well – all are prominent. The gymnasium was the cultural focus for the Greeks of the town. Always a conspicuous object of expenditure until its decline and disappearance in the Byzantine period, it provided educational facilities, both mental and physical, for those of the town's youth who would enter the gymnasial class – lecture halls and classrooms, ball-courts, a gymnasium (in the modern sense) and baths. The splendour of the circular example at Antinoopolis in the mid-third century is indicated by the use of gold-leaf in the repair of the roof of the colonnade and entrances.[57]

Public baths were also common and filled a real need for all sectors of the populace, since domestic supplies of water could only have been available for the wealthy or for large institutions like the monasteries. Oxyrhynchus had at least three sets of public baths in the Roman period and we hear of the construction of a new one in the fifth century.[58] In this setting social conventions were relaxed, drama, misdemeanour or tragedy common:

'To King Ptolemy, greeting from Philista . . . I am wronged by Petechon. For as I was bathing in the baths of the village . . . and had stepped out to soap myself, he being bathman in the women's rotunda and having brought in the jugs of hot water emptied one over me and scalded my belly and my left thigh down to the knee, so that my life was in danger.'[59]

The provision of water for these and other public facilities was expensive and labour-consuming as an account of the early second century from the town of Arsinoe shows: water was supplied to the baths, two public fountains, a brewery, the synagogue of the 'Theban Jews' and a 'house of prayer' from reservoirs which were equipped with an Archimedean screw, sixteen shadufs and two sakkiyehs worked for a total of over 1,300 night- and day-shifts in one month![60]

There were other facilities of a functional kind. Oxyrhynchus was not directly on the Nile, but on the left bank of a distributary channel, the Bahr Yusuf (Joseph's Canal). It had two small harbours, as well as a Nilometer and there will have been warehouses and storage buildings in this region and granaries in other parts of the town. Several towns, including Oxyrhynchus, had military garrisons at some point during the Roman and Byzantine periods and this will have entailed the construction of barracks to house them.

Public entertainment was also enormously important. The theatre at Oxyrhynchus had a capacity of about 11,000 and might be the scene of the occasional mass public meeting, if an emperor or a prefect arrived to be proclaimed, or the terminal point of a procession marking a religious festival and public holiday. More routinely, it would present spectacles of various kinds. Gymnastic displays by the ephebic youths,

84 Head from a statue. This Alexandrian head, from the first century BC, shows a mixture of Greek and Egyptian elements in the smooth face and unpolished curls.

athletic and artistic performances by the stars of the world-wide, travelling guilds or musical and dramatic performances of a more modest kind – mime artists performing a type of music-hall comedy, recitations of Homeric poems, singing and dancing, amateur chariot-races of the Greek type, for which prizes, as in modern horse-racing, were awarded to the owners of the teams.

By the sixth century Oxyrhynchus also had a hippodrome, supported by public tax, where Roman-style chariot races took place. The charismatic professional charioteers raced for rival teams, the Blues and the Greens, with local, religious and occasionally political associations and often incited their partisans to public violence. A circus programme of the sixth century shows that, between the races, the crowd was entertained by a procession, singing tightrope dancers, a gazelle and a pack of hounds, mimes and a troupe of athletes.[61] The prominence of this new and very popular form of entertainment says much about the diminished role of traditional Greek culture in the Byzantine period.

The villages show a much lesser degree of development and complexity in their public buildings, which naturally varied according to the size of the place. In the sizeable villages, like Karanis and Socnopaiou Nesos, the temple precincts were impressive and dominant and here the native Egyptian cults remained strongest, Socnopaios at Socnopaiou Nesos, Pnepheros and Petesouchos at Karanis, Socnobraisis at Bacchias (all versions of the crocodile god). The village of Dionysias in the Fayum shows, in the fourth century, a very impressive set of baths as well as a large barracks which makes it easy to see how the presence of a military unit dominated the social and economic life of the village. As the nuclei of the surrounding agricultural regions, the villages needed storage facilities for produce and the numerous large granaries at Karanis provide impressive testimony to the size, complexity and importance of such structures, which received and accounted for tax-payments in kind, as well as offering rented storage space to private individuals.

Entertainment facilities in the villages will have been limited. For major festivals or events villagers might go to the metropolis. Locally, the temple might come into use, or one of the larger private houses be made available. A letter of 245 BC requests the presence of a musician with Phrygian flutes and a character named Zenobius, who seems to be a drag-artist, with drum, cymbals and castanets who 'is wanted by the women for the sacrifice'![62] Documents of the Roman period show villagers hiring expensive entertainers from the metropolis:

'I wish to engage you with two other castanet dancers to perform at my house for six days . . . receiving between you for wages thirty-six drachmae a day and for the whole six days four artabae of barley and twenty pairs of loaves . . . and we will provide two donkeys for you when you come down and the same when you return.'[63]

No doubt, all this generated excitement in the otherwise toilsome routine of village life, but sometimes tragedy marred the fun. A report from the Oxyrhynchite village of Senepta:

'At a late hour yesterday, the sixth, while the festival was going on and the castanet dancers were giving their customary performance at the house of my son-in-law Ploution,

Epaphroditus his slave, aged eight, desiring to lean out from the roof of the same house and see the castanet dancers, fell and was killed.'[64]

As with public buildings, the gradual and haphazard growth of most such towns militated against systematic planning of residential areas. Towns were divided into districts, sometimes with particular ethnic or trade associations – at Oxyrhynchus, for example, there were quarters named after the Cretans, Jews, Gooseherds, Shepherds, Cobblers; streets took their names from prominent public buildings or the houses of individuals. The practical difficulties of finding one's way in such places which lacked maps, public transport and any sort of a postal system are illustrated by the following instructions for delivery of a letter in Hermopolis:

'Directions for letters to Rufus. From the Moon Gate walk as towards the granaries . . . turn left at the first street behind the Hot Baths . . . and go westwards. Go down the steps and up . . . and after the precinct of the temple on the right there is a seven-storey house and on top of the gatehouse a statue of Fortune and opposite a basket-weaving shop. Inquire there or from the concierge and you will be informed. And shout yourself.'[65]

As for the nature of the houses themselves, again, our information for the Roman period is far more comprehensive than for either the Byzantine or the Ptolemaic and, as in the case of public buildings, it shows signs of the highest level of prosperity

85   A house at Narmouthis (Medinet Madi). A very
palatial stone-built house of the Ptolemaic period in one of the
villages in the Fayum. Occupation lasted several centuries but
in the later period the accommodation was subdivided by mud-
brick partition walls.

attained in this millennium. In many places the small and fairly rudimentary houses of the lower social levels of the Ptolemaic period were replaced by structures of greater complexity, organised in more symmetrical blocks. But even then there are signs, at Philadelphia in the Fayum, for instance, of the Greeks of the Ptolemaic period introducing a chequerboard street layout and distinctive features of domestic architecture such as a double courtyard arrangement serving dining-room and apartment complexes, respectively. The wealthier Greeks might spend money on providing elaborate mosaics for the floor of a bath, or hire expert painters from Alexandria to decorate their houses. But much of what survives archaeologically from the villages of Roman period may rather reflect the native Egyptian tradition of housing, with a central open space providing light for rooms facing on to it. Many of these houses will have survived in adapted form into the Byzantine period but new building became much less substantial, more crowded, less symmetrically laid out with extensive re-use of materials from earlier constructions.

The vast majority of the population in the towns and villages spent the greater part of their lives in very modest accommodation. It is clear that most housing complexes were shared by a number of households and the bewildering pattern of fragmentation of ownership has already been noted. From this it naturally follows that many people did not live in all the houses, or all the parts of houses, which they owned. An owner might be able to rent out part of his property or he might capitalise on a vacant residence by giving the use of it to a creditor in lieu of interest on a loan, for example; otherwise it might be left empty or blocked up. One might suppose that hard times in a particular town, village or area would induce families to concentrate themselves (perhaps only temporarily from a long-term perspective) and to adopt a denser, more crowded and more economical pattern of residence. A partially preserved survey of one of the districts of Oxyrhynchus in the year 235 reveals an astonishingly high proportion of unoccupied dwellings, over 40 per cent.[66]

In periods of growth and prosperity, houses might spread upwards rather than outwards. A walled town would naturally encourage this; difficulty of communication would make for compactness, as would unwillingness to encroach on precious agricultural land. Very little is known about houses in the towns at any period. The seven-storey house in Hermopolis, mentioned above, was probably a tenement building of a type which suggests a comparison with the apartment blocks of imperial Rome. One would still expect to find a considerable range, from the grander urban villas down to the humble dwellings of small traders and artisans, which also served them as workshops. A glimpse of a luxurious residence is offered in a letter of the second century:

'The entrance and exit for all the work-people is at the side. But when we reach a fortunate completion the roof also will be made secure. A balustrade has been made for the stairway and another will be made for the porch and for the small dining hall. The beams of the windows in the great dining-hall have today been partly fixed. The second water-cooler is to be roofed over tomorrow.'[67]

A ground plan of a spacious house at Oxyrhynchus in the Roman period shows

86 A private house at Karanis. A view into a substantial
mud-brick house of the Roman period, showing the interior
walls with unusually regular brick courses. The niches beneath
the windows are surmounted by wooden lintels and will have
served as storage cupboards. The wall at the left contains a
shrine niche which has fluted columns, capitals decorated with
scrolls and a shell-shaped top.

three courtyards, one of which is labelled as an *atrium*, a vestibule of distinctively
Roman type.[68]

As for housing in the villages, the excavations carried out at Socnopaiou Nesos
and Karanis in the 1920s and 1930s by American archaeologists afford a very clear
picture of the development of domestic houses from the late Ptolemaic period
through to the middle of the fourth century AD. Here, as in many ancient sites,
rebuilding took place not after demolition of what was there, but on top of it, so
that an archaeological section reveals the nature of several continuous periods of
occupation, as well as modifications to individual buildings in those periods.[69]

The modest houses which predominate in the villages were generally built of
mud-brick, easily made from clay and straw, and were frequently extended, modified
or partitioned. In the smaller villages, two-storey houses seem to have been the
norm, though examples of three-storey dwellings are known.[70] Multiple dwellings
were often organised in *insulae* of up to a dozen units, but the individual houses
were of very modest proportions. The commonest arrangement consists of a floor
space of about sixty square metres, occupied by three rooms, one of which offers an

87 A courtyard at Karanis. Access from the house to the
courtyard is by a short flight of stone-covered steps. In the yard
there is a tall stone mortar and a storage jar sunk in the floor
and covered with a stone.

exit to the street, and a courtyard of about a quarter of the total floor area. Use of
stone blocks in domestic buildings is sparing and expensive, naturally more common
in the grander houses. Glazing is very rare indeed, but the use of wood in rafters,
floor-supports, stair-treads, cupboards, doorways, lintels and windows was very
common and, incidentally added greatly to the fire risk in these crowded residential
areas with very narrow streets and alleys.

The more substantial houses, which remained in use over a long period of time
had underground rooms with vaulted ceilings, a ground floor and a second, and
often a third, storey above, reached by staircases. The basement areas are often
divided into storage bins, which would hold the family's cereal stocks or other
foodstuffs, and the living accommodation on the other floors consisted of two or
three rooms of substantial size with mud floors, plastered walls which might be
decorated with paintings and niches used as cupboards or to hold small statuettes.

Just as important as the indoor facilities were those outside. Most houses had
courtyards and it was around these that much important domestic activity revolved.
They often contained animal pens, feeding troughs and mangers for livestock kept

by villagers – pigs, goats, chickens, geese. Sometimes large storage jars for water or grain are half-buried in the courtyard floor. Almost always there are clay ovens where bread would be baked and, with them, millstones for grinding the grain into flour, sometimes oil-presses as well. Also worth noting are the large communal dovecotes at Karanis – pigeons were an important source of both food and fertiliser. Altogether, these modest residences show a high level of domestic self-sufficiency, as is to be expected in villages which lacked the diversity of market and commercial facilities to be found in the larger towns.

Not that these villagers were unable to obtain a considerable variety of foodstuffs. For the very poor, we cannot doubt that the staple food was cereal, made into loaves. The historian Diodorus of Sicily marvelled at the economy with which the Egyptian peasants raised their children feeding them 'with plenty of boiled vegetables which are in ready and cheap supply; they give them those papyrus stalks which can be baked in the fire and the roots and stems of the marsh plants, sometimes raw, sometimes boiled and sometimes roasted.'[71] But beans and lentils were grown in considerable quantities in all areas and must have provided some variation in diet. As we move up the economic scale, the evidence for more variety becomes evident in the consumption of meat, fish, cheese, milk, wine, beer and a great range

88   The temple of Sobek and Horus, Ombos (Kom Ombo). The temple was constructed in the Ptolemaic and early Roman periods and was a popular resort of supplicants in search of healing, many of whom have left their mark in the numerous Greek graffiti scrawled on the walls of the temple. This unique relief, dating to the second century AD, illustrates a set of medical instruments of Roman type.

89   Miscellaneous objects from Karanis. A group of household objects photographed *in situ* in one of the private houses: a palm-wood door, a reed basket on top of a pot, a palm leaf basket resting on the pot, three smaller pots.

of vegetables. An account of the early Roman period which includes food eaten by artisans and children includes pickled turnips, salt, bread, beer, leeks, pigeon, asparagus, cabbage, relish, milk, barley-water, pomegranates, flour and chick-peas.[72]

Even if there was enough food to provide most people with the necessary daily intake of calories, there were other factors which militated against good health, particularly the spread of contagious disease and the many dangers in the contact with river-water. Diseases of the eyes and feet were particularly common and there was, for most people, little possibility of real medical attention. There were 'public doctors' in towns, but they appear mostly in the context of reports of accidents or death.[73] Traditional Egyptian medicine, which had a long history and was heavily tied in with religious institutions, can have borne little resemblance to anything approaching a public medical service. The Greeks brought their own medical practices and advances in medical science made in Alexandria might have made some impact amongst the urban elite but hardly in the villages. The Roman presence made little difference, except for the army medical services, which were, of course, not available to the civilian populace. Concern for the care of the sick which is evident in Christian sources led to the creation of new institutions but these were probably more like hospices than hospitals. Nevertheless, there are some indications that treatment could be had, as, for instance, in a letter of the late third century, probably written in Alexandria:

'I have been moved to write and tell you of my plight, how I was afflicted with illness for a long time so that I could not even stir. When the illness abated my eyes began to suppurate and I had granulations and suffered greatly, and other parts of my body were also affected, so that I nearly had to submit to surgery.'[74]

Elsewhere nostrums and folk-remedies were often the best that could be managed, as the prescriptions in medical handbooks show:

'For quartan fever: juice of silphium one obol, myrrh one obol. Another dose: hemlock three drachmae, henbane three drachmae, opium two drachmae, castor one drachma, black hellebore one drachma. Pound and work them up separately with water and make pastilles the size of an Egyptian bean, then dry in the shade and give them to the patient to drink, fasting, rubbing them in half a *cotyle* of raisin wine, having previously given him a bath two hours before taking; apply a warm bottle to the feet and cover him up with blankets.'[75]

As for material possessions, since it is difficult to establish any kind of a norm, we can merely indicate range and variety. A relatively wealthy man like Zenon, estate manager of Apollonius the finance minister in the third century BC, possessed an extensive wardrobe: one linen wrap, four winter cloaks, two summer cloaks, six winter tunics, five summer tunics, one outer garment for winter, one coarse mantle, two summer garments, one pair of pillow-cases, four pairs of socks, two girdles (or belts).[76] Lower down the scale, the contents of the trousseau described above[77] will represent the best and most treasured clothing and jewellery. A brief list of stolen property from a peasant of the first century might contain a large proportion of his worldly goods:

'120 silver drachmae . . . which I kept in a casket, a preparation of woof and warp for a cloak worth eighteen silver drachmae, a small wooden box in which were four silver drachmae, two tin drinking cups, a shovel, an axe, a mattock, a belt in which were four drachmae in copper, a flask in which was a half-chous of oil, a cook's kneading-trough, a basket of fifty loaves.'[78]

Along with the evidence for the range of trades and crafts practised in the towns and villages,[79] the objects of daily use found in the houses at Karanis and elsewhere give a good idea of the range of hardware in circulation and use. There are children's wooden toys, dice and other games, household furniture of wood – tables and writing desks, bedsteads and chests – baskets made of reed or palm leaves, cooking pots and bronze cauldrons, iron and wooden tools of all kinds, glass bottles and decanters (many of quite good quality), oil-burning terracotta lamps in profusion, combs and mirrors. The notion which we can obtain of the bric-a-brac of the Eygptian household is largely due to the sombre fact that when houses were abandoned or blocked up and built over, at least in Karanis, the inhabitants left much of it behind them.

This may show a healthy lack of emotional attachment to objects, the more startling when a human being turns out to be an object, as in a letter of condolence on the death of a relative: 'I too have had a loss, a young houseborn slave worth two

90 Selection of children's toys and games. Roman period, from the Fayum.

talents.'[80] But favourite animals attract some attention: 'Send warm greetings to your good wife and Julia and the horse' writes one correspondent, 'Send Soteris the puppy, since she now spends her time by herself in the country,' another.[81] And the wealthier, the more ostentatious, as is revealed by the verse epitaph inscribed by Zenon for his favourite Indian hunting-dog:

'A dog is buried beneath this tomb, Tauron, who did not despair in conflict with a killer. When he met a boar in battle, face to face, the latter, unapproachable, puffed out its jaws and, white with froth, ploughed a furrow in his breast. The other placed two feet about its back and fastened upon the bristling monster from the middle of its breast and wrapped him in the earth. He gave the murderer to Hades and died, as a good Indian should. He rescued Zenon, the hunter whom he followed and here in this light dust he is laid to rest.'[82]

It would be misleading to overemphasise the degree of self-containment and self-sufficiency in these households, villages and towns. We must ask to what extent the horizons of these people, from poor village peasants to wealthy town magnates, were bounded by the walls of the town or the limits of the village. The question has been answered in part by considering the geographical range of their economic relationships.[83] To complete the picture, attention may be given to the simple issue of movement – how far, why and by what means did people move about? But caution is needed here, for we can say nothing about those, probably the vast majority, who always remained within close range of their homes.

That said, however, it is obvious that movement within Egypt, in comparison to other parts of the ancient Mediterranean, was relatively simple – the major artery of communication offered cheap and easy transport and one could reach Alexandria by boat from Philadelphia in the Fayum, for instance, in four days.[84] There were, too, tributaries and canals which could also be utilised. In default of these the traveller had to fall back on slow and wearisome progress on foot or on the back of the ubiquitous donkey, or less commonly, by camel. But major roads, perhaps military in origin, developed to connect some of the main towns and there were local paths which might not be usable during and just after the time of the inundation: 'If the roads are firm I shall go off immediately to your farmer and ask him for your rents, if indeed he will give them to me,' writes an anxious woman from Oxyrhynchus around the year 200.[85] The hazards and frustrations of modern travel also have their counterpart:

'I have not been able to find a means of coming to you since the camel-drivers were not willing to go to the Oxyrhynchite Nome. Not only that but I came up to Antinoopolis to find a boat and I was unable to do so. So now I have made plans for my baggage to be sent to Antinoopolis and I'll stay there until I find a boat and then I'll sail.'[86]

Still more hair-raising experiences could be in store for the unwary: 'When we were in sight of home again, we fell into a brigand ambush . . . and some of our party were killed . . . Thanks be to the gods, I escaped, stripped naked.'[87]

One pattern of movement implied in our documents is from the metropolis into the rural areas of the nome and its scale naturally follows from the clear and plentiful evidence for town residents who owned land and other property in and around the villages of the nome. But it also follows from the variety of goods and services, social and economic, which the towns exported, like the entertainers of Arsinoe, described above, the delivery of agricultural machinery or weavers' implements from the metropolis to a village, or the reciprocity implied by the apprenticeship contract binding a child from the town to a weaver in a village.

Movement in the other direction was naturally necessitated by the role of the town as the social, economic and administrative centre of the nome. Taxes had to be taken there, surplus goods could be sold there, sometimes villagers are found residing in the metropolis, permanently or temporarily, occasionally they purchase or lease urban property. In addition, the nature of the agricultural economy dictated a certain amount of movement around the nome; villagers might be hired to labour in vineyards in a different village, those in charge of flocks of sheep might range over considerable areas to find pasturage. But such movement is casual and on a small scale. We might justifiably suppose that a predominant pattern of small-scale landownership and lease in the villages, together with the importance of the family unit and its patterns of inheritance, tended to render the majority of the village population static and this is reinforced by legal measures, increasingly frequent from the beginning of the second century, which tie the peasant to his place of origin, registration and tax-liability (*idia*).[88] So, for instance, the villagers of Theadelphia, complaining of their fiscal burdens in the early fourth century, pointed out that they

91   Detail of a house at Narmouthis (Medinet Madi). An unusual feature of construction; timber strengthening the angle of the walls.

knew of fellow-villagers who had run off to farm in other places and ought to be made to return.[89]

Movement also involved travel over greater distances. This is clearly implicit, for instance, in the seventh-century legal dispute discussed earlier.[90] Legal or economic relationships which extend over considerable distances might sometimes result from the permanent removal of a family from one area to another or from controlled instances of population movement. That this must have happened, for example, when the emperor Hadrian founded his new Greek city of Antinoopolis is indicated by the plentiful evidence for Antinoite citizens' connections with other towns and by the fact that they were granted specific exemption from compulsory public services outside Antinoopolis.[91] The possessor of a fragmentary letter announcing the accession to power of the usurper Avidius Cassius in the reign of Marcus Aurelius maintained households both in Antinoopolis and Oxyrhynchus.[92].

A similar phenomenon, common until the middle of the third century, is the ownership of land in the Nile valley by wealthy citizens of Alexandria. Some, no doubt, will have spent time at these estates. One way of explaining this absentee ownership is to suppose that Alexandrians bought land in up-river areas, another that these owners were wealthy townspeople of the valley who obtained Alexandrian citizenship and established a residence there. Undoubtedly both these things occurred, but the latter perhaps provides an easier explanation of the disappearance of the phenomenon after the third century – when Roman citizenship was universal there was no reason to seek Alexandrian citizenship as a stepping-stone to the higher status.

There is abundant evidence for a steady traffic down-river to the capital, for business, study or pleasure.[93] Sometimes people might do business en route: 'On my voyage to Alexandria . . . I reached Memphis on the fifteenth of the present month and seized the above-mentioned slave Euporos, from whom the whole truth respecting the aforesaid matter will have to be learnt.'[94] Trips were often necessitated by the need to appear in person at the prefect's tribunal, which could be a time-consuming business, or to exert pressure on some official. In the third century a father writes about his soldier son who wanted to move from a legion to a cavalry unit:

'So after many entreaties from his mother and sister to transfer him to Coptos I went down to Alexandria and used many ways and means until at last he was transferred to the squadron at Coptos. Though I longed to pay you a visit on the way up we were limited by the leave granted to the boy by the most illustrious prefect, and for that reason I did not manage to visit you.'[95]

Travel beyond the confines of Egypt was, of course, a different matter. In the Ptolemaic period, many of the Greek immigrants revisited and retained connections with their places of origin. In addition, the possession of an overseas empire will have given Greek administrative officers and their staffs the opportunity, not available to native Egyptians, for regular tours of duty in these places. More extravagant expeditions were the preserve of the powerful. Apollonius the finance minister of Ptolemy II Philadelphus made an official journey to the border of Syria to accompany

92 A passageway at Karanis. A passage with an arched ceiling which ran between two parts of a large granary. The courses of the bricks are marked by a white lime wash.

the princess Berenike to her marriage with Antiochus II and his estate manager Zenon visited Palestine in 259 BC.[96]

Again, in the Byzantine period, the more intimate setting of the eastern empire allowed travel to Constantinople, for the lawyer Dioscorus of Aphrodite to appear at the imperial court in 551, for instance.[97] Patriarchs, bishops and their supporters might also go there, with or without the assistance of the grain fleet, or anywhere else on church business. The intimate details of such journeys are revealed by the papers of one Theophanes, a lawyer and native of Hermopolis, who occupied a post on the staff of the prefect of Egypt in the 320s. In this capacity he made a journey to Antioch in Syria, perhaps in connection with financial preparations for the impending civil war of 324 between Constantine and Licinius. The journey from Pelusium to Gaza and then to Antioch via Askalon, Caesarea, Tyre, Sidon, Berytus and Laodicea took about two weeks and the expenditure of the entourage on food, wine (and snow to keep it cool!), baths, soap, papyrus, provisions for slaves was meticulously recorded in daily accounts which show that the average outgoings were between 2,000 and 3,000 drachmas per day.[98]

It may be merely coincidental that we have no record of anything on this scale during the period of Roman rule. But for humbler folk, at all times, there was red tape: 'In Ptolemaic times it was not permitted to sail from Alexandria without a pass . . . no-one could have sailed out secretly, since the harbour and other exits were kept closed by a strong guard . . . though now, under Roman possession it is much relaxed,' wrote the geographer Strabo in the reign of Augustus.[99] Application for a pass had to be made to the prefect: 'I wish, my lord, to sail out via Pharos. I request you to write to the procurator of Pharos to grant me clearance according to the usual practice.'[100] This writer was going home to Pamphylia. Others might seek to better themselves: 'Herminus went off to Rome and became a freedman of Caesar in order to take up official appointments,' but, unfortunately, no more details.[101] Pliny the Younger, in Italy, had an Egyptian therapist, a freedman named Harpocras.[102] Overseas posting on military service was more common. A letter home gives us a glimpse of the experience of a raw recruit of the second century AD, his pride in his new name and 'the emperor's shilling', the trouble he took to send back the ancient equivalent of a photograph for the mantelpiece:

'Apion to Epimachus, his father and lord, very many greetings. I thank the lord Sarapis that when I was in danger at sea he immediately saved me. On arriving at Misenum I received from Caesar three gold pieces for travelling expenses . . . I have sent you by the hand of Euctemon a portrait of myself . . . I pray for your health . . . My name is Antonius Maximus, my company the Athenonica.'[103]

In normal circumstances, Antonius Maximus would return home some twenty years later with an honorable discharge, a cash bonus which would allow him to buy a substantial plot of land, and Roman citizenship with its accompanying legal and tax privileges; in short, he would be a much bigger fish in his pond.

Cultural Patterns

Finally, let us turn our attention to some of the less materialistic developments in Egyptian society. Here, no comprehensive attempt can be made to describe Graeco-egyptian culture in all its aspects. Some, like popular entertainment, have already been discussed; others, like the development of art and architecture, can only be mentioned incidentally. More important, it should be emphatically asserted that no concept of the nature of this cultural amalgam can possibly ignore matters of religion; but this topic, although it touches on all other aspects in one way or another, requires separate discussion.[104] However, an analysis of some of the linguistic and literary elements may provide a useful background to it, and give a good picture of the cultural base in the towns and villages.

The major languages in use in this millennium in Egypt were Greek, Egyptian in the form of demotic, hieroglyphic, hieratic and Coptic, and Latin. Greek was in predominant use as a written language during the whole period. Demotic is extensively in evidence during the Ptolemaic and early Roman periods but gradually fades after the first century AD, finally to disappear in the middle of the fifth century. Hieroglyphic, which is used only in religious and ceremonial contexts, can without embarrassment (until the end of the third century) commemorate a Roman emperor as comfortably as a Pharaoh or a Ptolemy. A papyrus of 107 reveals the existence of five professional hieroglyph-cutters at Oxyrhynchus.[105] The latest known hieroglyphic inscription dates to 394.[106] Hieratic, likewise, remains in use in temple texts for the same period. Coptic, which is basically Egyptian written in the Greek alphabet with the addition of a few characters, begins to appear regularly towards the end of the third century, as the response of the Christian church to the need for a medium of communication with the Egyptian-speaking masses, and strengthens through the next three and a half centuries. Latin, on the other hand, was little used, although it became rather more current after the reign of Diocletian than it had been earlier.

These languages, except for hieroglyphic and hieratic, are all represented in business documents, in private correspondence and in literature. Greek is dominant in all three categories. Latin official documents, at least in the first three centuries AD, overwhelmingly tend to originate in the military administration and, in most cases, the writers of letters in Latin evidently learned it as a result of military service. A serving soldier from Karanis named Terentianus wrote to his father, a veteran soldier, sometimes in Greek, sometimes in Latin, and there are rare examples

93 Papyrus codex. This fragment of a miniature codex of first class quality from Antinoopolis dates to the fourth century and contains part of the Acts of St Paul and St Thekla, referring to Paul's arrival at Iconium. The material is thin and translucent and the script is of exceptionally fine quality.

of bilingual letters in Latin and Greek.[107] The use of demotic in official and private documents of the Ptolemaic period is very common. Its real importance has for too long been undermined by the tendency of scholars to concentrate their attention on Greek material and is perhaps only now beginning to be recognised. Its later counterpart, Coptic, also has this documentary role, but its main importance shows in the dissemination of Christian doctrine and in homiletic literature.

But all of these languages mainly existed where we cannot see them, at the spoken level. Many Egyptians clearly did not know Greek; many others, who operated mainly in demotic, learned it. Some Greeks learned to write Egyptian, but often for access to some specific skill or domain, as we have seen; perhaps more could understand a little of it. The same must have applied to Latin, though for far fewer people, as the letters of Terentianus seem to show. Coptic/Greek bilingualism is also very common, knowledge of Latin, Greek and Coptic less so, but a fourth-century monk is recorded as knowing all three languages and there is one example on papyrus of a trilingual glossary.[108]

When we come to consider the ability to read and write, we are, of necessity, dealing with a very much smaller number of people. The question of literacy in this culturally mixed society can be looked at from two points of view. First, what proportion of the population could read and write one or more of these languages and at what level of proficiency? Second, what kind of literature circulated amongst those who could read and write?

It is impossible to reach any firm quantitative conclusion about the numbers of the literate and any estimate as to whether it is likely to be a very small percentage or quite a large one is mere guesswork. There are obviously likely to have been more literate people in the towns than in the villages. Declarations in official Greek documents frequently state that 'X has written on my behalf because I do not know how to write.' This clearly refers to literacy in Greek and there are cases in which people who are manifestly able to write Egyptian are declared to be illiterate.[109] A small sample (about 1 per cent) of applications for the 4,000 available places on the roster of those entitled to free corn-distributions at Oxyrhynchus in the 260s and 270s shows that over two thirds of the applicants were illiterate in Greek.[110] It was apparently even possible for an illiterate to become a member of the town council.

If this proportion truly reflects the literacy rate of the male adult citizens of a metropolis at this period, the overall proportion will have been smaller. Women in traditional societies are less literate than men and Egypt was no exception; a woman petitioning for the right to exemption from legal guardianship uses the legitimate qualification of having three children and adds, to reinforce it unofficially, that she is also literate.[111] In the villages, the proportion will be smaller still. A man who held the bureaucratic office of village-scribe at Ptolemais Hormou in the Fayum in the second century was actually unable to write his own documents and the archive of over a hundred documents belonging to a farmer of Karanis, Aurelius Isidorus, in the early fourth century, shows clearly that he too was unable to write Greek; and his ignorance about his own age illustrates the high correlation between an illiterate population and one which tends to round off ages in fives and tens.[112]

It emerges, then, that no simple calculation is possible, especially when our Greek material defines literacy simply in its own terms. And a further complication is added by those whom we might call semi-literate, who describe themselves as 'slow writers'.[113] They could write a simple endorsement and signature at the end of a Greek document, in crude and laboriously formed letters, could possibly just about read the document, but were incapable of anything more difficult. For these people, and for the total illiterates, the means of coping with any necessary documentation lay in the existence of professional scribes, who would prepare written material for a fee, or in recourse to a literate relative or colleague who would write for them. But their illiteracy must have rendered them easy prey to exploitation or deception.

Even if the vast mass of the population was illiterate (which can only be a matter of speculation), it is still legitimate to consider the cultural level reached by the minority as an important facet of the society, a significant contribution to its development and evolution. And the particular fascination of Egypt lies in the distinctive characteristics of the different cultural threads, as well as their interaction.

The survival of hellenism in Egypt from the Ptolemaic period onwards owed a very great deal to Alexandria.[114] One aspect of this is its contribution to the diffusion and maintenance of Greek culture in the towns of the delta and the valley. Students could go, as to a great university centre, to sit at the feet of the most renowned teachers, but their education will have begun in the home town at about the age of

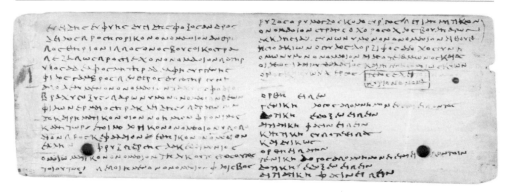

94 School exercise. One of a set of eight tablets fastened together by cords which belonged to a schoolboy named Epaphroditus. It contains a list of verbs, a phonetic classification of the letters of the alphabet, a series of gnomic questions and answers and notes on grammatical usages, including the nominative, genitive, dative, accusative and vocative cases for the singular and the dual.

ten. Sons, and occasionally daughters, of metropolites would generally be taught in schools which were essentially private, and the fruits of their early labours survive in examples of writing exercises on papyri or wooden tablets, through which they struggled to learn grammar, arithmetic, the principles of rhetoric and the works of the great authors.[115] A school textbook of the third century BC includes syllabaries, a list of the Macedonian month-names, numbers up to 25, names of divinities and rivers, proper names, a verse anthology, quotations from Euripides and Homer and two comic monologues.[116] An eleven-page student's notebook of the fourth century concludes with a maxim: 'Good luck to the owner and reader and even more to him who understands'![117]

It is interesting to note, however, that when, in the third century, the nome-capitals acquired some of the traditional Greek civic institutions, Oxyrhynchus, at least, in its aspiration to rival the great Greek cities, went so far as to appoint a 'public teacher' whose salary was paid by the town council. In theory at least, for his letter covering a petition to the emperors shows that all was not well: 'For though I was elected public teacher here by the city council, it is not at all the case that I receive the usual salary; on the contrary, if at all, it is paid in sour wine and worm-eaten grain; you yourself know how things are with us.'[118]

Primary education was not entirely confined to the Greek class; for practical ends, even a slave might be apprenticed to a writer of shorthand to learn the skill and qualify as a copyist. But with the decline of Greek civic institutions and the advance of Christianity, education with a different emphasis became an important feature of the Church and its teachers gave instruction in Coptic as well as Greek. By the late fourth century there are isolated examples of writing exercises which utilise biblical texts like the psalms.[119]

The arrival of the Greeks did not eradicate the existing patterns of demotic literacy and culture. We might expect to find them surviving most vigorously in the traditional Egyptian capital, Memphis, and in other centres of religious importance. But the publication of an increasing quantity of routine documentation and private correspondence in demotic, especially from the Ptolemaic period, shows that it did not merely survive in the hands of a few groups of professional scribes for use in special texts of a religious or medical nature. The existence of writing exercises, the numerous tax receipts and contracts, tend to suggest that written demotic was accessible to Egyptians in the same way, if not on the same scale, as Greek documents were to the Greeks.[120] And the common phenomenon of the demotic tax-receipt or contract with a Greek docket, or *vice versa*, shows how bureaucratic and social needs created an area of overlap within which both language groups could function.[121]

By the third century written demotic was evidently much less current and the fact that the Church found it desirable to transfer the Egyptian language into a medium which was visually akin to Greek is perhaps an important indication of what people were by that time accustomed to see, and evangelistic Christians were working with a body of theological and doctrinal material which was originally written in Greek.

The closest we can come to appreciating how education in Greek was reflected in routine matters is through the private correspondence of the literate, however unrepresentative they might be of the population at large. Many of them are inelegant, far from literary compositions, linguistically vulgar and syntactically imprecise. The content is frequently brief, banal and practical. Rare are the references to public events, or reflections on matters outside the daily routine. This has led some to conclude what might seem obvious, that most people in fact thought and wrote in clichés. On the other hand, it should be borne in mind that much of the content, outside the banal and polite formula, is often obscure to the modern reader and in a society where, although writing material was cheap and easy to obtain, delivery of missives was a chancy business, the paramount purpose of these letters was often a practical one. Reflection on the events of the time or moralising on the part of the writer was perhaps a luxury over which few would take trouble: 'Courage! Carry through what remains like a man! Let not wealth distract you, nor beauty, nor anything else of the same kind; for there is no good in them if virtue does not join her presence, no, they are vanishing and worthless.'[122] Expressions of such sentiments are relatively rare.

Another area in which such letters do sometimes transcend the banal is in their references to literature and books. Witness two postscripts to a letter of the Roman period from Oxyrhynchus: 'Make and send me copies of books 6 and 7 of Hypsicrates' *Characters in Comedy*. For Harpocration says they are amongst Polion's books. But it is likely that others too have got them. He also has epitomes of Thersagoras' work on the myths of tragedy,' and then, 'According to Harpocration, Demetrius the bookseller has got them. I have instructed Apollonides to send me certain of my own books which you will hear of in good time from Seleucus himself. Should you find any, apart from those which I possess, make copies and send them to me. Diodorus and his friend also have some which I haven't got.'[123] These items will certainly have come from Alexandria to a highly literate group of people, but there is some evidence for copyists and booksellers working in Oxyrhynchus and even

95 Terracotta figurine. An ornamental grotesque figure in the form of a tragic actor holding a theatrical mask in his left hand.

for traders, perhaps peripatetic, turning up in second century Karanis.[124] There, in the second century, an obscure and anonymous clerk, copying out a long list of tax-payers translated an Egyptian name in the list by an extremely rare Greek word which he can only have known from having read the hellenistic poet of Alexandria, Callimachus; he must have understood the etymology of the Egyptian name as well.[125]

The range of Greek authors whose works turn up on the papyri excavated in the towns of the Nile valley (especially Oxyrhynchus) is immense and spread through-out the millennium.[126] Homer is by far the most popular, and he was not only read, as we can judge from the fee of 448 drachmas recorded in a second-century account from Oxyrhynchus as payment to a Homeric reciter who would perform in the theatre.[127] The classical tragedians, writers of New Comedy like Menander, orators, philosophers, elegiac and lyric poets, historians and medical writers are all rep-resented. Then, too, there is a host of novels, prose romances, poems and treatises (like the work of the female writer Philaenis on the art of love, only preserved in tantalising fragments, one of which is headed 'On the Art of Making Passes').[128] Many of these were unknown in the classical tradition before their discovery in the sands of Egypt, many cannot be attributed even now to an author we can name, all had their span of glory when Greek culture flourished in the Nile valley.

In this small but committed reading public one might expect to find those who made the leap from reader to writer and there are, indeed, a significant few about whom something is known, such as Athenaeus of Naukratis, the author of a com-pendious collection of after-dinner stories and memorabilia (the *Deipnosophistae*). The fame of those literary figures who retained connections with their places of origin was important for the cultural atmosphere and reputation of the towns. In the fourth and fifth centuries, when Christianity was dominant on all fronts, Panopolis, in Upper Egypt, was still the centre of a flourishing circle of pagan Greek poets – Triphiodorus, Pampremius, Nonnus, Cyrus – who travelled far and wide in the eastern empire and achieved considerable reputation and sometimes high office. The tradition might well have been a long one, for Herodotus remarks on Panopolis' leaning to Greek culture in the fifth century BC.[129] There were others too from the same general area, Olympiodorus of Thebes, Christodorus of Coptos, Andronicus of Hermopolis. Later still, in the mid-sixth century, Dioscorus of Aphrodite, who was certainly a Christian, tried his hand at writing verses in Greek – with no great success in the judgement of posterity which has dubbed them 'wretched unmetrical effusions.'[130]

Latin literature is naturally much less in evidence in Egypt, though several of the literary men mentioned above show signs of familiarity with it. Of the well-known writers, Virgil is the most popular and a few papyri of works of Cicero, Juvenal, Livy, Lucan, Sallust and Terence just about complete the roster.

The Egyptian tradition in literature, most vigorous in the Ptolemaic period, is represented by a large number of works in demotic. The genre most commonly found is the romantic tale, exemplified by several story-cycles. These are always set in the native, Pharaonic milieu and typically involve the gods, kings and queens, princes and princesses and others of high status. Romance and magic, the gods and the underworld, the trials and combats of heroic figures all have their role in these tales. One of the best known involves Prince Khamwas, a son of Ramses II, and his attempt to gain possession of a book of magic written by the god Thoth which had been taken to the grave by an earlier prince, Naneferkaptah.[131] Another important genre is the Instruction Text, the best known that of Ankhsheshonq, a list of moralising maxims, composed, as the story goes, when the central character was languishing in prison for having failed to inform the Pharaoh of an assassination

96 Excavations at Oxyrhynchus, c. 1900. The rubbish tips of ancient towns were plundered for fertiliser (*sebakh*) by the modern inhabitants and the resulting casual finds of papyri eventually led to systematic excavation of such dumps at the turn of the century. The town of Oxyrhynchus has proved by far the most productive of such sites.

plot to which he was privy. The tone of the reflections is wry and practical: 'You may trip over your foot in the house of a great man; you should not trip over your tongue; do not open your heart to your wife, what you have said to her goes to the street', and so on.[132]

Almost all the texts of demotic literature were copied in the Ptolemaic or the early Roman period and many will have been composed then. From the second and third centuries AD there are examples of Greek translations or adaptations of Egyptian literary works which is an important clue to the existence of a Greek-speaking readership, perhaps one of which a part had some demotic ancestral memory.[133] This in itself does not quite constitute a merging of the Egyptian and Greek literary traditions, but it points the way forward to the role of Coptic literature, much of which uses the themes and substance of Christian material written in Greek. The important differences between Coptic and hellenised Greek Christianity must not be minimised, but the literature is one important area of fusion and overlap.

The existence of two distinct cultural traditions in the pre-Christian period is clear. What are we to make of their interaction? As we have seen, some people moved in both worlds. Even in the fourth century AD a Panopolite family which boasted 'Greek' orators and poets held religious offices in Egyptian cult.[134] From the Ptolemaic period onwards, the demotic literature shows signs of the influence of Greek literary themes and motifs. The reverse is much less obvious, despite the translation of demotic works into Greek. By way of comparison, we may point to the survival of the distinct Egyptian and Greek traditions of temple-building, or domestic architecture and contrast some works of art in which there are clear signs of fusion (strikingly so, again, in the Christian period). So the degree of interaction is diverse and uneven, not amenable to any rule of thumb. Historically speaking, the cultural development is layered and, in the Graeco-roman period, very mixed. Even in 1863 an English observer, Lucie Duff Gordon, could remark that: 'This country is a palimpsest in which the Bible is written over Herodotus and the Koran over that. In the towns the Koran is most visible, in the country Herodotus.'[135] As the quotation implies, the mixture is nowhere more clearly to be seen than in the multifarious aspects of religion, to which we now turn.

97 The Temple of Horus, Apollinopolis Magna (Edfu).
This beautifully preserved temple is a Ptolemaic rebuilding of an older structure which was begun in 237 BC and completed in the mid-first century BC. The two most conspicuous elements in the Horus-myth are depicted in detail in the temple's interior reliefs – the victory of Horus over Seth, his uncle and destroyer of his father, and his companions.

6

Gods, Temples and Churches

The religion of Egypt and its people must not be sharply distinguished from that which modern experience has taught us to identify as the secular and it is, in many ways, the touchstone of the character of this civilisation during the millennium which we are considering. Changes occurred as the centuries rolled by, but they were gradual and unobtrusive, each supervening feature, cult or practice accommodating in some way to what was already there. The legacy of the resultant blend, a unique and subtle interlock of different characteristics and influences, could be observed by an English resident in the nineteenth century:

'Nothing is more striking to me than the way in which one is constantly reminded of Herodotus. The Christianity and the Islam of this country are full of the ancient worship and the sacred animals have all taken service with the Muslim saints. At Minieh one reigns over crocodiles; higher up I saw the hole of Aesculapius' serpent . . . and I fed the birds – as did Herodotus . . . Bubastis' cats are still fed at the Cadi's court at public expense in Cairo and behave with singular decorum when the "servant of the cats" serves them their dinner. Among gods, Amun-Ra, the sun-god and serpent-killer calls himself Mar Girgis (St George) and is worshipped by Christians and Muslims in the same churches, and Osiris holds his festivals as riotously as ever at Tanta in the delta, under the name of Seyd el Bedawee. The fellah women offer sacrifices to the Nile, and walk around ancient statues in order to have children. The ceremonies at births and burials are not Muslim, but ancient Egyptian.'[1]

It is, of course, possible to identify the source of many of the different elements and influences in the pagan amalgam – Egyptian, Greek, Jewish, Oriental, Roman – but such an enquiry will be of little use without some notion of the ways in which they remained distinct, the areas in which overlap, complement, juxtaposition and blend can properly be observed and a sensitivity to the fact that the whole amalgam was the unique product of its various parts, sometimes isolated, sometimes interacting. It must be appreciated that, as a direct consequence, Egyptian Christianity, which forms the subject of the final part of this chapter and of our period, had many important characteristics which distinguished it from Christianity in other parts of the Mediterranean world.

The range of institution and practice which we are to consider, in both the pre-Christian and the Christian centuries, is immense. It reaches from the highest and most formalised levels of state cult and ritual down to informal and primitive rites and superstitions and embraces everything in between. At the apex we shall observe the rulers embedding themselves in, or helping to mould, the religious establishment: Alexander the Great revealed by the oracle at Siwah as son of Amon; Ptolemy II Philadelphus establishing official cult for himself and his wife/sister Arsinoe II; his immediate successors introducing their own cult of the Benefactor Gods; Roman emperors worshipped as gods and portrayed in traditional style on Egyptian temple reliefs; patriarchs and bishops struggling to establish their own brand of Christian 'orthodoxy'. At the base of the pyramid we shall find primitive piety and superstition: the innumerable prophylactics in the form of amulets or crude terracotta figurines of the popular deities; the routine supplications to the divine powers; prayers and spells in the hearts and mouths of the hopeful and the oppressed, the lustful and the vindictive; those who hope to avoid retribution by swearing to abstain from violating the sacred animals, those who attempt to avert government oppression by hedging themselves about with the protection of the divine. In between, the ubiquitous institutions and practices of the towns and villages: the temples of the crocodile god, Sobek, in the villages of the Fayum; the priests and cult-associations who performed the daily rituals and tended the sacred precincts; the local officials presiding at festivals and sacrifices; the innumerable burials of sacred animals; the various associations and bands of votaries of the gods in the temples; and later, in the Christian era, the burgeoning of the local churches and their clergy, the piety and asceticism of the numerous communities of monastics.

Pagan Religions

We must begin with the survival of traditional Egyptian religion. It is beyond the scope of this book to describe in any detail a complex phenomenon which is extremely difficult to understand and is, in any case, the proper preserve of the expert on Pharaonic Egypt. It would be a misleading oversimplification to list the principal Egyptian deities, their attributes and their local associations, for they defy orderly description, but we must take account of the abundant evidence for the way in which the Greeks identified and viewed them. Modern European and North American scholars working in all periods of Egyptian history are, willy-nilly, influenced by their inheritance of the Greek intellectual tradition. However inappropriate such cultural imperialism may be to the study of the Pharaonic or Islamic periods, the political imperialism imposed on Egypt during the Greek, Roman and Byzantine periods was a real and significant fact which profoundly affected its

98   The Temple of Amon, Thebes (Luxor). Roberts' sketch of the first pylon shows how little of the entrance was clear in the mid-nineteenth century. The mosque which can be seen in the left-hand corner of the peristyle court is still *in situ* and its sanctity has precluded complete excavation of this part of the temple.

99   The Temple of Amon, Thebes (Luxor). The outer face
of the first pylon of the temple shows scenes illustrating the
battle of Qadesh (thirteenth century BC). The missing obelisk at
the west of the entrance is now in the Place de la Concorde,
Paris. The temple is surrounded by houses of the Roman
period and the complex was turned into a military camp in
about AD 300. See Plate 34.

religion and culture and so cannot justifiably be put aside. It is therefore legitimate
to attempt to see, on the one hand, what the Greeks made of Egyptian religion and,
on the other, the ways in which its fundamental characteristics (inescapably defined,
as we must admit, in 'European' terms) changed and adapted to the alien cultural
presence.

At the most formalised level, Egyptian religious institutions and practices are
dominated by the great temples of the traditional gods. Despite the tendency of
modern historians to locate them in the context of the Pharaonic period, it is
important to emphasise that many of the most impressive of these monuments were
extensively embellished, or even constructed *de novo*, in the Ptolemaic and Roman
periods. Important additions were made, for instance, to the great complex of the
Temple of Amon at Karnak under the Ptolemies; the Temple of Horus at Edfu is
basically a Ptolemaic reconstruction, the Temple of Isis at Philae and the buildings
surviving at Denderah, Kom Ombo and Esna are all substantially from the Ptolemaic
and Roman periods. To recreate their dominance in the landscape, the modern
visitor to Luxor (ancient Thebes) can easily find the now dilapidated remains of the
broad sphinx-lined avenue that led from the massive temple complex at Karnak
down to the Temple of Luxor (both temples of Amon); as he approaches he will
pass, on his right, a modest brick shrine built in the reign of the emperor Hadrian.
Within the Luxor temple itself, amongst other things, he might observe an altar
with an inscription dating to the reign of Constantine and, in one of the rooms

beyond, the faded remains of wall-paintings which show that, in about 300, it served as a cult-centre and perhaps the throne-room of the Roman emperors. Whilst the expert on Pharaonic Egypt can rely upon his knowledge of criteria of artistic style and presentation, the layman might be forgiven for thinking that the scenes of rulers and rituals carved on many of the walls and columns of the temples mentioned above portray the Egypt of the Pharaohs. In fact, the rulers are Ptolemaic kings and Roman emperors: the latest emperor whose cartouche appears in a temple relief is Decius (249–51), at Esna; the elaborate rituals on the walls of the Temple of Horus at Edfu illustrate the victory of Horus over his uncle and destroyer of his father, Seth, the marriage of Hathor and Horus, the annual coronation ceremony which symbolised renewal of the monarch's power and presuppose the ancestral memory of the traditional gods and their mythology – but they were inscribed in the Ptolemaic period.

From the earliest days of Ptolemaic dominance, preservation of the traditional institutions of Egyptian religion was fundamental. The decree promulgated on March 7, 238 BC at Canopus in the Delta provides eloquent testimony:

'The high-priests, the prophets, those who enter the holy of holies for the robing of the gods, those who wear the hawk's wing, the sacred scribes and the other priests who have assembled from the temples throughout the land . . . declared: since King Ptolemy, son of Ptolemy and Arsinoe, the Brother-sister Gods, and Queen Berenike his sister and wife, the Benefactor Gods, constantly confer many great benefactions on the temples throughout the land and increase more and more the honours of the gods and show constant care for Apis and Mnevis and all the other famous sacred animals in the country at great expense and outlay, and (since) the king on a campaign abroad brought back to Egypt the sacred statues that had been taken out of the country by the Persians and restored them to the temples from which they had initially been taken . . . be it resolved by the priests in the country to increase the honours which already exist in the temples for King Ptolemy and Queen Berenike, the Benefactor Gods, and to their parents the Brother-sister Gods and to their grandparents the Saviour Gods, and (be it resolved) that the priests in all the temples throughout the land should also be called priests of the Benefactor Gods and should be inscribed in all public documents, and that the priesthood of the Benefactor Gods should also be engraved on the rings they wear; and (be it resolved) that in addition to the four tribes of the body of priests living in each temple which exist at present another one should

100 **Temple of Sarapis, Thebes (Luxor).** A modest shrine, mainly brick-built, set in a housing complex of the Roman period which fronts the avenue of the sphinxes leading to the entrance of the Temple of Amon. The temple was dedicated in the reign of Hadrian. At the rear is a headless statue of Isis.

be designated, to be called the fifth tribe of the Benefactor Gods . . . a public religious assembly shall be celebrated every year in the temple and throughout the whole country in honour of King Ptolemy and Queen Berenike, the Benefactor Gods, on the day when the star of Isis rises, which the holy books consider to be the new year'.[2]

This decree, like the Rosetta stone some forty years later, was to be inscribed in hieroglyphic, demotic and Greek and consecrated in temples of the first, second and third rank.

The traditional religion could accommodate Egypt's new rulers without awkwardness, on the face of it, except for the occasional xenophobic outburst.[3] If the emperor Augustus openly scorned to sacrifice to animals, religious stelae nonetheless show him doing just that. The iconography of the presentation of the last of the Ptolemies, Cleopatra VII, shows clear parallels with that of the most renowned female Pharaoh before her, Queen Hatshepsout (18th Dynasty, *c.* 1479–1458 BC). And some four hundred years after Cleopatra's death, in 373 in the tidal wave of Christianisation, a graffito written by a priest (*pterophoros*) of Isis records that he took the trouble to have a statue of her covered in gold.[4] There is one additional dimension. Alongside all this, new and separate shrines dedicated to the cult of the rulers sprang up; a temple of Arsinoe II at Theadelphia, a temple of Ptolemy I Soter at Coptos (the right to certain revenues from which was the subject of a lengthy legal dispute in 160), and many more.[5] These would provide a focus for the loyalty of the Greek subjects and prestigious priesthoods for them to parade; the eponymous priesthoods of Alexander and the Ptolemies at the Greek cities of Alexandria and Ptolemais were reserved for Greeks, though their transliterated names and titles appear in demotic documents as well. More remarkably, an innovation after the death of Arsinoe II in 270 BC provided that her cult statue was to take its place in Egyptian temples, next to that of the local god. The later cult of Roman emperors, with its own temples, the Caesarea, fits into this scenario without difficulty. At the same time, the monarch becomes a conspicuous and dominant figure in temples of the Roman gods. An account of 215 from the Temple of Jupiter Capitolinus at Arsinoe records receipts from 'the price of iron removed . . . from the machine constructed to facilitate the erection of the divine colossal statue of our lord the emperor Severus Antoninus' (Caracalla).[6]

The traditional cults of many of the Egyptian gods had universal significance throughout the land, not incompatible with particular idiosyncrasies in their different local manifestations. Amon, Hathor, Anubis, Thoth, Isis, Osiris and Horus are ubiquitous and prominent. The goddess Isis, wife of Osiris and mother of Horus, was exceptional in that her cult (in a form broadly describable as a mystery religion) aroused widespread interest outside Egypt, reaching all parts of the Mediterranean world during the Roman period and making a notable impact on art and literature. Plutarch wrote a learned monograph on the subject of Isis and Osiris and in *The Golden Ass*, a racy novel set in northern Greece in the middle of the second century AD, the author Apuleius describes how his hero, Lucius, was redeemed through initiation into the mysteries of Isis. In Egypt itself, the goddess was a natural figure for identification with female members of the Ptolemaic dynasty – Arsinoe II and Cleopatra VII are the most prominent examples.

But for the perspective of the masses of ordinary folk our most valid impression of the nature of Egyptian religious institutions the Graeco-roman period must be based on the temples of the towns and villages of the valley. In the villages, particularly, we can expect to find the foundations of the popular religion surviving in a form that was, relatively, least affected by the invading culture and then only gradually.

The number and dominance of the shrines in a small village might cause some surprise. Ptolemaic Kerkeosiris, with a population of about 1,500 in the second century BC, had thirteen Egyptian shrines: two devoted to Isis, three to Thoth, two to Thoeris and one each to Petesouchos, Orsenouphis, Harpsenesis, Anubis, Bubastis and Amon.[7] Other documents record shrines of the Greek gods Zeus and the Dioscuroi (Castor and Pollux).[8] In order to get some idea of the physical presence of such foundations, we have to go to the Fayum village of Karanis in the second century AD. There, in a settlement whose population was probably of the order of 4,000, two major temples were uncovered. The northern temple has three pylons and three courtyards, of which the third contains a hidden altar-sanctuary. The southern one, which is better preserved, was the nucleus of a precinct covering an area of some 75 by 60 metres (the temple itself measures approximately 15 by 22 metres). By way of comparison, it might be noted that at Tebtunis, which can hardly have been much bigger, the main temple precinct measured about 60 by 112 metres.[9] The stone-built southern temple at Karanis is approached by a flight of steps and a platform and consists of a series of small rooms (including perhaps a library and an oracle) surrounding two courtyards, the second with a sanctuary, housing an altar and the image of the god. Within the precinct wall there was a

102 **Karanis, the north temple**. The entrance is approached from an elevated platform. Both the temples in Karanis are stone-built and contrast with the mud-brick houses around them.

101 **Statuette of the goddess Isis**.

great variety of buildings, some for the use of priests and other cult officials, others perhaps providing accommodation for visitors seeking oracles or interpretation of dreams or for the sick, in the case of temples which were traditional centres of healing. Yet other buildings functioned as market stalls or workshops – village temples are known to have been centres for small scale industry such as weaving and brewing. Altogether, it is easy to see how such an institution played a vital role in the physical, social, religious and economic life of the village.

The southern temple at Karanis was devoted to the cult of the crocodile god Sobek (in Greek, Souchos), appearing here in the dual form of 'Pnepheros and Petesouchos'. This deity was particularly popular in the Fayum villages (though not exclusive to them) and emphasises the mixture of reverence and fear which the animal inspired – religious lore connected it with the primordial creative forces – and at Tebtunis allegedly tame representatives of the species could be produced for an eminent visitor to feed:

'Lucius Memmius, a Roman senator, who occupies a position of great dignity and honour, is making the voyage from Alexandria to the Arsinoite Nome to see the sights. Let him be received with special magnificence and take care that . . . the customary tit-bits for Petesouchos and the crocodiles, the necessaries for the view of the labyrinth, and the offerings and the sacrifices be provided.'[10]

An integral part of the cult was the mummification of dead crocodiles and an extensive necropolis adjoined the precinct at Karanis. The similar example at Tebtunis is full of interest, not only for the excavators' observation of the conditions but also as an illustration of the role which chance played in the search for papyri at the turn of the century:

103　Karanis, Temple of Pnepheros and Petesouchos.
The main entrance of the southern temple.

'The tombs of the large Ptolemaic necropolis adjoining the town proved in many instances to contain only crocodiles and on Jan. 16, 1900 . . . one of our workmen, disgusted at finding a row of crocodiles where he expected sarcophagi, broke one of them in pieces and disclosed the surprising fact that the creature was wrapped in sheets of papyrus. As may be imagined, after this find we dug out all the crocodile tombs in the cemetery; and in the next few weeks several thousands of these animals were unearthed, of which a small proportion contained papyri. The pits were all quite shallow, rarely exceeding a metre in depth, and the crocodiles were sometimes buried singly, but often in groups of five or ten or even more, and with their heads pointing generally to the north. To the votaries of Sobk this mummification of his sacred animal must have been a labour of love, for besides quantities of the full-grown specimens, tiny crocodile mummies were found, in addition to numerous sham ones, which had the shape of a crocodile, but contained only a bone or some eggs, or sometimes merely a figure of a crocodile in stone or wood.'[11]

This aspect of the treatment of the crocodile is by no means unique. Other necropoleis up and down the valley reveal mummification and burial of sacred animals on a truly staggering scale. At Memphis, apart from the sarcophagi of the Apis bulls in the Serapeum, there are huge burial galleries for baboons and falcons, the latter identified with Horus and represented by upwards of half-a-million specimens; the demotic archive of Hor reveals details of the ibis-cult (the bird identified with the god Thoth-Hermes) at the same place, the accretion of a total of more than four million burials in annual mass interments of over 10,000 birds which involved ritual processions of the priests to the burial galleries.[12] The scale of such activity, both in farming live birds and treating dead ones provided plenty of work for tenders and embalmers of species of animals and it indicates that it would be misleading to see them simply as tokens of the divinity of some higher power. There

104 North Saqqara, the ibis galleries. The south ibis courtyard is the find-spot of the archive of the priest Hor. The catacomb consists of a wide main gallery flanked by a series of narrower side galleries. The pots in which the ibises are buried are uniform in size and manufacture, although the quality of mummification varies. Evidently a range of specimens of varying cost was available for purchase nearby. See Plate 20.

was perceived to be some essentially divine quality in the animal itself and this is surely the light in which we should interpret the universal representations of the gods with animal heads, Thoth with the ibis head, Horus the falcon, Hathor the cow, Bastet the cat or lioness, Thoeris the hippopotamus and so on. The sacrosanctity of the animals was observed not merely in the temples and necropoleis. The historian Diodorus records that he personally witnessed an unfortunate member of a Roman embassy lynched in Alexandria by an angry mob after having accidentally killed a cat; and in AD 46 fourteen fishermen of the Fayum swore an oath to the effect that they never had been, nor would be, engaged in catching the sacred fish called oxyrhynchi and lepidoti, which they described as 'images of the gods.'[13]

Even small temples, like the south temple at Karanis, which was principally devoted to a single cult, were by no means universally exclusive of other deities. Several images of Harpocrates, the infant Horus, who is often depicted standing dominant on the backs of two crocodiles, were found in the precinct. An altar in the north temple carries a representation of the combination divinity Sarapis-Zeus-Amon-Helios, who may be the principal object of cult, but there is also a statue of Isis and representations of the crocodile god in another name, Socnopaios. The sharing of temples is a very common phenomenon, especially by the Roman period when we frequently encounter priests, for example, of 'Thoeris, Isis, Sarapis and the gods who share the temple.'[14] The gods mentioned above do not exhaust the roster even for a small village like Karanis. Other Egyptian deities attested there are Anubis, Apis and Imhotep and there are representations of, or references to, the Greek gods Demeter, Dionysus and Aphrodite. The larger and more cosmopolitan the place, the greater the variety would be, the larger and more diverse the number of temples. In the Roman period at Oxyrhynchus the following temples and cults have been identified: Egyptian – three temples all shared by Zeus-Amon, Hera-Isis and Atargatis-Bethynnis (of Syrian origin), the great Serapeum, two temples of Isis (one of which was in the Serapeum), a temple of Osiris, four temples of Thoeris;

105 Head of the god Sarapis.

106 Relief of Aion. The relief of the deity Aion, found at Oxyrhynchus, is part human, part animal; the lion's head has a nimbus, each hand holds a key, the right has a torch, between the thumbs is a bolt of lightning. The divinity developed as a personification of the notion of eternal Time. Sometimes identified with Sarapis and with the solar deities, it found its way into gnosticism and into Mithraism, as being almost identical with the Mithraic personification of time.

Greek – Demeter, Kore, the Dioscuroi, Dionysus, Hermes, Apollo, Agathos Daimon, Neotera, Tyche; Roman – Jupiter Capitolinus and Mars.

The importance of the cult of the god Sarapis, from the reign of the first Ptolemy onwards, is perhaps our best starting point in attempting to explain the nature of this curious amalgam of religious practices. Its appearance almost certainly springs from a consciousness of the need to put Egyptian religious traditions and characteristics into a form which was comprehensible to Greeks. Behind it lay the notion that the sacred Apis bull, an old and clearly traditional Egyptian institution, in some way merged its divine characteristics with those of the god Osiris when it died. Ultimately, it became enormously popular and temples of Sarapis spread all over Egypt, but the cult was particularly prominent at Alexandria and at Memphis where the remains of the huge Serapeum and the series of massive sarcophagi of the dead Apis bulls can still be seen. Its universal popularity is underlined by a graffito from the Kalabsha temple, beyond the southern frontier, of the second or third century AD written by an Egyptian: 'Give special consideration to the ancestral gods and revere Isis and Sarapis the greatest of the gods, saviours, good, kindly, benefactors.'[15] In one of the earliest Greek papyri known, a woman with a Greek name, Artemisia, daughter of an Egyptian, calls upon Oserapis (a demotic form of the name) to bring a curse upon the father of her daughter who had denied the child a proper burial and funerary gifts.[16]

The significance of Sarapis for the Greek-speakers and their descendants is only one aspect of a complex reaction to Egyptian religion which has several important, perhaps contradictory, facets. There is the open acceptance by the Greek inhabitants of the efficacy of the local deities: Greeks went to the temple of Hatshepsout to receive oracles; a certain Nearchos had a favourable response from the oracle of Amon and carved the names of his friends on the monuments for everlasting supplication; another text proclaims: 'I, Spartacus, son of Phaedrus, have come to Abydos. Save me, Osiris.'[17]

An aspect of the response which is more difficult to understand fully is the nature of the identifications which the Greeks made between Egyptian gods and those in their own tradition: Amon and Zeus, Horus and Apollo, Thoth and Hermes, Aphrodite and Hathor, Ptah and Hephaestus and so on. It is misleading to think of a simple equivalence, like that between Zeus and Jupiter in the Greek and Roman pantheons, because different identifications were current at the same time in different, or even the same, places, as is amply demonstrated by the complexity of some of the forms in which Isis 'of the many names' is addressed in a Greek invocation of the second century: 'at Sebennytos inventiveness, mistress, Hera, holy; at Hermopolis Aphrodite, queen, holy; at Diospolis Parva ruler . . .; at Athribis Maia, supporter'.[18] The places named include Rome, Greece, Asia, Syria, India and Persia and Isis' powers affect not only the waters of the Nile but those of the Ganges too. It would be incorrect to say that Isis was, in her essential nature, a syncretistic fusion or blend of all of these deities; the preservation of the numerous different forms suggests, rather, the reverse. If there is an explanation it is perhaps to be found by seeing such

107 Wall-painting from Karanis. A painting on the eastern side of a niche in the southern wall of house dating to *c.* 50 BC–AD 50, representing the Thracian god Heron, whose cult appears at several of the villages in the Fayum (temples are known at Magdola and at Theadelphia). As a sun-god he is connected with Horus/Apollo and Amon-Re and as a god of war with Ares and Herakles.

108 Temple of Horus, Apollinopolis Magna (Edfu). The hypostyle hall.

expressions as embodying characteristics of two very different traditions: the Greek, which liked the nature of its gods to be well-defined and the Egyptian, in which this was unnatural. The nature of the Egyptian gods was much more fluid and their characteristics could be combined or linked, in a more or less transient manner, at different times and in different places. Thus, such characterisations as that of Isis cannot be explained satisfactorily only in terms of one tradition or the other and the blend only makes sense if it is seen as an irrational (in modern terms) product of the overlap between two religious traditions, where the Greek-speakers, from whom our evidence is mainly derived, transposed Egyptian religious phenomena into the Greek milieu.

This sort of thing evoked from outsiders responses which varied between veneration and scepticism. Lucian, the satirist of the second century AD who held a position on the staff of the prefect of Egypt at some point during his career, imagines the following dialogue between *Momos* (Blame) and Zeus:

'**M.** You there you dog-faced, linen-vested Egyptian, who do you think you are, my good man, and how do you consider yourself to be a god with that bark of yours? And what does this fancily painted bull of Memphis mean by accepting homage, giving oracles and having prophets? I am ashamed to mention ibises and apes and goats and other far more ludicrous creatures who have been smuggled out of Egypt into heaven, goodness knows how. How

109 Socnopaiou Nesos, the temple precinct. The precinct is surrounded by a mud-brick wall of massive proportions. The complex of structures in its north-west corner may be a banqueting hall or residence-block for priests or attendants in temple service.

can you bear, gods, to see them worshiped on equal terms, or even better, with yourselves? And you, Zeus, how can you put up with it when they stick a ram's horns on to you?

Z. These things you say about the Egyptians are truly shocking. Nevertheless, Momos, the majority of them have mystic significance and it is quite wrong for one who is not an initiate to mock them.'[19]

The veneration is evident as early as the fifth century BC in Herodotus' account of Egypt and, centuries later, in that of Diodorus of Sicily and in Plutarch's monograph on Isis and Osiris.[20]

Outside the areas of overlap, there are religious institutions and practices which more clearly preserve their own traditions, though not unaffected by their surroundings. Thus we can find Greek cult at Theadelphia in temples of the Dioscuroi, Demeter and of Zeus of Labranda, cult of the Thracian rider-god Heron at Karanis (clearly a predecessor for similar Christian representations of saints on horseback), and cult of the dead Antinous at Hadrian's foundation of Antinoopolis. In the Roman period, apart from the Caesarea, temples of the Roman emperors, which have already been mentioned, there is a temple of Jupiter Capitolinus at Arsinoe, celebration of the Capitoline games at Oxyrhynchus, an isolated example of a Roman veteran celebrating the Saturnalia.[21] Other 'foreign' religions, too, leave their mark. The Jews preserved their own traditions and synagogues, despite their tenuous survival during the second and third centuries; the temple of Isis at Philae contains a shrine of the Ethiopian god Mandulis; within the precinct of the Serapeum at Memphis there was a sanctuary of the Syrian goddess Astarté. Despite the clear signs of racial and cultural distinctions which have been noted in the social context, it is not apparent that the proximity of these various religious institutions was in itself the cause of any real awkwardness or tension in normal circumstances, even though they might become the focus or the medium through which such tensions were expressed.[22] Perhaps the clearest statement of a definition of a religion as alien to the Egyptian tradition comes, paradoxically, from a Greek papyrus of the second century AD: 'these practices were alien from those of the native Egyptians, but they were nonetheless carried on; yes, they are carried on even now; and hymns are sung in a foreign tongue . . . and sacrifices are offered of sheep and goats, quite opposite to the native rites.'[23] We cannot exclude the possibility that these words describe Greek cult rather than some outlandish foreign import!

This might reasonably be taken as a hint that the traditional Egyptian religion did preserve its ancestral integrity in some way which was not totally undermined or diluted beyond recognition by the growth and mixture of the extraneous elements which have been described. There were still five hieroglyph-cutters practising their craft at Oxyrhynchus in 107 and it is certainly unsafe to assume that the significance of the tradition in which they worked was not generally understood.[24] One thing which certainly did change was the power and influence of the religious foundations. At the higher political and economic levels, the temples and priests of the Ptolemaic and Roman periods were hardly a shadow of what they had been under the Pharaohs. Their land and wealth was seriously reduced in scale and from the beginning of the second century BC they were slowly but surely reduced to complete subjection to the secular authority; in the reign of Hadrian their administration was centralised under the control of a 'High-priest of Alexandria and all Egypt', who was in fact a civil bureaucrat of equestrian rank. By the early Roman period, they were supported either by small grants of revenue-producing land or by direct subvention (*syntaxis*), sometimes supplemented by income from commercial activities and the sale of religious offices. An annual account of the temple at the village of Socnopaiou Nesos records expenditure of over 10,000 drachmas and it may be supposed that its income was of the same order of magnitude; inventories of temple property do not suggest that they made great profits or were richly endowed with precious objects.[25]

Despite all this, the character of the Egyptian priesthood remained distinctive, as is shown by a description written by an author of the first century, who was himself both an Egyptian priest and a Stoic philosopher (an unlikely combination in modern eyes). After describing the ascetic way of life, devotion to contemplation and abstinence from various prohibited foods, he goes on to the essential rituals of purification preceding participation in sacred rites:

'Then they spent a number of days in preparation, some forty-two, others more, others less, but never less than seven days. And during this time they abstained from all animal food, from all vegetables and pulse, but above all from sexual intercourse with women, for (needless to say) they never at any time had intercourse with males. They washed themselves three times a day with cold water, viz., when they rose from bed, before lunch and before going to sleep . . . Their bed . . . was woven from the branches of the palm-tree and a well-smoothed cylindrical piece of wood was their pillow. They exercised themselves in enduring hunger and thirst and paucity of food during their whole life.'[26]

The regulations of the emperors' Special Account show how such distinctions were embedded in Roman administrative practice, making compulsory the shaving of the head and the wearing of linen clothes and forbidding Egyptian priests to engage in commercial transactions.[27] Candidates for the priesthood had to submit to circumcision, furnish documentary proof of their priestly pedigree and prove ability to read the sacred texts in hieratic and demotic.

The preservation of this 'caste system' in the priesthood, despite the fact that the offices which were originally hereditary eventually came to be saleable to persons of the right class, is very important and distinguishes Egyptian priests sharply and recognisably from priests of Greek cults. The many surviving funerary stelae of the family of the high-priests of Memphis in the Ptolemaic period clearly convey the impression of wealth and status but they disappeared with the advent of Roman rule. There were still large numbers of Egyptian priests in the Roman period (the small village of Tebtunis had fifty in the second century), but there was probably a marked decline in their status.[28]

The priests received salaries for their service and were divided into tribes and distinguished in grades according to function as prophets, robers, sacred scribes, wearers of the hawk's wing, singers of hymns, and so on. The prophets and robers

110 Narmouthis (Medinet Madi). The avenue leading to the temple at the Fayum village of Narmouthis.

were responsible for the performance of the daily liturgy in the temples. This involved ritual bathing, as a prelude to entering the sanctuary of the temple, where the image of the god was kept and from which all except the priests were prohibited, purifying, robing and crowning the image and providing it with a ritual meal. The sacred scribes were charged with the erection of hieroglyphic inscriptions and book-keeping in the temple. Other attendants called *pastophoroi*, who were not priests, were responsible for bearing the shrine of the god in processions at festivals.

Numerous other groups of votaries connected with the upkeep of cults were attached to temples, the sweepers who erased the footsteps of the priests as they left the sanctuary, libation-pourers, lamplighters, those who looked after sacred animals, alive and dead, possibly temple prostitutes in some places. Some of these, at least in the Ptolemaic period, probably fell into the general category known as 'sacred slaves' (*hierodouloi*). They are particularly interesting because, in spite of the name, they were not slaves in the literal Greek sense, but people who voluntarily bound themselves in service to the god, as a demotic dedication by a female sacred slave from the temple of Soknebtunis at Tebtunis shows:

'I am your servant together with my children and my children's children; I shall not be able to be free in your temple for ever and ever. You will protect me, keep me safe, keep me sound, protect me from every male spirit, every female spirit, . . . drowned man, . . . dead man, . . . man of the river, . . . demon, . . . monster.'[29]

This dedicant bound herself for a period of ninety-nine years and undertook to pay

111 **Ibis sarcophagus**. This unique object of the Ptolemaic period comes from the massive ibis catacombs at Tuna-el-Gebel (Hermopolis West). It is an ibis-shaped coffin with a hollow body and a lid in its back through which the body could be inserted. The legs, neck, head and bill are made of silver, the eyes are glass with rims of solid gold.

a monthly 'rent of service.' The example underlines the fact that women were not excluded from such groups and there were also some specific priesthoods reserved for them.

All this shows that there was clearly an important sense in which the sacred rites and institutions were isolated from the laity. The priests at Socnopaiou Nesos in the second century celebrated a total of 153 festival days annually in their temple.[30] But at some point during these festivals, they and their attendants would bring out the image of the god and parade it before the public, thronging the forecourts of the temple and the streets leading to it. These were the only occasions on which ordinary people were offered direct access to the image; spectating, rather than active participation in the rite, was the institutional way in which the laity was made conscious of the celebration of its gods. The priests and other devotees were the intermediaries between the layman and his god. For the latter a form of contact with the gods in their temples was available in various ways. A petitioner of the second century BC complains of an assault made on him 'while I was in the great temple of Isis here (i.e. at Kerkeosiris) for devotional purposes on account of the sickness from which I am suffering.'[31] They might come to seek oracular responses or to take advantage, when harassed, of the personal protection offered to those remaining within the precincts of certain temples.

The contrast between Egyptian and Greek (and, we should add, Roman) cult in respect of the nature of the clergy is made explicit in one of the regulations of the emperors' Special Account, which states that in Greek temples private individuals were permitted to take part in religious rites.[32] Greek priests were laymen in the sense which those of Egyptian cult were not and their offices were essentially of the same status and character as a civic magistracy – they were often appointed for a fixed term and they tended to come from the wealthy elite. Thus, direct supervision of the revenues and property of the Temple of Jupiter Capitolinus at Arsinoe in the third century was in the hands of a high-priest who was also a town-councillor.[33] In these cults bureaucratic officials could make libations and sacrifices, as a strategos is recorded to have done in a Caesareum and in a gymnasium in 242; but the same document records that he was merely a passive spectator at a procession in honour of Isis.[34] Another strategos was supplied with a list of objects for sacrifice to the river-god Nilos, a deity who became particularly popular in the Roman period: 'one calf, two jars of sweet-smelling wine, sixteen wafers, sixteen garlands, sixteen pine-cones, sixteen cakes, sixteen green palm-branches, sixteen reeds likewise, oil, honey, milk, every spice except frankincense.'[35] Here, as in the case of Sarapis, we can see a cult with obvious non-Egyptian characteristics, the association of Nymphs in it and the divine personification of Abundance (*Euthēnia*), which makes it quite distinct from the ancestral Egyptian worship of Ha'py, the deity associated specifically with the river's inundation. But alongside the new, certain traditional practices survive, notably the sacrifices which the Roman prefects of Egypt made to the Nile, as the Pharaohs had done, and their avoidance of sailing on the river when it was rising.[36]

For ordinary people, experience of the divine in all its ramifications was most emphatically not limited by the precincts of a temple or the liturgy of the priest; these were, for them, merely one aspect of a world in which the supernatural was

112 Palestrina mosaic (detail). Depiction of an Egyptian temple complex with the gods in front of the pylon.

113 Wall-painting from Karanis. A painting on the back of a niche in the southern wall of house shows Isis suckling Harpocrates, the infant Horus. The depiction of the facial features has obvious similarities with the style of many of the mummy portraits from the Fayum; the treatment of the subject is evidently a forerunner of the Christian portrayal of the virgin and child.

184

completely natural. An insight can perhaps be gained from a modern perception of the role of religion in a primitive village in southern Italy in the 1930s:

'In the peasants' world there is no room for reason, religion and history. There is no room for religion because to them everything participates in divinity, everything is actually, not merely symbolically, divine: Christ and the goat; the heavens above and the beasts of the field below; everything is bound up in natural magic. Even the ceremonies of the Church become pagan rites, celebrating the existence of inanimate things, which the peasants endow with a soul, and the innumerable earthy divinities of the village.'[37]

This should lead us to avoid analysing Egyptian paganism in terms of faith and belief, or describing it as void of intellectual and spiritual validity, for this would be to force it into modern categories which do not apply. Something of the flavour of the intellectual literature on the subject which was current in the later part of our period can be gained from an arcane collection of semi-philosophical treatises on the divine which survives under the name of the *Corpus Hermeticum*.[38] The content includes revelatory discussions of the mystical nature of the divine and evidently reflects a rationalisation, in a rarefied form, of common experience and folklore in the guise of popular Greek philosophy; the name indicates the attribution of this body of religious lore to Hermes, identified with Egyptian Thoth, the scribe of the gods and the inventor of writing. The philosophical content itself is a mixture of Egyptian, Judaic and Greek traditions and any modern attempt to unscramble a coherent theology or message is doomed to failure. We can perhaps come closer to the spirit of the whole pagan amalgam by appreciating the numerous, varied and subtle ways in which the consciousness of the divine manifested itself amongst the hellenised and native Egyptians.

The presence of the gods – Egyptian and Greek – was an integral part of the various social units which have already been described, first and foremost the household. They are pictured on mural decorations, their statues stand in the niches set in the walls of living quarters, extending their protective powers to the inhabitants. Innumerable statuettes of deities have survived, like those of Isis suckling Harpocrates found at Karanis, and many must originally have belonged in a domestic context. Marriage contracts specify, among the items of dowry, statues of Hathor-Aphrodite; a document from Oxyrhynchus records a complaint about the theft of a gold statue of Bes, the very popular dwarf god, whose domain was the household and who offered particular protection to women in childbirth.[39]

The humbleness of the context did not necessarily reduce the level of sanctity or respect, as an official letter of 241 BC shows:

'Several of the houses in Crocodilopolis which had formerly been used for billeting have had their roofs demolished by the owners who have likewise blocked up the doors of their homes and built altars against them; and this they have done to prevent them being used for billeting . . . write to Agenor to compel the owners of the houses to transfer the altars to the most convenient and conspicuous places on the house-tops and to rebuild them better than they were before.'[40]

114 Plaque in relief. A depiction of the household god Bes, also the protector of women in childbirth. He is usually portrayed as a dwarf with a mask-like face carrying a sword in his hand; he also often has a crown of feathers and a lion's mane.

115 Mummy of Irtyertia. This splendid mummy of the Ptolemaic period from Panopolis describes its subject as Great Setem Priest, Celebrant and Royal Acquaintance; his mother Tanafereti is described as House Mistress and Singer of Min (Pan) and six generations of his family are listed. It illustrates the strength of the native religious tradition in well-to-do Egyptian families of the period.

Private worship in Greek cult might be considerably more formal than this, involving shrines, sacrifices and cult banquets. Aline, the wife of the Apollonius who was involved in putting down the Jewish revolt of 115–7, wrote to her husband: 'I have received an oracle from the Dioscuroi on your estate, and their shrine has been built and Arius, the limb-maker, is attending to their cult.'[41] The limbs mentioned here are models, probably in terracotta, used for votive offerings.

One context in which the human relationship with the divine is central is the attitude and the practices surrounding death. When it is mentioned in the Greek documents, consciousness of the departure from the terrestrial life is often explicit and matter-of-fact: 'this will be my chief desire, honourably to protect you both while you live and after you have departed to the gods.'[42] The visible memorials – tombs, stelae, inscriptions – are not the only form in which a man might wish to be remembered, as a will of the mid-second century indicates: 'My wife, and after her death my son Dius, shall give to my slaves and freedmen for a feast which they shall hold beside my tomb every year on my birthday one hundred silver drachmae wherewith to furnish it.'[43]

For the survival and adaptation of the ancestral Egyptian rituals and practices, the archaeological remains offer the most vivid picture we can obtain. Numerous mummies from the Ptolemaic and Roman periods, some as late as the fourth century AD, show the care and expense which was lavished upon those who could afford the embalming, the elaborate bandaging, the highly decorated woven mummy-cloths, the very lifelike portraits painted in encaustic on wooden boards set into the head-piece of the mummy or the gilt masks which served as headpieces, the painted boxes which contained ritual texts to accompany the deceased on his journey. The rich might be laid in massive stone sarcophagi, set in lavishly decorated tombs; the more modest might afford a ceramic coffin; the poor would end up simply as plainly bandaged mummies, soaked in pitch and consigned, with a label bearing the name of the deceased, to a communal pit or graveyard.

The traditional rituals have their origin in the Pharaonic period, their modification and dilution was a slow and gradual process. The long and detailed hieratic text known as *The Book of the Dead*, which illustrates the various stages and processes in the journey of the deceased and accompanied him on it, was certainly still being copied for current use in the Ptolemaic period.[44] We should perhaps not be too ready to conclude that it, or the custom of providing food-offerings, implies universal belief in something like a modern notion of the afterlife. A unique funerary stela of a lady of priestly family named Taimouthes, from the first century BC, suggests something rather different in the address to her widower:

'Cease not to drink, to eat, to get drunk, to enjoy sex, to make the day joyful, to follow your inclination day and night; do not allow grief to enter your heart . . . The West land is a land of sleep and of darkness, a place whose inhabitants lie still. Sleeping in their form of mummies, they do not wake to see their brothers; they are conscious neither of their father nor their mother; their heart forgets their wives and their children.'[45]

116 Stele of That-i-em-hetep (Taimouthes).

117 The Wardian tomb. The right-hand wall of the L-shaped tomb-decoration of the Roman period from Alexandria contains a herm probably representing the god Pan in a rustic setting. See Plate 54.

The Egyptian deities most closely associated with death, principally Osiris, god of the domain of the dead, and Anubis, the jackal-headed god who presided over the rituals of embalming and mummification, appear ubiquitously in tomb-paintings and on shrouds. On the third century grave-stela of a small child with the Roman name C. Julius Valerius we find representations of Anubis as the jackal, of Horus as the falcon and of Isis-Nemesis, the protectress of the dead, as the griffin.[46] Even in the catacombs at Alexandria, which might be expected to show the highest degree of hellenisation, the traditional Egyptian deities preside over the rituals portrayed on the walls of the tomb, the ancestral emblems – the sun disk, the uraei, the feathers of Ma'at – are present. But the Greek influence is also there, strikingly. On either side of the entrance to the most lavish of these chambers, which is surrounded by scores of small, plain niches for the bodies of the poorer members of the family or association to which the complex belonged, stand statues of man and wife; the torsoes are carved in the unmistakable Egyptian posture, but the heads are just as unmistakably Greek. No less striking, and quite unlike anything in the native Egyptian tradition, are the numerous poignant and arresting mummy-portraits of the Roman period from the Fayum.

There is ample material which allows us to appreciate the extent to which the divine was embedded in the everyday thoughts, words and actions of the living people. The gods were alive in the names which people commonly used, not only theophoric combinations like Petosiris (gift of Osiris), Isidorus (gift of Isis), Theodorus (gift of god), but also in undiluted form – Isis is used as a personal name and Horus is very common indeed among both Greek and mixed families. Expressions such as 'with the help of the gods', 'if the gods keep me safe', 'if the gods are willing' and so on are commonplace and unremarkable. So too are the official formulae in which the gods and rulers appear. A Greek-speaker may swear an oath by 'King Ptolemy, Queen Arsinoe and your spirit (*daimōn*)' or a prayer may be offered by a non-Greek writing in Greek 'to all the gods and the *daimōn* of the King for your health'; in 30–29 BC the temple lamplighters of Oxyrhynchus swore an oath to perform their duty 'by Caesar (i.e. Octavian) god and son of a god.'[47] Writers frequently invoke specific deities, Greek and Egyptian, by name in order to enlist their help or protection; a notable instance occurs in a letter to Aline, wife of Apollonius, which calls upon 'Aphrodite Tazbes', certainly a hellenisation of one of the forms of the goddess Hathor.[48] Stereotyped wishes for good health are also abundant: 'I pray for your health with your children, whom may the evil eye not harm, and I make supplication for you every day before the Lord God Sarapis, praying for you and all your household the best of things.'[49] The fact that such expressions are conventional does not mean that the actions did not occur; travellers writing from Alexandria, in particular, frequently make it clear that they had literally visited the great Serapeum in order to make their supplications.

From this it is but a short step to another facet of this continuum of relationships with the divine – amulets, spells, curses, oracles, horoscopes, magical formulae and the like, which are, in turn, related to practices closely connected with temple foundations such as the interpretation of dreams and the Egyptian medical arts. The notion of a clear antithesis between religion and magic has no place here – witness the Egyptian priest Hor: 'I petitioned four magicians . . . (but) not one of them gave judgement on the utterance which concerns these things except the magician of Imhotep, son of Ptah, to whom appeal is made throughout the two lands because of his magic-making (?).'[50] The divine encompasses both beneficent and evil powers in a way which cannot be explained in terms appropriate to Christian dualism. The powers of the gods are the given fact; most, like Isis, are beneficent, some, like Pan, identified with the Egyptian Min, the god associated with the desert, are feared. They, and a whole array of other numinous entities (some of whom may be called 'demons' if we strip the word of its modern connotations of evil) had to be worshipped, enlisted, placated, averted as the situation demanded. The liturgy in the temple is the highest and most formal social expression of these relationships. The terms 'superstition' and 'magic' denote an array of practices through which the relationships were expressed on a more accessible level, enabling those without access to inner temple or priestly office to manipulate divine powers and spirits in order to cope with their daily circumstances.

Amulets in the form of stones inscribed with apotropaic messages or symbols, brief texts on papyrus which could be rolled and worn on the person would ward off disease or the evil eye. Practical guidance could be obtained from deities in the form of oracular responses to questions: 'O Lord Sarapis Helios, beneficent one. Is it fitting that Phanias my son and his wife should not now agree with his father and make a contract? Tell me this truly. Farewell.'[51] Or an answer: 'Concerning your enquiry: you are in good health; what you long for night and day will be yours; the gods will show you the way to what you desire and your life will get better and you will have the means to lead a happy life.'[52] Numerous examples of horoscopes obtainable from expert astrologers indicate the conviction that the movement of the planets influenced human affairs and might affect the efficacy of magical rites. Spells might be employed to procure an object of love or lust, curses to discomfit a rival or an enemy.[53] Local practices passed easily into the common experience of the Greek-speakers and thence, as we shall see, into the Christian milieu. A Ptolemaic stela from the Serapeum at Memphis with a striking mixture of Greek and Egyptian features has an inscription proclaiming: 'I interpret dreams, being in possession of instructions from the god. With good fortune. This interpreter is a Cretan.'[54]

Folklore of this kind developed its own compendious literature. Greek handbooks of medicine and collections of love-spells have already been mentioned. The roster of magical papyri from Egypt includes several which are written in both Greek and demotic (as well as Coptic examples from the Christian period); some are evidently parts of very long compilations and many are copiously illustrated. Apart from offering formulae which were supposed to affect another human in some specific way, they are also replete with elaborate rituals, often involving priests, designed to enable the magician to communicate with supernatural powers in order to obtain aid or answers to questions. Such books are unlikely to have been in general circulation; they were probably accessible only in libraries or collections maintained (often in temples) by magicians or doctors to whom the man in the street would apply for the prescription appropriate to his needs. This will certainly have helped to preserve the mystique of these arcane practices, but the professionals were not averse to claiming 'Royal Appointment', as is neatly shown (despite its undoubted falsity) by a story based on the Hadrian's meeting with an Egyptian poet:

'An incense offering was shown by Pachrates, the prophet of Heliopolis, to King Hadrian as a demonstration of the power of his magic. By it he brought a man to the spot in a single hour, he made him take to his bed in two hours, he killed him in seven hours, and caused a dream to come to the king himself. Hadrian marvelled at the prophet and ordered his salary to be doubled.'[55]

Official disapproval, which was reinforced by sanctions and was quite clearly genuine, was evinced by the emperor Septimius Severus in 199:

'Therefore let no man through oracles, that is, by means of written documents supposedly granted under divine influence, nor by means of the parade of images or suchlike charlatanry, pretend to know things beyond human ken and profess (to know) the obscurity of things to come, neither let any man put himself at the disposal of those who enquire about this or answer in any way whatsoever.'[56]

The effect must have been scarcely, if at all, noticeable.

Egyptian Christianity

Christianity arrived early in Egypt from Judaea, encouraged, no doubt, by the presence of a large hellenised Jewish community in Alexandria, the first natural base for propagation of the new faith. Not for the first time, the matrix of coexisting

118 The martyrdom of St Thekla. The account in the Apocrypha tells of the arrival of St Paul at Iconium, his conversion of Thekla to chastity, her condemnation to death and deliverance and her final martyrdom at Seleucia. The much embroidered version of the Acts of St Paul and St Thekla seems to have been very popular in Egypt. The carved limestone relief represents her death in the arena. See Plate 93.

institutions and practices in Egypt began to adapt from the middle of the first century AD onwards, to the intrusion of something new and different, something which fed on and grew into the existing social and religious relationships. But elements of paganism survived for several more centuries, some absorbed into an increasingly Christian society, others struggling to remain distinct.

Apart from the tradition of the foundation of the Church of Alexandria by St Mark, which is now generally regarded as a fiction, little can be said about the growth of Christianity during its first century. Indeed, it makes virtually no impression on our sources except for those later writers clearly influenced by pro-Christian propaganda. In Egypt, where the religious amalgam had constantly been enriched and modified by diverse influences, there was perhaps less hostility to it than elsewhere in the Roman empire. The earliest copy of a New Testament text so far known is a fragment of the Gospel of St John which was probably written during the second quarter of the second century.[57] But for a hundred years after that, beyond the identification of a handful of remains of Christian books, it is virtually impossible to chart its spread in the Nile valley independently of the later pro-Christian writers.

The middle of the third century saw the first reliably documented official persecutions of Christians in Egypt. Under the emperor Decius people were required to produce documentary proof of the fact that they were not practising Christians and several of these declarations have survived:

'To the commissioners of sacrifices at Oxyrhynchus from Aurelius Gaion, son of Ammonius and Taeus. It has always been my habit to make sacrifices and libations and pay reverence to the gods in accordance with the orders of the divine (i.e. imperial) decree, and now I have in your presence sacrificed and made libations and tasted the offerings with my wife, my sons and my daughter, acting through me and I request you to certify my statement.'[58]

A few years later in the reign of the emperor Valerian, the government legislated to punish Christian clergy and to deprive the Church of its property. But these sporadic pogroms clearly did not prevent the growth of Christianity and the development of the Church, which remained unthreatened for the most part.

Persecution was formally suspended under the next emperor, Gallienus and was not systematically resumed until the Great Persecution of Diocletian began in 303. Egypt is said to have suffered particularly severely in this episode, not least because one of its prefects, Sossianus Hierocles, was a notorious anti-Christian. Eusebius of Caesarea, in his History of the Church describes the headlong rush to martyrdom in the Thebaid:

"As soon as sentence was given against the first, some from one quarter and others from another leapt up to the tribunal before the judge and confessed themselves Christians, unconcerned in the face of terrors and the varied forms of tortures, but speaking without dismay and boldly of the piety towards the God of the universe, and receiving final sentence of death with joy and laughter and gladness; so that they sang and sent up hymns and thanksgiving to the God of the universe even to the very last breath.'[59]

Our meagre documentary record is less dramatic. Admission of Christianity could be avoided: 'It became known to us that those who present themselves in court are being made to sacrifice. I made a power of attorney in favour of my brother.'[60] But churches were closed down; a declaration of 304 submitted to an official by a reader (*lector*) of a former village church stated that bronze objects in its possession had been yielded for confiscation.[61]

Under these circumstances it is hardly surprising that Christians are not conspicuous in documents of the second half of the third century, for they certainly would not be inclined to advertise their affiliation. There are only a couple of clear instances of people designated as Christians in official documents.[62] The rest is question, inference or conjecture. How numerous were the Christians around AD 300? How long did it take for them to achieve a majority? Even after the Edict of Toleration in 311 and Constantine's subsequent recognition of the Church's right to property and status, which allowed it to enhance the organisation of its administrative structure and to acquire considerable wealth, it was probably a matter of gradual growth rather than a deluge. Christians who had hitherto been covert could now come out into the open. The adoption of more recognisably Christian names is an indicator, but precise quantification is very difficult.[63]

Whether or not Constantine had it in mind to make Christianity the official religion of the empire, it is certain that in Egypt pagan religion and its institutions were only slowly eclipsed. Even in the mid-fourth century there are clear signs of its survival in the army, where it would certainly have been easily eradicated, had that been official policy, and plenty of examples of priests of Greek and Egyptian cult. But towards the end of the century signs of persecution of pagans by Christians appear. During a visit to Egypt in 385 the praetorian prefect of the east, Maternus Cynegius closed the temples and forbade sacrifices to Zeus. In 391, Theophilus the Patriarch of Alexandria attempted to convert a temple of Dionysus in Alexandria into a church. Rioting between pagans and Christians ensued, the former occupying the great Serapeum; when the Christians took it the statue of the god was assaulted – and a swarm of rats issued forth. The subsequent destruction of the temple was certainly advertised by Christians as symbolic of a great victory (just as the story of the rats supported their desire to show the decadance of paganism) and the same year saw the beginning of legislation which aimed to outlaw pagan rites and close the temples. It was clearly not completely effective. The activities of Shenute, Abbot of the White Monastery in the first half of the fifth century, include an episode in which he was prosecuted by pagan priests for a raid on their temple in which an image of the god Pan and a book of magic were stolen; on another occasion he addressed a reply to a pagan landowner at Panopolis who had protested against a raid on his house by Shenute and his monks.

Nevertheless, by this time the strength of Christianity was clearly visible except among the tribes of the southern regions who were converted in the mid-sixth century. The landscape was now dominated by the great churches and monasteries. The ruins of the enormous and magnificent Church of St Menas south of Alexandria, a very popular object of pilgrimage in antiquity, testify to the scale of building in the fifth and sixth centuries. But the archaeological record of the earlier stages of development is sadly lacking. In the third century, Christians will have met for

119 Granite shrine. The granite monolithic shrine, made to house a sacred bird or animal was dedicated to Isis by Ptolemy VIII. It was discovered lying on its side among the ruins of the Coptic Church at Philae where it had been used as an altar base.

prayer in converted house-chapels, a single example of which, consisting of an altar sanctuary and two longitudinal rooms for worshippers, has been identified in the Bahria Oasis.[64] A document of the 290s shows that the town of Oxyrhynchus then had two churches which may well have been of this kind but there is no indication of their scale or character.[65] After Galerius' Edict of Toleration in 311 references to town and village churches are naturally more common but there is no information about physical detail before the fifth century. It seems, on the whole, more likely that the earlier buildings were modest in plan and structure than that they exemplified the great basilical churches of the later period, with the threefold division of the main longitudinal axis and the apsidal recess at the end. Pagan temples, Greek and Egyptian, were also increasingly occupied by Christians and adapted to their worship, although they were not suitable for conversion into churches in their entirety. Many still exhibit the Coptic crosses carved on their walls and an inscription records the dedication, with the collaboration of the king of the Nubades, of part of the Temple of Dendur in the middle of the sixth century: 'By the will of God and the command of the King Eirpanome and Joseph, the exarch of Talmis, and by our receiving the cross from Theodorus, the bishop of Philae'.[66] Similarly, in Hermopolis a Temple of Amon was inhabited by Christians and had part of its interior turned into a chapel, whilst a new church was built in the fifth century on top of an earlier temple of Ptolemy III and Berenike.

Hand in hand with physical growth went the development of the Church's administrative organisation, more visible from the reign of Constantine. Certainly, the hierarchical principle, with the bishop at the apex, will have existed from the time of the earliest Christian groups. The process by which the bishops of individual towns and the churches and clergy in their areas were subordinated to the authority of the Patriarch of Alexandria was a gradual one, to all intents and purposes complete by the sixth century. But it had involved a good deal of tidying up and formalising of the position of local institutions which were part of a rather haphazard growth, ultimately making more effective the powers which were latent in the Alexandrian Patriarchy.

Nevertheless, as far as most bishops were concerned, Alexandria was a long way off and their own powers in the appointment and control of their clergy were very important. Priests were appointed jointly by the bishop and other priests of the community; deacons and lower orders, sub-deacons, readers and minor functionaries and administrators (including women who could be admitted to positions as high as the diaconate), were directly appointed by the bishop. His powers of patronage were undoubtedly strengthened by the attractiveness of clerical positions; apart from the stimulus of religious vocation, there were salaries and the humbler functionaries would benefit from certain tax exemptions. A declaration from the early fourth century casts an interesting light on the relationship between a deacon and the bishop who appointed him, evoking comparison with apprenticeship and labour contracts from an earlier, pagan context: 'Whereas I was today ordained into your service as deacon and made a declaration to you, so that I should be inseparable (?) from your bishopric, for this reason I agree by this contract not to leave your side nor to (migrate to the office?) of bishop or priest or (any cleric?) unless your agreement is obtained, because I make the contract on these conditions.'[67]

The churches and their clergy were not the only institutions through which the growth of Christianity was expressed. The proliferation of monastic communities (of both men and women), so numerous and conspicuous after 400, particularly as strongholds of native Egyptian loyalty to the Monophysite doctrine, can also be traced back to the fourth century. The biography of the founding father of monasticism, St Antony (*c.* 251–356) is not untouched by romanticism, but there is no doubt that it was Egypt's most original contribution to Christianity and there is clear documentary evidence for organised monasteries in the last decade of Constantine's reign.[68] The so-called Antonian communities owed their origins to the desire of individuals to congregate about the person of a particularly celebrated ascetic in a desert location, building their own cells, adding a church and a refectory, then towers and walls to enclose the unit. Other monasteries, called Pachomian after Pachomius, the founder of coenobitic monasticism, spread after *c.* 321 and were planned and envisaged from the start as walled complexes with communal facilities. The provision of water-cisterns, kitchens, bakeries, oil-presses, workshops

120   Aswan, Monastery of St Simeon. The compound is built on two levels, covers an area of about 90 × 100 m and is surrounded by a wall over 6 m high. At the northern end of the upper enclosure is a two-storeyed residence with a large, cell-lined hall on the upper level.

(in which basket-making figured prominently), stables and cemeteries, the ownership and cultivation of land in the vicinity made these communities self-sufficient to a high degree. But it need not and should not follow that they were entirely divorced from involvement with the nearby towns and villages.[69] Indeed, many of the stories in the *Lives of the Desert Fathers* clearly indicate extensive contacts and it is quite likely that many monastery churches were open to the local public for worship.

The nature of the organisation of these monasteries is somewhat anomalous. In principle they were subjected to the authority of their local bishop, in fact this was not easily exercised. They elected their own councils of priors and their principals (abbots or abbesses). Some, like the legendary Shenute, the Abbot of the White Monastery near Sohag in the late fourth and early fifth centuries, were very powerful figures indeed who, with the potentially violent support of large numbers of fanatical brethren, found defiance easy and exercised their influence well beyond the confines of their monastery walls. The evidence for the administration of an early Meletian monastery shows clearly, again, that there was no rigid separation between village priesthood and membership of a monastic community:

'Aurelius Pageus, son of Horus, of the village of Hipponon . . ., priest, to the priors of the monastery of monks called Hathor . . . Whereas . . . I desire to make a journey . . . to Caesarea to fulfil the orders given, it is necessary for me to appoint a deputy in my place until my return; therefore I gathered round the monks of our monastery in the presence of Patabaeis, priest of Hipponon and Papnutius, the deacon of Paminpesla and Proous, former monk and many others . . .; and they approved . . . Aurelius Gerontius my full brother as a person fitted to occupy my place temporarily until my return.'[70]

This recurring feature is perhaps easier to understand in the context of the fact that early evidence for monks shows them not only living communally, but also individually or in small groups within the towns and villages, a particularly dis-

121 Wooden frieze. A fourth- or fifth-century portrayal of the entry of Christ into Jerusalem on a lintel from the Church of al-Mo'allaqa (Cairo). The representation of the entry takes place within the walls of the city and Christ is portrayed without beard or nimbus. The Greek inscription above refers to Christ as 'He in whom dwells the fullness of Divinity.'

reputable category, according to St Jerome.[71] These monks will have been constantly visible to the laymen around them and participated actively in the life of the community. Their distinctive style of dress and appearance, their reputation for asceticism invites a natural comparison with the description of the priests of pagan Egyptian cult and perhaps offers the most obvious explanation for the fact that the origins of monasticism were uniquely Egyptian.

The early evidence for the ownership of wealth and property by churches and monasteries gives more than a hint of what was to turn, by the beginning of the fifth century, into a very powerful economic force indeed. Constantine not only made it legal for them to hold property but also made provision for grants to churches and by the sixth century there is clear evidence that they were entitled to some proportion of the taxes paid by local landowners, instanced in payments to village churches made by a supervisor of the Apion estates in the Oxyrhynchite Nome and shipments of grain to monasteries.[72] As for property, there were precious objects in the churches, money acquired through bequest, possession of houses, shops and workshops of various kinds, but above all a massive income from the ownership of estates, some exploited directly, others rented out to tenants, which necessitated the appointment of a multitude of estate supervisors and administrators and the acquisition of boats to transport produce.

Although it is hardly possible to draw up a balance sheet, the total income of Christian foundations will certainly have more than sufficed for the construction and upkeep of buildings and the payment of salaries to the clergy, who were generally by no means averse to self-enrichment. These items probably account for the major proportion of expenditure, but the Church was also committed to the maintenance of hospices of the sick and charitable foundations, to regular subventions for the support of the poor and the widowed: 'The holy church to Peter, administrator of the church of St Kosmas. Provide for Sophia, widow, from the coats you have one coat for good use, total: 1 coat only.'[73]

The good works upon which the church lavished part of its wealth were certainly a conscious corporeal reinforcement of the hold which it exercised over the minds and spirits of its adherents. Any attempt to trace, in a brief compass, the development of that theological, spiritual and doctrinal hold is bound to be an oversimplification of a very complex history. From one viewpoint, that of the Church establishment, it might appear deceptively straightforward. Thus, we can say that in the second century Christian theology will have developed along various lines which were heavily influenced both by the Jewish exegetical tradition and by ideas current in Greek philosophical thought, worked out principally in the Platonic tradition. The crucible in which these elements mixed in the first instance was cosmopolitan Alexandria, whence they were eventually diffused in the rest of the land. From the last quarter of the second century, influential Christian thinkers began to elicit from the mélange of theology, philosophy and practice, a notion of orthodoxy, the three main elements in which were the formation of the Canon of the New Testament, the doctrine of apostolic succession and acceptance of the episcopal organisation of the Church. As these foundations became more central to the political development of the Church, so it became increasingly possible for the establishment to define as heretical those sects, practices and beliefs which rejected some or all of them. Thus, the issue of the relationship between orthodox and heretical Christianity has no contemporary application to any historical context before about AD 180.

The history of the political and doctrinal struggles within the Church during and after the fourth century has largely been written in terms of the disputes over the nature of God and Christ and the relationship between them, and through the eyes of the victors. But these were not the only challenges which orthodoxy had to remove. To mention only the most obvious, Christian gnosticism and Manichaeism, about which more will be said below, represent important strands of deviation from what became the orthodox dogma. But even during the gradual rejection of these elements, the triumph of orthodoxy in Egypt is not a simple matter because in the fifth and sixth centuries, there was still a vast range of shades of commitment and belief, still a fundamental division between the Monophysite Christians (traditionally identified with the native Copts) and the Chalcedonian (hellenised) Church.

Some patterns in the development of Christianity in the fourth, fifth and sixth centuries seem, nevertheless, to emerge with relative clarity. The promulgation of Christian doctrine by the translation of biblical and exhortatory texts into the Coptic language from the late third century onwards made it available to Egyptian speakers in large numbers and it was they, ultimately, who underpinned the strength of the Monophysite Church. It may well be that the Church's numerical gain of adherents in the fourth century lay predominantly in this area. Christianity had earlier made some impact on the hellenised elite and it continued to convert them into the Church and the monasteries surely, but perhaps more slowly. Alongside the chasm between Monophysite and Chalcedonian Christians, paganism survived with some vigour among the hellenised Egyptians into the fifth and even sixth centuries: the literary men in Panopolis, the philosophers in Alexandria are its most conspicuous representatives. Shenute, as we have seen, was not slow to identify and attack his local pagans. Some tried Christianity and did not like it; a document of 426 records the apostasy of a town councillor who had been a Christian but had reverted to a pagan circle.[74] If we want to stress the ways in which this relatively neat picture can

122 Medallion. The representation on this sixth-century tunic decoration is of a stylised figure in a chariot drawn by bulls. The crossed nimbus suggests that it might be a representation of the Ascension of Christ.

be reinforced without discomfort at the mundane level we can highlight various phenomena: the vast increase in the number of biblical texts (Greek and Coptic) in circulation; the appearance of conventional Christian formulae in letters; the standardised abbreviations of sacred names; the stereotyped invocations of the Holy Trinity in both Greek and Coptic papyri; regularisation of the liturgy and of the calendar of festivals observed in the local churches. But if we pursue the theme from Christianity's grass roots, we shall find that it was, even in the later centuries of our period, still far more heterogeneous than all this would lead us to think and that it continued to accommodate a great variety of diverse strains and influences, shades of commitment and belief; some antagonistic to others, some complementary, some overlapping – in fact, a picture of much the same kind as we have sketched in describing the amalgam of paganism.

It is not possible in a brief compass to analyse, or even to list, all the elements in this picture. A summary account might justifiably concentrate upon two of the most important and vital strains, Manichaeism and Christian gnosticism. A feature central to both (though there are important deviations) was the emphasis on dualism – the struggle of good against evil: for the Manichaeans, a perpetual war between Light and Dark worked out in terms of the immediacy of the physical universe, the Dark constantly invading the Light, man being a mixture of both and thus containing the seeds of his own salvation. For them the crucifixion of Jesus could not be a unique event, merely one manifestation of this struggle. For the gnostics, the material world was to be rejected as evil; knowledge of the divine was reached through knowledge of the self and the implication of divine essence in the human self naturally led to charges that gnostics put themselves on a par with divine beings. It is not difficult to see the grounds on which such beliefs were anathematised by the powers which represented what developed into catholic orthodoxy.

There is no doubt, however, that both gnostics and Manichaeans formed relatively strong elements in Egyptian Christianity. The Manichaeans, followers of the Persian prophet Mani (216–76) were important enough to elicit a swingeing condemnation from a bishop of the late third century and to be outlawed by the emperor Diocletian in a letter issued at Alexandria, probably in 302, which ordered that their books should be burned.[75] Lycopolis was one of their main centres and there is continued evidence of their presence through the fourth into the fifth century and beyond: a cache of Coptic translations of liturgical and homiletic texts of the fourth century, the sensational discovery of a minute and beautiful codex in Greek of the fifth century containing a *Life of Mani*, a Greek translation of an Aramaic original.[76] The Manichaeans were certainly unpalatable to the Church establishment; amongst the plentiful evidence that they were seen as a dangerous subversive force are the characteristically vigorous attacks on them made by Shenute, which contain accusations that they rejected fundamental beliefs – the virgin birth, the resurrection, Jesus' miracles. But they themselves had no doubt of the fact that they really were Christians, as the Life shows: 'He said in the gospel of his most holy hope: "I, Mani, the apostle of Jesus Christ through the will of God, the Father of Truth from whom I was born."'[77]

The strength of gnosticism amongst Christians was equally sensationally highlighted by the discovery of a Coptic gnostic library at Nag Hammadi in 1945, a

123 Leaf of a codex from Nag Hammadi.
The page contains the end of the *Apocryphon of John* and the beginning of the *Gospel of Thomas*, both in Coptic. The former recounts the revelation by the resurrected Christ to John son of Zebedee in a mythological framework which is comparable to that in the early part of the book of Genesis and describes the creation, fall and salvation of humanity. The *Gospel of Thomas*, translated from the Greek is attributed to Didymus Judas Thomas (identified in some eastern traditions as the twin of Jesus) and contains traditional sayings, prophecies, proverbs and parables of Jesus.

collection of texts concealed in an earthenware pitcher.[78] It is uniquely important because it is the only evidence for gnostic Christian theology and thought which is not derived from attacks made on it by its adversaries. The range of the literature is astonishing: mythological and magical texts, poetry, philosophical tracts and, above all, a copy of the Gospel of St Thomas, a secret, 'heretical' gospel which did not find its way into the Canon of the New Testament; some of the 'Sayings of Jesus' which it records had come to light fifty years earlier in one of the first published papyri from the town of Oxyrhynchus.[79] Not only do these documents allow us to reconstruct a 'gnostic New Testament' with its own Gospels, Acts, Epistles and Revelations; the variety of the literature is such as to make it seem likely to have belonged to several different religious groups but if, as is possible, this cache was originally part of a monastery library it suggests great catholicity of reading within one group or community.

Recent debate about these remarkable texts has given much attention to the question of whether or not they are, in fact, closer to the original spirit of Jesus' teachings than catholic Christianity later became. Whatever the answer, there is, again, no doubt that the people who read these texts firmly considered themselves Christians. The intellectual background, which can be traced back to the second century, owes a great deal both to the Jewish and to the Greek philosophical tradition. The development accommodates a range of sophistication and variation in thought which ascends from simple folklore, magic, revelation through popular

Neo-platonic thought to a highly developed rationalisation which can only have meant anything to the literate and well-educated minority. Not even the fundamental dualism was a common feature of all gnostic thinkers and their reading was wide enough to include, as the Nag Hammadi library shows, portions of the mystical, revelatory *Corpus Hermeticum*.

The survival of elements from the mixed pagan background emerges in other striking ways, too. Coptic Christianity developed its own distinctive art, but much of it was pervaded by the long-familiar motifs of Greek mythology, coexisting with representations of saints, virgin and child, Christian parables and decorative styles which owe a great deal to both Greek and Egyptian precedents. Pagan habits survived in other forms, too. Papyri from the Christian centuries continue to yield amulets, oracles, spells and magical texts of various kinds; the modern inclination to label these as 'gnostic' might seem to be too formal a categorisation and one which their readers and writers would have found mystifying. The juxtaposition of

124 Biercloth. This fifth-century textile from Panopolis is a striking example of Coptic artistry in the illustration of Greek mythological themes. The female figure is Artemis, the male may be Actaeon, Orion or Meleager. The small nude dancing figures are woven in purple over a background of tendrils on the borders or within a scroll in the median band.

different elements is perhaps more incongruous in hindsight than it would have been at the time. 'Hor, Hor, Phor, Eloei, Adonai, Iao, Sabaoth, Michael, Jesus Christ. Help us and this house. Amen.' runs a Coptic Christian magical invocation of the fifth or sixth century, mingling pagan, Jewish and Christian elements.[80] The establishment Church would hardly find a place for this in official doctrine or practice, but it nevertheless survived. Christianity engulfed its pagan precedents slowly and untidily. Rigid barriers cannot be appropriate in defining the perspectives of the masses. Even if the political and military victory of Islam over Christianity was clear and decisive, it was only so from one point of view. Victory over the minds of men is another matter.

125 Alexandria, the Tegran Tomb. Despite the fact that the upper classes of the Alexandrian population were thoroughly hellenised, the richly decorated tombs of the Roman period which held their corpses are dominated by the traditional motifs of Egyptian funerary art. In this scene from the second-century Tegran tomb the mummified corpse is laid on a bier; the figures of the two mourners are connected with the goddesses Isis and Nephthys, as are the two mourning kites; and on the side walls are two figures of the dog-headed Anubis. For the mummy-wrapping, see Plate 78.

7

Alexandria, Queen of the Mediterranean

The City

There is no more impressive and majestic reflection of the achievement of the Greeks in Egypt than the great city which bore Alexander's name. It dominated the eastern Mediterranean world politically, culturally and economically for six-and-a-half centuries and rivalled the new eastern capital of the Byzantine empire, Constantinople, for another three. For the most part insulated from the political convulsions of the Hellenistic kingdoms, later protected by the penumbra of the Roman peace and far removed from the disturbances of barbarian invasion, Alexandria had the freedom and the stimulus to develop into a spectacularly beautiful city. By the middle of the first century BC Diodorus of Sicily could describe it as 'the first city of the civilised world, certainly far ahead of all the rest in elegance and extent and riches and luxury.'[1] Materially enriched by the exploitation of its enormous potential for maritime trade and culturally unrivalled as the fountainhead of the Greek literary and intellectual tradition for more than a millennium, Alexandria was truly the queen of the Mediterranean.

It is hardly credible that this can literally have been part of the vision of its famous founder when he chose the site near the Egyptian village of Rhakotis, which was to remain the enclave of the native Egyptian inhabitants of the city. Alexander's motives and intentions are recorded only in sources which clearly benefit from hindsight. The traditional date for the foundation is April 7, 331 BC. Plutarch's *Life of Alexander* has the king visited by a venerable prophet in a dream, quoting a Homeric reference to the island of Pharos, enough to convince Alexander that he had found the right site:

'Since there was no chalk available, they used barley meal to describe a rounded area on the dark soil, to whose inner arc straight lines succeeded, starting from what might be called the skirts of the area and narrowing to the breadth uniformly, so as to produce the figure of a military cloak. The king was delighted with the plan, when suddenly a vast multitude of birds of every kind and size flew from the river and the lagoon on to the site like clouds; nothing was left of the barley meal and even Alexander was much troubled by the omen. But his seers advised him that there was nothing to fear (in their view the city he was founding would abound in resources and would sustain men from every nation); he therefore instructed his overseers to press on with the work.'[2]

After an initial sojourn at Memphis, Alexander's body found its last resting place in the greatest of the many cities he founded; our latest record of a visit to the site of the tomb, which has defied all subsequent attempts at identification, concerns the Roman emperor Caracalla in 215; he followed this act of homage to Alexander with a systematic massacre of the youth of the city.[3]

By about 320 BC Alexandria had displaced Memphis and become the new capital of the Ptolemaic kingdom of Egypt. But its position within Egypt was nevertheless always slightly anomalous. As a thoroughly Greek city, with an outlook and a culture alien to the native Egyptian tradition, it resembled an accretion rather than an integral part, even though it was endowed at first with a dependent territory in the surrounding delta lands; this was later assimilated to the rest of the delta and administered as an independent nome, except for properties owned by residents of

126 Alexandrian coin. The emperor Hadrian is shown in a chariot holding an aquila in his left hand. The personification of Alexandria meets him, her head covered in an elephant skin. The coin celebrates the visit of Hadrian to Egypt in AD 130.

Alexandria. The Bithynian orator Dio of Prusa, in a public speech made in Alexandria, probably in the reign of Vespasian (AD 69–79), went so far as to describe Egypt as a sort of 'appendage' of the city, presumably making some concession to his audience's viewpoint, but this was not mere sophistry for the Roman prefect was regularly and officially described as 'prefect of Alexandria and all Egypt'.[4] However it was always the administrative hub of the country, first the nerve-centre of the Ptolemaic kingdom whose magnificent palace complex, later known as the Brucheion, was adorned and embellished by successive monarchs of the dynasty; the buildings subsequently became the headquarters of the Roman prefects until their destruction during the occupation by the Palmyrenes in the early 270s; but Alexandria remained the seat of Egypt's government and administration throughout the Byzantine period.

The planning and layout of the city are associated with the name of the most famous architect of the day, Dinocrates of Rhodes, but the early stages of its physical growth cannot be traced with any certainty, apart from the construction of a few outstandingly imposing buildings. A vivid general impression of its splendours can be obtained from the long eye-witness description given by the geographer Strabo, who was a friend of the Roman prefect Aelius Gallus, and visited it during the first decade of Roman rule:

127 Alexandria, 'Pompey's Pillar'. David Roberts' sketch of the misnamed monument, which still stands where it was erected in front of the Serapeum *c.* AD 299, just after the recapture of the city by the emperor Diocletian from the usurper Domitius Domitianus.

'The whole city is criss-crossed with streets suitable for the traffic of horses and of carriages, and by two that are very wide, being more than one plethrum (*c.* 30 metres) in breadth; these intersect each other at right-angles. The city has magnificent public precincts and the royal palaces which cover a fourth or even a third of the entire city. For just as each of the kings would for love of splendour add some ornament to the public monuments, so he would provide himself at his own expense with a residence in addition to those already standing so that now, to quote Homer "there is building after building". All however are connected with the Harbour, even those that lie outside it . . . The so-called Sema (tomb) is also part of the royal palaces; this was an enclosure in which were the tombs of the kings and of Alexander'.

After describing the harbour and its surrounding buildings – theatre, temple of Poseidon, Caesareum, Emporium, warehouses and ship-houses, he continues:

'Then there is the suburb Necropolis in which are many gardens and tombs and installations suitable for the embalming of corpses. Within the canal there is the Serapeum and other ancient precincts which have been virtually abandoned because of the construction of new buildings at Nicopolis; for example, there is an amphitheatre and a stadium and the quin-quennial competitions are celebrated there, while the old buildings have fallen into neglect. In a word, the city is full of dedications and sanctuaries; the most beautiful building is the gymnasium which has porticoes over a stade (*c.* 175 metres) in length. In the middle (of the city) are the law courts and the groves. There is also the Paneum, an artificially made height, conical in shape and resembling a hill and ascended by a spiral stair. From the top one has a panoramic view of the whole city lying below.'[5]

Alexandria long continued to excite the admiration of the ancients. When the Arab general 'Amr entered with his army in 642 the invading throng gazed in wonder at the width and grandeur of the intersecting streets and shielded their eyes from the dazzle of the marble. Apart from the magnificently decorated subterranean burial chambers of the Ptolemaic and Roman periods, little remains today of the splendours of this city. But they are perhaps not completely irrecoverable even now; excavations undertaken in recent years at Kom-el-Dik, near to the centre of the city, afford a glimpse of some of the grand buildings of the later Roman period, a theatre, a set of baths, and a school in an area which must have been a gymnasium complex, an important centre of leisure and cultural pursuits.

For knowledge of most of the major structures we have to rely upon our ancient witnesses. The great lighthouse designed in the early Ptolemaic period, dedicated by one Sostratus of Cnidus (perhaps more likely the sponsor of the project than its architect) and known as the Pharos was one of the wonders of the ancient world. It stood on the site now called Fort Qait Bey, at the end of a causeway which divided the two great harbours of Alexandria, and was built in three storeys, the first square, the second octagonal and the third cylindrical, reaching a height of about 120 metres. The fire which burned within it was magnified and projected by a re-flecting mechanism and could be seen from an immense distance out to sea.

Another notable building of the Ptolemaic period, much embellished and recon-structed in the Roman era, was the great Serapeum, standing near the site of 'Pom-pey's Pillar', whose destruction in 391 has already been described. This grew even-tually into a great complex of buildings set on a platform, a central shrine adorned with marble columns and statuary, with outer colonnades linking it to a library which was an offshoot of the main library of Alexandria. It was certainly rivalled eventually in scale and splendour by the Caesareum begun by Cleopatra and completed in the reign of Augustus, as the description by the Alexandrian Jewish writer Philo makes clear:

'For there is elsewhere no precinct like that which is called the Sebasteum, a temple to Caesar-on-shipboard, situated on an elevation facing the harbours renowned for their excellent moorage. It is huge and conspicuous, decorated on an unparalleled scale with dedicated offerings, surrounded by a girdle of pictures and statues in silver and gold, forming a precinct of enormous breadth, embellished with porticoes, libraries, chambers, groves, gateways, broadwalks and courts and adorned with all the most extravagant fitments.'[6]

In front of it stood two great obelisks, which remained *in situ* until the late nineteenth century; one of them can now be seen on London's embankment, the other in Central Park, New York.

As in all the great cities of antiquity, some of the buildings of an earlier age were gradually adapted to changing circumstances. Strabo noted how the new constructions of the early Roman period in the area of the legionary barracks, known as Nicopolis, diminished the focal role of the Ptolemaic palace area. The eventual dominance of Christianity was to exert an even more striking effect on the face of the city. On the site of the old Serapeum, for instance, stood a Church of St John the Baptist. The Caesareum was one of the great buildings which survived long after its original function became obsolete (in fact, until the early tenth century). The emperor Constantine dedicated it as a Church of St Michael and in the middle of the fourth century it became the official seat of the Patriarch of Alexandria; it was damaged in riots between pagans and Christians in 366, restored in 368; in 415 it witnessed a brutal Christian attack on a female teacher of pagan philosophy named Hypatia who was stripped naked and dragged through the streets until she died; on

128 The Pharos beaker. This colourless glass vase, of Alexandrian manufacture, illustrates the famous lighthouse but the three stories are not shown in accurate detail. The Pharos is attached to a fortification wall and above its tower is a colossal male statue, probably representing Zeus Soter, with an oar or rudder resting in the crook of his left arm to signify maritime power.

September 14, 641 it was the destination of a great procession and the scene of a service of thanksgiving for the triumphant return of the Patriarch Cyrus. From the early fourth century onwards the city had accommodated the new buildings demanded by the Christian faith and by the time of the Arab conquest it was adorned with as many splendid churches as it had earlier had pagan temples; notably the Church of St Mark, the traditional founder of Christianity in Egypt, those of SS Theodore and Athanasius and many more. Of these virtually no trace remains today.

By the middle of the first century BC the population of this great city was reckoned by Diodorus of Sicily at 300,000 'free residents', a figure which should perhaps be extrapolated to an overall total of around half-a-million.[7] Little is known of the physical conditions in which these people lived. The account of Caesar's war against Pompey refers to the elaborate labyrinth of cisterns which supplied the populace with fresh water and the crowding of the domestic buildings may be inferred from part of the 'city law', of the third century BC, which includes a regulation prescribing a space of one foot between houses![8] Dinocrates' original plan will certainly have been based on a rectilinear grid of intersecting streets and the inner city was girdled by an encircling wall on three sides. Although residential accommodation must soon have spread beyond the wall, the bulk of the population will have been compactly housed within it. Little is known about the domestic architecture. Wealthier residents might have owned more spacious houses of the peristyle or urban villa type. The one substantial arachaeological relic of domestic building in the city lies in a small area close to the theatre and dates to the late Roman and Byzantine periods. It reveals relatively modest structures, composed of several stone-built units. One example consists of two ranges of residences separated by a central court, with commercial premises at street level and living quarters above linked by an external wooden gallery. How much of the city remains unrecovered can be

129   Alexandria (Kom-el-Dik), the town-houses. The block of houses consists of two ranges of modest units facing each other across a central axis. It was built in the third century and shows some affinities with the apartment-blocks at Ostia in Italy, but differs in being built of local limestone rather than brick.

gauged from a chronicle written by a Patriarch of Antioch in the twelfth century, but probably referring to the fourth century, which describes Alexandria as the greatest of the cities of the inhabited world and enumerates within it 2,478 temples, 6,152 courts, 24,296 houses (this figure may reckon multiple residences as single units), 1,561 baths, 845 taverns and 456 porticoes.[9]

Social Life

The city was divided into five 'quarters' designated by the first five letters of the Greek alphabet. One of these (Delta) and a substantial part of another (Beta) was monopolised in the early Roman period by the very large and important Jewish community of Alexandria. Native Egyptians were concentrated in the west, around the site of the old village of Rhakotis. The other residential areas will have contained the majority of the Greek or hellenised population of the city. The immigrants attracted to the new city in the early Ptolemaic period were drawn from many areas of the Mediterranean world; from Thrace, Macedonia and mainland Greece, from the Aegean islands, the coastal cities of Asia Minor, from Persia, Syria and Judaea. Even Sicilians were represented if we can take literally the vivid scene in an *Idyll* of Theocritus, probably written in the 270s BC, in which two loquacious women attend a festival of Adonis: a bystander complains at them, 'My good women, do stop that ceaseless chattering – perfect turtle-doves – they'll bore one to death with all their broad vowels' and one of them replies, 'It's Syracusans you're ordering about and let me tell you we're Corinthians by descent like Bellerephon. We talk Peloponnesian and I suppose Dorians may talk Dorian.'[10] The flow of immigrants probably never dried up completely. Later on Romans or Italians were perhaps attracted by trade or stayed on after completing military or administrative service; in addition to all these, Dio of Prusa catalogues Libyans, Cilicians, Ethiopians, Arabs, Bactrians, Scythians and Indians.[11] And there was also, of course, a steady influx of Egyptians from up-country, ready to seize the opportunities offered by trade, commerce or, after several decades of Ptolemaic rule, by the gradual opening up of official positions to non-Greeks.

By no means of all of these residents were entitled to claim the privileges of free citizens of Alexandria. The model of the Greek city dictated that such privileges and status would be quite severely restricted. How the original composition of the citizen body was determined we do not know, but the designation of the citizen by enrolment in a tribe and a deme, with distinctively Greek names, is commonly found on documents and inscriptions. From this citizen body almost all Egyptians would be excluded in the early period, though it later became increasingly possible for individuals to attain entry and subsequently, in some cases, Roman citizenship. The Jews were also systematically excluded, although they possessed their own particular (though lesser) privileges which, amongst other distinctions, marked them off from other sections of the populace. Clearly, some were attracted to hellenisation by the Greek institutions around them. A famous letter of the emperor Claudius to the Alexandrians contains an admonition that:

'the Alexandrians show themselves forbearing and kindly towards the Jews, who for many years have dwelt in the same city, and dishonour none of the rights observed by them in the worship of their god but allow them to observe their customs as in the time of the deified Augustus, which customs I also, after hearing both sides, have confirmed. And, on the other hand, I explicitly order the Jews not to agitate for more privileges than they formerly possessed . . . and not to force their way into the games of the gymnasiarchs or *kosmētai*, while enjoying their own privileges and sharing a great abundance of privileges in a city not their own and not to bring in or admit Jews from Syria or those who sail down from Egypt.'[12]

The privileges enjoyed by the members of the Greek citizen body were clearly substantial and jealously guarded. Not merely the right to participate in Greek games, but official recognition of superior status to Egyptians and others, certain reductions in tax liability, guarantees of better treatment under a judicial structure which systematically linked social status and legal privilege, the possibility of a share in the largesse which might be offered to the citizens by a monarch or an emperor. Roman emperors judged it politic, especially when they were new to the throne, to protect them:

130 Alexandria (Kom-el-Shuqafa), the catacombs. This extensive complex of underground burial chambers dates from the second century AD and shows a combination of Egyptian and Greek elements. In the foreground is the exit from the shaft down which the corpse would be lowered to its destination in the burial chamber. At the higher level there was a rotunda entrance and a banqueting hall for relatives and friends of the deceased. Behind the pillared vestibule lies the burial chamber in which there are three rock-cut niches with false sarcophagi and bas-relief wall-decorations showing traditional Egyptian deities attending the corpse.

'(Being well aware of) your city's outstanding loyalty towards the emperors, and having in mind the benefits which my deified father conferred on you . . . and for my own part also . . . having a personal feeling of benevolence towards you, I have commended you first of all to myself, then in addition to my friend and prefect Pompeius Planta, so that he can take every care in providing for your undisturbed tranquillity and your food supply and your communal and individual rights.'

wrote the emperor Trajan in AD 98.[13]

All this was the model – ultimately derived from the character of the free cities of old Greece and Asia Minor – for the groups of Greek settlers in the other towns of Egypt and the other so-called Greek cities, Naukratis, Ptolemais and, later Antinoopolis. It carried with it, too, certain distinctive features of civic governmental structure, peculiar to Alexandria and the Greek cities. Thus the constitution of Alexandria established at its foundation will have made provision for the existence of a town council and colleges of elected magistrates (gymnasiarchs, *kosmētai*, *exēgētai*) who were responsible for the limited degree of civic autonomy which the monarchs allowed – supervision of the citizen roll, presentation of a limited range of business to the citizen assembly, administration of local revenues, festivals, games, public facilities and so on,

The council, above all, was the focus of prestige through which the elite satisfied local political ambitions but at some point during the Ptolemaic period (perhaps in the mid-second century BC) Alexandria lost its civic council, possibly in reprisal for public disorderliness or vociferous opposition to the monarch. The Alexandrians petitioned the emperor Augustus for its restoration on the grounds that it would safeguard the imperial revenues and protect the purity of the Alexandrian citizen body against contamination by 'uncultured and uneducated' infiltrators (probably a veiled reference to the Jews).[14] The attempt clearly failed for although the letter of

131 Alexandria (Kom-el-Shuqafa), male statue.
The wall-niches on either side of the vestibule contain statues, one male and one female, presumably representing the principal members of the family or group to whom the catacomb belonged. The stance and clothing are traditionally Egyptian in style; the modelling of the head is clearly Greek.

the emperor Claudius promised to look into the matter again after reiterated requests, it was not until 200 that Alexandria was given permission to reinstitute its council; and the privilege was considerably diluted by the fact that at the same time it was extended to the nome-capitals in the delta and the valley.

Whatever small degree of independence and prestige the restoration offered was fairly shortlived; by the end of the third century effective control of civic affairs devolved more and more upon officials appointed by and responsible to the central imperial authority. The weight of monarchical or imperial authority must always have been evident in the presence of the machinery of the Ptolemaic bureaucracy and the city-garrison, then the retinue of the Roman prefect, the legionary camp and the Alexandrian arm of the Roman imperial navy, but the civic authority had retained some degree of immunity and independence from it. In the Byzantine period control was exercised by the prefect and his staff and there was scarcely even lip-service to the fiction of freedom. If the descendants of the civic aristocrats of earlier centuries had ambition for public position they now satisfied it by obtaining lucrative posts in government service, where they had plenty of opportunity to oppress their less fortunate fellow-citizens.

Throughout almost the whole of our period the methods and instruments of control were of the utmost importance for the Alexandrian mob was notoriously volatile and violent. Early in the period, Theocritus' Syracusan ladies can compliment Ptolemy II Philadelphus for having made the streets safe: 'Nowadays no ruffian slips up to you in the street Egyptian fashion and does you a mischief – the tricks those packets of rascality used to play.'[15] This, however, is literature not fact and the factual record from the end of the third century BC onwards is horrific.

Some of the incidents reported appear trivial in themselves, for instance the stoning of the Roman prefect Petronius in the reign of Augustus or the vengeance wrought in about 59 BC on a member of a Roman embassy who accidentally killed a cat, witnessed by the historian Diodorus of Sicily.[16] But the not infrequent failure to control the mob could and did have far-reaching political consequences. The root of troubles changed in the course of time. During the last two centuries of the Ptolemaic period the Alexandrian mob played an important part in dynastic intrigue within the ruling house. It ensured the accession of Ptolemy V Epiphanes against a palace clique led by the courtier Agathocles and his sister. In the early 160s BC it was incited by a certain Dionysius Petosarapis to attempt the murder of Ptolemy VI Philometor on the grounds that he was planning to murder his brother Euergetes, the people's favourite. In 80 BC it dragged Ptolemy XI Alexander II out of the palace to the gymnasium and assassinated him, having been enraged by the murder of his wife after only nineteen days of a joint reign; and during the reign of Ptolemy XII Auletes it displayed violent and implacable hostility to his pro-Roman sympathies and manoeuvres.

Little wonder, then, that the Roman emperors were at pains to appear conciliatory, albeit that the velvet glove concealed the iron hand in the form of a strong legionary force stationed virtually within the city at Nicopolis. But in the early Roman period there were still notable examples of violence, most of them internal and occasioned by the hostility of the Alexandrian Greeks, aided by the Egyptian rabble, to the large Jewish population of Alexandria, perhaps particularly in reaction to the tend-

132 Alexandria (Kom-el-Dik), the baths. The large and impressive brick built baths of the third century AD lay close to the theatre and were supplied by an adjacent complex of water cisterns. On the highest of the three levels is the cold bath; beneath it is the warm bath and at the base is the steam-bath. The excavation reveals the underground columns of the hypocaust.

ency amongst the Jews to hellenise. Philo gives a graphic description of the violence perpetrated in the reigns of Tiberius and Gaius against the Jews and their synagogues by groups of Alexandrian Greeks organised in guilds and cult associations: houses were overrun and looted, victims were dragged out and burned or torn limb from limb in the market-place.[17] Rival delegations went to Rome to plead their respective cases. Philo, who was himself a member of the Jewish embassy, describes how his party pursued the deranged emperor Gaius from Rome to the Bay of Naples and waited for a hearing whilst the emperor enjoyed himself in his seaside villas.[18] Predictably, no coherent reaction was forthcoming until his successor Claudius attempted to pour oil on the waters.[19]

More generalised dissidence on the part of the Alexandrian Jews is evident in the riots which occurred in sympathy with the outbreak of revolt in Judaea in AD 66 and necessitated punitive action by two Roman legions and extra drafts of troops from Libya. Fifty years later, the much more serious and widespread Jewish revolt led to the massive depletion of the Alexandrian Jewish community, an event from which it took a very long time to recover.

The attitudes of the hostile Alexandrian Greeks appear in a vivid and curious form. In the late second and early third centuries Alexandrian nationalism is expressed in a literary compilation of fictional 'Martyr-acts' which purport to record encounters, in a form which is evidently based on genuine documentary reports of such proceedings, between Alexandrian dissidents and Roman emperors.[20] The historical dates of these episodes range from the reign of Tiberius (14–37) to that of Commodus (180–192); the earlier examples are pervaded by expressions of anti-Jewish feeling on the part of the Alexandrian Greeks and involve real persons known to have been involved in the disturbances against the Jews. Thus one Isidorus before the emperor Claudius:

'My lord Caesar, what do you care for a twopenny-halfpenny Jew like Agrippa? . . . I accuse them (i.e. the Jews) of wishing to stir up the entire world . . . They are not of the same nature as the Alexandrians, but live rather after the fashion of the Egyptians ... I am neither a slave nor a girl-musician's son but gymnasiarch of the glorious city of Alexandria, but you are the cast-off son of the Jewess Salome!'[21]

Isolated incidents such as Caracalla's massacre of the Alexandrian populace in 215 might partly explain the hostility, but apart from this it is difficult to see what underlay such an upsurge of nationalistic feeling, reflected generally in the abusive tone adopted towards the emperors – Commodus, for example, is described by an Alexandrian as tyrannical, boorish and uncultured in a text which makes no reference at all to the Jews.[22] But, from the point of view of the literary genre, it is interesting to note how close these compositions are in form and style to the records of Christian Martyr-acts.

Reports of violence continue throughout the later centuries of our period. A visitor in the third century writes to his parents at home in Oxyrhynchus: 'things have happened the like of which hasn't happened through all the ages. Now it's cannibalism, not war ... So ... rejoice the more, my lady mother, that I am outside the city.'[23] In the Byzantine period, with the decline of the gymnasia as focal points of Greek culture, the emphasis shifted to the amphitheatre, the Roman-style chariot races and the potentially violent factions of supporters whose muscle could be mobilised for political purposes, threatening the city's food supply from up-river and imperilling the position of the civil or ecclesiastical authorities in the city; there is no doubt, for instance, that the factions of Alexandria played an important role in the revolt of Heraclius against the tyrant Phocas in 609.

But the most common theme of the urban violence in this era is linked with the struggles between pagans and Christians, as in the events which led to the destruction of the Serapeum in 391. In the disturbances of 412–5, which culminated in the murder of the pagan teacher of philosophy, Hypatia, the hostility of the Christian mob was directed at her because she was suspected of having undue influence with the civil prefect. In these episodes the revived Jewish community makes an interest-

133 Alexandria (Kom-el-Shuqafa), burial niches. In the corridors leading off the main burial chamber were scores of *loculi* built to hold the humbler members of the family or group to which the catacomb belonged. The names and ages of the deceased were marked in red paint on the stone slabs which sealed the niches.

ing re-appearance; the violence began when the Alexandrian Christians attacked the Jews in the theatre on the Jewish Sabbath and was escalated by the influx of monks from the surrounding areas.[24] The catalogue of atrocities could easily be extended. Alexandria remained a place where the mobilisation of mass violence was relatively easy and effective, whatever was the issue, real or imaginary, at stake. 'Egyptian' Christians could be incited to violence against 'Greek' pagans just as easily as Alexandrian 'Greeks' against Jews.

The most obvious feature of Alexandrian social life which contributed to this ugly characteristic was the vibrant interest in public entertainment and spectacles. The theatre and the hippodrome frequently figure in such events and the Alexandrian populace was, in fact, notorious for its addiction to such pastimes. In the speech which he delivered at Alexandria Dio of Prusa devoted a good deal of attention to

134 Alexandria (Kom-el-Dik), the theatre.
The magnificent auditorium of the theatre was adorned with columns of Italian marble at the rear. It was probably originally constructed in the third century AD and later modified. Sixth-century graffiti carved on the seats reveal a connection with the Blue and Green factions associated with the popular rival teams of charioteers in the hippodrome.

this unseemly frivolity and his remarks find curiously striking contemporary parallels. Particularly popular were the citharodes, who played the harp and sang: 'a potpourri of effeminate songs and music-hall strummings of the lyre and the drunken excesses of monsters which, like villainous and ingenious cooks, they mash together in their own recipes to excite their greedy audiences.'[25] As for the audiences: 'you sit dumbfounded, you leap up more violently than the hired dancers, you are made tense with excitement by the songs . . . song is the occasion of drunkenness and frenzy . . . if you merely hear the twang of a harp-string, as if you had heard the call of a bugle, you can no longer keep the peace.'[26] The Alexandrian theatre claques had their own trademarks too – the emperor Nero is said to have been so captivated by the rhythmic applause of some Alexandrian sailors from the fleet which had just put into Italy that he sent for some more.[27] Hardly more elevated in tone and content than the performance of the singers, dancers, acrobats and jugglers were the vulgar dramatic pieces known as mimes. The mimes of Herodas, composed early in the Ptolemaic period and containing references to contemporary Alexandria, survive on papyrus and are excellent examples of the genre; sketches and dialogues populated by jealous, adulterous or unsatisfied wives, pimps and prostitutes, tradesmen and truant schoolboys.[28]

The grisly connection between such diversions and public violence is made explicit by Philo in a description of a show in the Alexandrian theatre:

'The first spectacle, lasting from dawn till the third or fourth hour consisted of Jews being scourged, hung up, bound to the wheel, brutally mauled and haled for their death march through the middle of the orchestra. After this splendid exhibition came dancers and mimes and flute-players and all the other amusements of theatrical contests.'[29]

As for the hippodrome and its chariot-races, Dio of Prusa thought this perhaps a necessary evil because of the 'moral feebleness and idleness of the masses,' but disapproved heartily of the drunken excesses of the spectators: 'not a man keeps his seat at the games; on the contrary you fly faster than the horses and their drivers, and it is comical to'see the way you drive and play the charioteer, urging the horses on and taking the lead and falling off.'[30] It is hard to overemphasise the importance of the hippodrome in the Byzantine period, when the leading charioteers were public celebrities, those who bred horses for racing were granted privileges of tax exemption and the claques of rival supporters could make or break a prefect, a Patriarch or even an emperor.

No less important in its own way was the public ritual, including games and processions, associated with the many and varied Alexandrian religious cults. From the beginning of the Ptolemaic period innumerable temples, shrines and priesthoods developed, celebrating some of the traditional gods of old Greece, Zeus, Dionysus, Aphrodite, the Egyptian or Graeco-egyptian deities, Isis, Sarapis and Anubis, as well as the deified members of the ruling house and Alexander in particular, whose priesthoods carried great prestige. The importance of the public spectacles associated with such cults is illustrated by the extravagance of the great procession of Ptolemy II Philadelphus described by Callixeinus of Rhodes; here cult of Dionysus is the focal point and the floats exhibited extravagant scenarios of the god and his cult-

135 Alexandria (Kom-el-Dik), inscription from the theatre. The block of stone discovered in the theatre carries two incised drawings of charioteers belonging to the Green team. The inscriptions read 'Long live Doros' and 'Long live Kalotychos'. The schematic representations, which were cut at different times, show the victorious drivers in their chariots each drawn by a pair of horses. The lower charioteer is represented in full face, whilst the horses are in profile. His right hand holds a whip, the left a palm and crown as well as the rein.

followers, the grape harvest, an enormous golden phallus fifty metres long with a gold star three metres in circumference at the end, to emphasise the priapic aspect of his worship.[31] Contemporary Alexandrian literature gives us the excited reaction of Theocritus' two Syracusan ladies, who escape from their humdrum world of shopping, clothes and baby-minding, to the visual delights of a festival of Adonis in the royal palace, as they admire the intricately woven tapestries depicting the god: 'the figures stand and turn so naturally, they're alive. not woven . . . how marvellous he is lying in his silver chair with the first down spreading from the temples, thrice loved Adonis, loved even in death.'[32]

The advent of Roman emperor-worship brought no fundamental change here – Augustus might appear as Zeus Eleutherios Sebastos, an Augustan guild of imperial slaves might be found, Germanicus might issue an edict forbidding the Alexandrians to worship him as a god, but these are differences of detail, not kind. The impact of Christianity was a different matter. Apart from anything else, it broke the importance of priesthoods and cult-associations connected with pagan religion, and with them an important network of social structures. It could neither tolerate nor accommodate emperor-worship or any other pagan cult from a theological standpoint, though it might promiscuously adapt pagan literary or artistic motifs. Paganism maintained its precarious survival in intellectual and literary circles where its adherents were easily identified and often persecuted after the mid-fourth century. The social importance of these groups is clear, but limited. The Alexandrian mob of the Byzantine period found its opiate not only in chariot-races but in popular Christianity and it would pack the great churches to be inspired by the sermons of its ecclesiastical leaders. When the powerful and charismatic fourth-century Patriarch Athanasius returned from one of his several periods of exile, the scene was likened by Gregory of Nazianzus to the entry of Christ into Jerusalem. The citizens of Alexandria poured out to welcome him, 'like the river flowing back on itself, all the way from the city to Chaireum, a day's walk away and more . . . shouting and dancing in front of him. He was acclaimed not only by the throng of children but by a polyglot mob shouting now in unison now in antiphony, vying to outdo each other. I forbear to mention the applause of the whole populace, the outpourings of myrrh, the all-night revels, the illumination of the whole city, the public and private feasts and all the other ways in which cities make public display of their joy.'[33]

Economic Life

Throughout the whole of our period Alexandria remained the most important commercial city of the Mediterranean world. The encomium of Dio of Prusa, even though addressed to an Alexandrian audience, is not exaggerated or tendentious:

'Not only have you a monopoly of the shipping of the entire Mediterranean because of the beauty of your harbours, the magnitude of your fleet, and the abundance and marketing of the products of every land, but also the outer waters that lie beyond are in your grasp, both the Red Sea and the Indian Ocean . . . The result is that the trade, not merely of islands, ports, a few straits and isthmuses, but of practically the whole world is yours. For Alexandria is situated, as it were, at the crossroads of the whole world, of even its most remote nations, as if it were a market serving a single city, bringing together all men into one place, displaying them to one another and, as far as possible, making them of the same race.'[34]

This position Alexandria owed to its natural advantages. There were two magnificent harbours, the Great Harbour to the east and the Eunostus (Harbour of Fortunate Return), with a smaller, artificially excavated harbour at its rear, to the west. The harbours were separated by an artificial dyke, the Heptastadium, linking

136 The Sophilos mosaic. The mosaic, of the second century BC, bears an idealised portrait personification of Berenike, wife of Ptolemy III Euergetes, with a headdress in the form of a ship's prow which may be intended as a symbolic reference to Ptolemaic domination of the seas.

the mainland to the island of Pharos on which the famous lighthouse stood. These accommodated an immense volume of maritime trade with the Mediterranean world and also made Alexandria an important centre of the shipbuilding industry. To the south of the city, Lake Mareotis, which itself had a harbour on its northern shore, was linked by canals to the Canopic branch of the Nile delta, giving access to the river valley. Not only did this make available to Alexandria as much of Egypt's domestic produce as she required – the large-scale transport of grain from the valley was, of course, absolutely essential to feed the city's populace – but it also linked her, through the important entrepôt of Coptos to the ports of the Red Sea coast and a network of trading relations with India and Arabia, which reached its apogee in the Roman period. Great though the volume of imports through this route was, it was outweighed, as Strabo noted, by the volume of exports which Alexandria despatched to the south.[35]

The Nile thus became one of the great trading arteries of the classical world. To the Meroitic kingdom in the south went silver- and bronze-ware, lamps, glass, pottery, wines, olive oil, reaching as far as Sennar, south of Khartoum, where bronze lamps of the first or second century have been found. Ivory, myrrh, spices, silver and gold were to be seen in profusion at Hiera Sykaminos on the southern border, on their way down-river. Under Roman rule the roads which connected the ports of the Red Sea coast to the Nile, directing goods to Coptos and thence down-river to Alexandria, were developed. In the later period the contacts through these regions to the kingdom of the Axumites tended to take over from the Nile route to Meroe as these regions were increasingly disrupted by the local tribes. The Romans did not, of course, invent these contacts; their chronological span is neatly indicated by the activities of a pious and curious Christian merchant of the sixth century named Cosmas Indicopleustes (Sailor of the Indian Sea). He recorded an inscrip-

137 Alexandrian coin. The Pharos represented as a square tower seen at an angle, surmounted by an open latticed circular lantern. On the summit is a statue of Isis Pharia holding a sceptre, on either side of the lantern a Triton. Reign of Antoninus Pius.

tion giving an account of the Third Syrian War of Ptolemy III Euergetes which he discovered during a trip to a Adulis, the main port in the Axumite kingdom and, in the Roman period, an entrepôt of major importance for the profitable trade in ivory.[36] More adventurously, Ptolemy VIII had been responsible for despatching an expedition to discover the route to India. This included a character called Eudoxus of Cyzicus who was visiting the Ptolemaic court; he returned from the trip with a cargo of precious stones and perfumes, which the king immediately confiscated; somewhat later, after the death of Ptolemy VIII, Eudoxus went again, stayed away for some eight years, and was again deprived of his profits by the reigning king when he returned.[37]

It is worth noting that the Alexandrian stimulus to trade and commerce did have some important and beneficial side effects which were non-pecuniary. From the reign of Ptolemy VIII, for instance, we have a work written by Agatharchides of Cnidus, *On the Red Sea*, in which he made use of information available in the royal archives in Alexandria as well as eye-witness reports from merchants. An anonymous Alexandrian merchant is responsible for a work written in the latter half of the first century AD, the *Periplus Maris Erythraei* (*Voyage round the Red Sea*), which remains our most detailed literary source for the study of Roman trade with the east.[38] There are thus important links between the vibrant commerce centred in Alexandria and the intellectual and literary activities which will be considered in the final part of this chapter.

The resulting influx of wealth, both public and private, into the city was enormous. It was not only a proportion of Egypt's massive surplus of grain which found its way through Alexandria to the Aegean, then to Rome and Constantinople, despatched under government supervision by contract with the shippers of the Alexandrian grain fleet. Indigenous products, most notably glass, textiles, luxury goods and papyrus, found ready markets in the east and the west and the latter, at least, continued to do so for centuries after the Arab conquest.

Individual merchants were able to make themselves extremely rich and powerful. Perhaps not always on the scale of the great landowner, though there must have been many, like Ptolemy II Philadelphus' minister Apollonius, who made money both from land and from trading ventures far afield. The wealthy merchant and usurper of the third century, Firmus, who has already been described,[39] is perhaps fictional and almost certainly not typical but he is nevertheless a credible figure. Hagiographical sources of the Byzantine period show, for instance, an Alexandrian

138 Head of Augustus. This beautiful bronze head displays the finest characteristics of Alexandrian craftsmanship in a style which is entirely Greek. It perhaps found its way to Meroe, where it was discovered, as a result of one of the Ethiopian raids or Roman counter-measures of the 20s BC.

139 Fragment of a wine-jar. Characteristic of the Ptolemaic period are wine-jugs of blue faience decorated with reliefs portraying members of the royal family, in this example Cleopatra I, wife of Ptolemy V Epiphanes, dressed as the goddess Isis. The reliefs are sculpted in the Greek idiom, but the notion of portraying contemporary persons as objects of religious cult is not a traditional Greek one.

merchant in the Spanish trade who was able to bequeath 5,000 gold *solidi* to each of two sons and another who, after returning down-river with three ships loaded with imported goods, distributed all his wealth, amounting to 20,000 *solidi* (about 275 pounds of gold) to the poor of Alexandria. [40] In the latter case, as in many others, the influence of the church is evident and its enormous wealth, though primarily land-based, was certainly much increased by revenues from commerce and trade. Its leaders were frequently able to exert political pressure through economic control, of the transport of grain for example, and a fourth-century Patriarch, George, one of the rivals of Athanasius, is said to have maintained a local monopoly in nitre, papyrus, reeds and salt.[41]

All this represents the apex of an economic pyramid whose base consisted in the organisation and labour of a very large number of poorer and humbler people. Apart from the structure of the transportation services, best known in the late Roman and Byzantine periods when they were operated through guilds of ship-owners, their captains and agents, there is little evidence for the details of the organisation of industry and commerce. A general picture is given by an undoubtedly spurious 'Letter of Hadrian' which is more likely to be a reflection of conditions in its author's day (the late fourth century) and firmly indicates that Alexandria did not have an unemployment problem:

'The people are most factious, vain and violent; the city is rich, wealthy and prosperous, in which no-one lives in idleness. Some are glass-blowers, some are making paper and others are engaged in weaving linen; everybody at any rate seems to be engaged in some craft or profession. The gouty, the circumcised, the blind all have some trade. Not even the maimed live in idleness. They have only one god – Mammon. Christians, Jews, everyone worships this divinity. Would that this city were endowed with better morals – it would be worthy of a city which has the primacy of all Egypt in view of its size and prosperity.'[42]

This passage mentions three of the most famous Alexandrian products, glass, paper and linen, all of which were exported far and wide. The best Alexandrian glassware, in particular, was of very fine quality indeed and Strabo notes that the properties of the vitreous earth which was used enabled the glass-blowers to achieve polychromatic effects which could only be done elsewhere by a blending process.[43] Although a guild of glassworkers is known at Oxyrhynchus,[44] it seems likely that much of the household ware found in the valley (notably at Karanis in the Fayum) was of Alexandrian manufacture.

Alexandria was the headquarters of the papyrus industry for the whole of the Mediterranean world. An anonymous geographer of the fourth century AD states that it was manufactured nowhere else at all, but there was certainly a good deal of production for local use in the towns of the delta and the valley.[45] The marshes and swamps of the delta were the habitat for the raw material which was processed at Alexandria and exported both in the form of writing material and manufactured books.[46] Details of the organisation of the industry are completely unknown, though it is most likely that at all periods it was a mixture of small and large private enterprises operating under varying degrees of government control. Certainly, in the Roman period, land on which papyrus grew could be privately owned. Weaving, too, was common all over Egypt but there were Alexandrian specialities in methods of weaving and dyeing and imported silk from the east is said to have been rewoven at Alexandria.[47]

Also of particular importance was the manufacture of drugs, perfumes, jewellery and works of art. For these many of the raw materials came along the trade routes from the east and were manufactured at Alexandria for export. No doubt the former was stimulated by the vitality of medical science in the capital. The value of the precious unguents in the manufacture of perfumes is stressed by the conditions in which the factory workers operated – wearing only masks, veils and loincloths and being stripped and searched on leaving work.[48] Jewellery was wrought from gold, silver and a great variety of precious gems. A document of 18 BC records the transfer of a goldsmith's workshop and a technique for covering triumphal statues at Rome is said to have been borrowed from Egyptian silversmiths.[49] Alexandrian cameo work, too, was particularly fine. Such products need to be considered not

140 Alexandrian coin. The Serapeum is shown as a portico with 2 Corinthian columns supporting a pediment; there is a statue of Sarapis inside, his right hand touching the Caesareum, represented as a small shrine with 2 columns supporting a pediment bearing an inscription represented by dots. Reign of Trajan. See Plate 105.

merely as objects of commerce but as works of art and Alexandria was certainly a very important centre for a wide range of artefacts, although nothing is known about the way in which artists organised their operations. The output, in particular, of Alexandrian mosaicists and sculptors in bronze has left a prominent mark, sometimes very far afield. In the Ptolemaic and Roman periods the orientation of style and motif is, as we might expect, Greek rather than Egyptian; not until the emergence of Coptic art in the Byzantine period is there any significant sign of fusion of the two traditions.

Intellectual Life

Any discussion of the history of literature, ideas, scholarship and science between the Hellenistic and Byzantine periods would find it necessary to refer to Alexandria far more often than any other city in the Mediterranean. There is virtually no area of intellectual activity to which she did not make a major contribution and in several

141　**Alexandria (Kom-el-Dik), a school**. This unique building which lies close to the theatre and the baths consists of three elements. In the centre is a main lecture hall, with the lecturer's seat at the centre of the short range at the top; the rooms on either side are smaller and may be subsidiary classrooms or preparation rooms – the one on the left is square-ended, the one on the right horseshoe-shaped.

spheres her role was paramount. Modern fashion and taste has most frequently turned its attention to the early part of the Ptolemaic period when the patronage at the royal court was in its heyday and attracted the presence of leading poets, men of letters, scholars and scientists from all over the Greek world. The household names of this era – Callimachus, Apollonius of Rhodes, Theocritus, Euclid, Eratosthenes – are not matched in the later centuries, but it would be seriously misleading to imagine that the continuators of the tradition were of little or no importance. Scholars of the later ages turned their attention to more esoteric and less attractive subjects of study, notably Platonic and Aristotelian philosophy, but their achievements were remarkable, nevertheless, and they played a major role in keeping their tradition alive until the very end of the Byzantine period, and beyond. The fourth-century historian Ammianus Marcellinus was in no doubt about the importance and vitality of intellectual life at Alexandria in his day:

'Even now in that city the various branches of learning make their voice heard; for the teachers of the arts are somehow still alive, the geometer's rod reveals hidden knowledge, the study of music has not yet completely dried up there, harmony has not been silenced and some few still keep the fires burning in the study of the movement of the earth and stars; in addition to them there are a few men learned in the science which reveals the ways of fate. But the study of medicine – whose support is much needed in this life of ours which is neither frugal nor sober – grows greater from day to day, so that a doctor who wishes to establish his standing in the profession can dispense with the need for any proof of it by saying (granted that his work itself obviously smacks of it) that he was trained at Alexandria.'[50]

The environment was of prime importance. Early in the Ptolemaic period, probably under Ptolemy I Soter, the Museum (literally 'Shrine of the Muses') was established within the palace area. Strabo, who saw it early in the Roman period, described it thus:

'It has a covered walk, an arcade with recesses and seats and a large house, in which is the dining-hall of the learned members of the Museum. This association of men shares common property and has a priest of the Muses who used to be appointed by the kings but is now appointed by Caesar.'[51]

Little is known of its later history. The emperor Claudius enlarged it (and also arranged for annual public readings of his histories of Carthage and Etruria!); Hadrian visited it in 130 and disputed with its leading lights; in 215 Caracalla, in the aftermath of his massacre of the Alexandrian populace, abolished the common meals and attacked the Aristotelian philosophers amongst its members.

There was certainly an admixture of non-scholar members in the Roman period when membership carried the privilege of maintenance at the public expense and tax concessions – it was granted not only to intellectuals and literary men but also as a reward to distinguished public administrators and even renowned athletes. The last scholar-member of whom we have any record is Theon, father of Hypatia, a distinguished mathematician who was active in the second half of the fourth century AD.[52] By that time, other institutions of learning, which, unlike the Museum, offered instruction to students, filled its role, notably the university and the Christian Catechetical School; and from the first century BC onwards there had existed important philosophical schools which were essentially private enterprises, run by distinguished teachers and unsupported by public money.

The Great Library of Alexandria was indispensable to the functioning of the community in the Museum. It also was within the palace quarter and was probably founded by Ptolemy I, although his son significantly enlarged it. At some point, perhaps during the Ptolemaic period, it spawned a daughter library which was located in the Serapeum. Collection of books for the Great Library during the Ptolemaic period was voracious and assiduous – at its height it probably numbered close to half-a-million papyrus rolls, most of them containing more than one work. But during Caesar's Alexandrian war against Pompey a significant proportion of the collection is said to have been destroyed in a fire, perhaps in the store houses rather than the main building.[53] The loss must have been partly compensated by Antonius' gift to Cleopatra of the contents of the library of the kings of Pergamum, said to number 200,000 volumes.[54] The Great Library itself might have perished in the destruction of the palace quarter in the early 270s and the daughter library during, or soon after, the destruction of the Serapeum in 391. Neither seems to have been in existence at the time of the Arab conquest.

Until the middle of the second century BC the extent of Ptolemaic patronage guaranteed a very lively milieu indeed, marked by intellectual creativity hardly matched in later periods. Men of talent were attracted from all over the hellenised Mediterranean, some to be tutors to members of the royal family, like Philitas of Cos and Strato of Lampsacus. Others enjoyed the benefits offered at court without such duties. One such was the Syracusan poet Theocritus, fulsome in his praise of the patronage offered by Ptolemy II Philadelphus: 'No man comes for the sacred contests of Dionysus who is skilled in raising his voice in sweet song without receiving the gift his art deserves and those mouthpieces of the Muses sing of Ptolemy for his benefactions. And what could be finer for a wealthy man than to win a fair reputation among mortals?'[55] Although writers of prose works made their mark in historical and geographical writing, it is the poets of third-century Ptolemaic Alexandria who have best earned the admiration of posterity. The *Idylls* of Theocritus, apart from their own considerable merits, are particularly important as models for Latin bucolic poetry. Apollonius of Rhodes wrote an epic in traditional form on the subject of the voyage of the Argo. He engaged with Callimachus of Cyrene in a celebrated and probably exaggerated personal and intellectual quarrel turning on the merits of traditional epic as against those of a more refined and learned genre, briefer and more varied in content. Callimachus reveals great innovative talent as an exponent of the latter. The theme of the four books of *Aetia* (Causes) is the origins of surviving local customs, especially religious; the debt to royal patronage is implicitly acknowledged in a poem on *The Deification of Arsinoe* and another, *The Lock of Berenike*, elaborates the conceit that a lock of hair, dedicated to Aphrodite by the wife of Ptolemy III in thanks for his return from the Third Syrian War, disappeared and was rediscovered among the constellations by the astronomer Conon.

The erudition and refinement of Alexandrian literature is in keeping with the aura of scholarship in the Museum and the Library. A few in the distinguished series of directors of the Library were themselves creative writers – Apollonius of Rhodes resigned the directorship in about 245 BC, to be succeeded by the geographer Eratosthenes. It is disputed whether Callimachus ever held the post but, at all events, he was responsible for a monumental and painstaking biographical and bibliographical catalogue of authors and works in 120 books. This is merely one episode in a long tradition of sustained and accurate scholarship. Successive librarians, of whom the most eminent were Aristophanes of Byzantium and his pupil Aristarchus in the first half of the second century BC, maintained a programme of collating and interpreting the texts of the great classical Greek authors, introducing order, analysis and criticism to the Homeric epics, the lyric poets, historians, dramatists and many more. Both produced extremely important editions of the *Iliad*; Aristophanes developed systems of critical and lectional signs for use in texts and Aristarchus did pioneering work on Greek grammar as well as producing commentaries and critical editions. In short, these and other scholars laid the syste-

142   Poems of Bacchylides. Bacchylides was one of the most important of the Greek lyric poets of the fifth century BC, but his work was almost unknown until the discovery of this papyrus of the second century AD, which contains 20 of his poems. The roll, as reconstructed, contained 39 columns of writing and measured approximately 4.5 × 0.25 m.

matic basis for the survival of this great corpus of literature into later antiquity and beyond.

The orientation of this literary and scholarly activity may seem to be obsessively Greek and it is true that the theme and content of the works of the Alexandrian poets, for instance, owe little or nothing to any Egyptian context outside Alexandria. But something needs to be said about literature of a less refined and sophisticated kind. There are the characteristically Egyptian folk-tales and romances which exist in both demotic and Greek versions and survived long into the Roman period, and thus must have had a Greek readership.[56] The evidence of the desire and need to transmit the native Egyptian historical tradition into Greek, brought the native Egyptian priest Manetho to write three volumes in Greek on the history and religion of Egypt, probably early in the reign of Ptolemy II Philadelphus. Finally, there is the influence of the Jewish community in Alexandria, which increased considerably in size and importance in the reign of Ptolemy VI Philometor. To this milieu and probably to this period belongs the so-called *Letter of Aristeas*, which recounts the story that Ptolemy II Philadelphus requested the despatch of seventy Jewish scholars from Jerusalem to Alexandria in order to translate the Pentateuch into a Greek version for deposit in the collection of the Great Library.[57] The theme is elaborated with descriptions of the sumptuous gifts sent by Philadelphus to Jerusalem, of the city of Jerusalem itself and of the banquet in Alexandria lasting seven nights during which the king interrogated the translators. Many of the details must be fictional and the whole composition is highly tendentious but two things are certain: one is that it originated in Jewish circles in Alexandria and the other is that the Pentateuch was actually translated into Greek at Alexandria during the Ptolemaic period.

The Alexandrian achievement in scientific fields under the early Ptolemies was no less impressive than in literature (nor are the two areas unconnected). Great advances were made in pure mathematics, mechanics, physics, geography and medicine, to which a brief and eclectic summary cannot do justice. The achievement of Euclid, working in Alexandria *c.* 300 BC was, in effect, to systematise the whole existing corpus of Greek mathematical knowledge and to develop the method of proof by deduction from axioms. Archimedes worked for some time in Alexandria in the third century BC and is said to have invented the Archimedean screw when he was in Egypt;[58] more important still were his original researches into solid geometry and mechanics. Ctesibius, who was active in the reign of Ptolemy II Philadelphus, is credited with the invention of a water-clock and a pressure pump. The application of mathematical principles to practical issues and problems lay at the very core of the advance in scientific knowledge. If further illustrations were needed we could point to Eratosthenes: his famous assessment of the circumference of the earth was based on a geometrical calculation from observation of the length of the shadows cast at noon on the day of the summer solstice at Alexandria and at Syene, which he assumed to lie on the same line of longitude; the degree of accuracy achieved in the result is uncertain only because we cannot determine with precision what unit of measurement he used. He also appears to have been the first to attempt a map of the world based on a system of lines of latitude and longitude. The temptations to erect barriers, between disciplines or between eras, should be resisted. In the middle of the first century AD Hero of Alexandria produced important works on pneumatics and the construction of artillery and automata and all the advances mentioned point forward, over 400 years, to the colossal achievements of Claudius Ptolemaeus, who worked in Alexandria *c.* 150, in the fields of mathematics, astronomy, optics, music, geography and cartography. That the same goes for medical science, is emphasised by the words of Ammianus Marcellinus.[59] The foundations had again been laid in the Ptolemaic period. The names of the most distinguished physicians include Herophilus and Erasistratus, both at work in the third century BC, who did a great deal to establish the nature of the nervous, digestive and vascular systems. The price of such scientific progress might seem high: the monarchs are said to have provided criminals from their prisons for experimentation and vivisection.[60] The names of these pioneers are perhaps less familiar than that of one of their successors, the greatest physician of classical antiquity, Galen of Pergamum – he too received his training in the medical schools of Alexandria in the middle of the second century AD.

The roster of great names and great achievements peters out somewhat after the middle of the second century BC. Internal troubles at the Ptolemaic court connected with the accession of Ptolemy VIII in 145 BC forced some distinguished scholars to leave and it is possible that the Ptolemaic loss of power and prestige abroad was accompanied by a failure to attract intellectually distinguished visitors. Be that as it may, there appears to have been something of a revival in the last few decades of the dynasty, when we can adumbrate the origins of a great tradition in a field in which Alexandria had not been distinguished under the earlier Ptolemies – philosophy. This owed a good deal to external circumstances; one of the results of the first war of Mithridates of Pontus against Rome (89-5 BC) was that Athens, hitherto the epicentre of philosophical studies, had witnessed an exodus of philosophers, several of whom subsequently settled in Alexandria. The most influential was one Antiochus of Askalon, whose pupil Dion died in Rome in 57 BC, where he was participating in an ambassadorial visit by a hundred leading Alexandrians to protest against the re-instatement of Ptolemy XII Auletes. Dion himself was a Platonist, an affiliation which represents the most important strain in Alexandrian pilosophy for the next four centuries. Such labels are, however, often confusing in some respects for the philosophical ambience was very mixed and distinctions between different schools of thought were not rigid. Another distinguished pupil of Antiochus was Arius Didymus, labelled as a Stoic, who developed a close personal relationship with Octavian at Rome in the 30s BC and returned with him to Alexandria after the battle of Actium; Octavian is said to have decided to spare the city and its inhabitants on three grounds – the reputation of its founder, its size and beauty and as a favour to his friend Arius.[61]

The presence of great names inevitably attracted disreputable lesser fry; in the first century Dio of Prusa was scathing in his condemnation of the street-philosophers, the Cynics who 'gather in groups at street-corners, in alleyways and at temple gates and play upon the credulity of lads and sailors and a crowd of that sort, stringing together rough jokes and much gossip and badinage that reeks of the market-place . . . and accustom thoughtless people to deride philosophers in general.'[62] But there was no lack, then or later, either of respectable and popular teachers – of whom the unfortunate Hypatia was one – or of serious philosophical thinkers. The most

143 Limestone relief. A slab in the form of a niche, probably portraying the birth of Venus. Fifth or sixth century. The posture of the goddess emphasises the ubiquity of conventions in the iconography of 'pagan' and Christian elements in Coptic Christian art.

interesting figure in the early Roman period is the prolific Jewish writer Philo, a member of a wealthy hellenised Alexandrian family.[63] In his case the social and cultural context was crucial, for it produced a scholar deeply immersed in Platonic philosophy and interested, above all, in applying it to the Jewish Old Testament tradition. It appears that his familiarity with the latter was largely through the medium of the Greek translation of the Septuagint, for his knowledge of Hebrew does not seem to have been profound.

Such cross-fertilisation could hardly have taken place anywhere else and the result was the creation of a new intellectual current which was particularly important as a precursor of the vital interaction in the following two centuries between Platonist philosophy and Christian theology. One factor which may have contributed indirectly to this was the decline of the hellenised Jewish intelligentsia in Alexandria after the revolt of 115–7. The effect which Greek thought had on Christianity in the first century of its existence came primarily through the medium of hellenised Jews like Philo. Whether or not there was a vacuum to be filled, it was the crucial influence of the currents of Greek philosophical thought which helped to draw the developing Christian doctrine away from the strictly Jewish exegetical tradition which had given it birth. Alexandria therefore occupied a unique role in the history of Christianity – without it, the development of Christian thought would have looked very different indeed.

This line of development leads directly from Philo to the great Christian thinkers of the second and third centuries. The foundation of the Catechetical School at Alexandria in the second half of the second century provided the necessary focus. Its first head was Pantaenus, said to be a convert from Stoicism, his pupil and successor in 190 was the bishop Clement who fled under threat of persecution in 202 and he in turn was succeeded by Origen, whose tenure was interrupted temporarily in 215 when he left during the carnage created by Caracalla and permanently in 230 when he went to Palestine. All three were steeped in the Greek philosophical tradition, drawing on Stoicism for their ethical and moral speculation, on Platonism for their metaphysics and Aristotelianism for their logic. Origen is, in many ways, the most interesting of the three, combining intellectual fervour and rigorous scholarship with extreme personal asceticism (he is said to have submitted to voluntary castration in order to be able to teach women without incurring suspicion).[64] He also took the trouble to learn Hebrew, which enabled him to compile a critical synopsis of the various versions of the Old Testament. He wrote an important treatise on philosophical and doctrinal matters, but his unique and lasting contribution to Christianity lay in his exposition and exegesis of the Scriptures. Over a century later, one of his successors as head of the Catechetical School, Didymus the Blind (*c.* 313–98), whose pupils included Gregory of Nazianzus and St Jerome, was still working in the Origenist tradition and writing learned commentaries on books of the Old Testament.

Origen might well be described, although it does not remotely do justice to the breadth of his interests and influence, as a Christian Neo-platonist. Platonism was without any doubt the dominant force in third century philosophical thought in Alexandria and pagan and Christian thinkers alike were immersed in it, often in a common context. A warning against the danger of drawing too rigid a division between pagans and Christians comes in the person of a mysterious but very influential teacher named Ammonius Saccas; he was perhaps a son of Christian parents who apostasised to paganism. He numbered among his pupils not only Origen but also the most profound and influential of all the pagan neo-Platonists, Plotinus, who came from Lycopolis in Upper Egypt and studied in Alexandria with Ammonius for about eleven years in the 230s and 240s.[65]

One thing which pagan and Christian Neo-platonists did tend to share was a hostility towards the other most prominent feature of philosophical thought at Alexandria in this period – gnosticism. Something has already been said about the importance of this in a later and perhaps less rarefied context.[66] Its main proponents in second-century Alexandria, Valentinus and Basilides, were active *c.* 130–160 and it is clear that although the strains of Christian doctrine which eventually became a more or less coherent orthodoxy viewed them as heretical, they considered themselves, and would have appeared to pagans, as Christians. Their intellectual fervour, passionate dualism, belief in the centrality of man in their system and claim to have access to knowledge (*gnōsis*) by revelation evoked strong antipathy, particularly from Christian thinkers (and even the pagan Plotinus indulged in rare polemic against them). But for the fortuitous find of the Nag Hammadi library of gnostic texts, we should know of them only from their opponents, whose inclination must have been to suppress or minimise their importance. But even this cannot wholly conceal the vitality of a tradition in Christian thought which, again, draws very heavily on the Jewish and hellenistic intellectual background in Alexandria.

The later history of philosophical thought in Alexandria is no less important, although by the fourth century its seminal contributions to Christianity had been made. Almost all the important Platonist and Aristotelian philosophers of the fifth and sixth centuries, several of whom were also literary scholars, studied at Alexandria at one time or another, including Proclus, the *doyen* of the Athenian Academy. After his death in 485, as the influence of Athens declined that of Alexandria increased, dramatically so after 529 when Justinian closed the Academy at Athens and forbade the teaching of 'pagan philosophy'. But the writing and teaching of Platonic and especially Aristotelian philosophy continued at Alexandria into the seventh and

144 Relief of St Menas.
The marble relief shows the saint between two camels. Menas was a much revered figure who became an ascetic and was martyred in the reign of Diocletian. His church, built in the mid-fourth century to the south west of Alexandria (Abu Mina), became a centre of miracles and pilgrimages. 'Menas flasks', embossed with the figure in the same attitude as on this relief and made to carry sacred healing water, have been found all over the eastern Mediterranean.

eighth centuries, ultimately transmitting the tradition to the custody of the Islamic world.

After 529 the leading lights of Alexandrian philosophy presumably either were or became professed Christians, like John Philoponus (c. 490–570) who wrote commentaries on works of Aristotle. Prior to that, pagans and Christians had co-existed in the discipline, although the tradition of hostility between them is often sharply illustrated. Proclus, for instance, wrote a polemical work in eighteen books against the Christians and was in turn attacked by John Philoponus who tried to show that Proclus was ignorant and stupid in matters of Greek scholarship as well.[67] On the other hand there is no doubt that both pagans and Christians studied, for the most part peaceably, in the same schools and personal connections could transcend religious differences. The pagan teacher Hypatia numbered among her pupils and admirers Synesius of Cyrene, who became a bishop, perhaps after conversion later in life; but he remained deeply imbued with pagan Greek culture and retained his admiration for her to the end.

The Byzantine period also saw a revival of the Greek literary tradition in Egypt and Alexandria again made its distinctive contribution. This was, however, a far different world from that of Ptolemaic Egypt. The literature still shows clear signs of being in the tradition which goes back to the poets of hellenistic Alexandria and classical Greece, though there are also now clear indications of familiarity with Latin poetry. 'The Egyptians are mad about poetry, but have no interest in any serious study,' remarked Eunapius of Sardis, writing *c.* 400.[68] By this time open-handed royal patronage, the Museum and the Great Library had long disappeared. The poets of the later age were scholars and teachers as well, making their living from pedagogy and from writing commissioned encomia or narrative poems on militaristic or political subjects for important public figures. Few of them were Alexandrians; Palladas, a writer of epigrams, and Claudian are the only ones certainly known to have been natives of the city and the latter pursued his art (in the form of Latin epic) at the court of the emperor Honorius in Rome. The remainder came, not from the Mediterranean cities, but from Upper Egypt, and particularly the area of the Thebaid around Panopolis; for most of them, too, Alexandria was both a cultural centre in its own right and a stepping-stone to wider travels to Constantinople and other cities of the east.[69]

Few literary critics would favourably compare the often contrived, florid and overblown productions of these writers with the poetry of the earlier age. The phenomenon is important nonetheless, not least for the fact that the literature works with the genres, themes and motifs of the pagan Greek tradition, with little or no concession to the contemporary, predominantly Christian, context. Some of the men of letters, indeed, were not only pagans but combative and militant pagans who, perhaps not surprisingly, sometimes became central figures in the intimidation and persecution of Christians. There is an instructive story involving Horapollon, a poet-scholar of the late fourth century from the region of Panopolis, who wrote commentaries on Sophocles, Alcaeus and Homer and taught not only in Alexandria but in Constantinople as well. A pupil named Paralius became disenchanted with paganism, taunted his teacher over his pagan beliefs and announced his intention to convert to Christianity; whereupon Horapollon's other pagan pupils chose a moment when their teacher was not there and there were few Christians present and beat him within an inch of his life.[70]

The golden age of these pagan literary figures was certainly the first half of the fifth century. It is possible to discern traces of antecedents in the previous century or so (and perhaps even a feeble flicker later on), but the efflorescence and coherence for even a relatively brief period demands some explanation; perhaps the most persuasive is that it was a reaction to the official outlawing of pagan religious practices in 391 – what was left of the pagan tradition had to express itself in a form which was legally permissible. Its decline after the middle of the fifth century perhaps merely reflects the inexorable advance of Christianity. The family of Horapollon might exemplify it; a son and grandson remained staunch pagans, until the latter experienced a sudden conversion to Christianity at the end of his life.

The Alexandrian contribution to the intellectual history of the ancient world stands in no need of defence or apologia. A satirist of the third century BC might mock the members of the Museum as 'well-propped pedants who quarrel endlessly in the Muses' bird-cage,'[71] and the Byzantine poets might seem like anachronistic pedants who could produce adulatory verse to order. But from the beginning to the end of its unique history Alexandria promoted the spread, survival and augmentation of the classical Greek tradition, just as it promoted trade and commerce, in two directions. The literate public of the eastern and western Mediterranean alike used and read texts and commentaries on classical authors made in Alexandria. Alexandrian hellenistic poets, in particular, enlarged the horizons of Greek poetry (even if their work is sometimes dismissed as 'inferior' to that of epic and lyric poets of the classical age) and exercised an enormous influence on the development of Roman poetry and, indeed, on that of European literature after the Renaissance.

For the Greek elite of the towns of the delta and the valley, too, it was the ultimate source of their reading matter, which has left its legacy to posterity in the shape of several thousands of literary texts on papyrus. In the first place these have allowed modern scholars to reconstruct the literary tastes of this small but important reading public and occasionally to resurrect important lost works of literature, such as several of the comedies of Menander, or an unknown work of the lyric poet Archilochus.[72] Second, they yield uniquely important information about the way in which Alexandrian scholars edited the classical authors and thus help to fill a major gap in the textual history of this literature between the time of its composition and its appearance in the manuscripts from western Europe. Finally, they allow us to appreciate one of the most important ways in which Egypt as a whole made its contribution to the world of classical antiquity: the seeping and pervasive influence which could give an intelligent and cultured man the means to proceed to a powerful and respected position in the Roman or Byzantine world at large; or create the fertile ground from which an Egyptian town like Lycopolis could send Plotinus, one of its brightest sons, to Alexandria and thence to Rome, to become one of the major intellectual figures of later antiquity.

Epilogue

If Byzantium's surrender of Egypt to the Arabs in 642 marked the end of an old era and the beginning of a new, it must nevertheless not be seen as an impermeable divide between two periods in the history of civilisation in the Nile valley. The changes in the political map of the eastern Mediterranean which were the consequences of the westward advance of the forces of Islam did not by any means eradicate all traces of the preceding epoch. Administrative, social, economic, cultural and religious continuities can be traced through the early centuries of Arab rule in Egypt but there was also much that was new and unfamiliar. An appreciation of the impact of these changes, which lie beyond the scope of this book, requires a sensitivity to the way in which expansion and domination by a new political power may absorb and adapt to existing patterns and an awareness of the underlying structures of the society in question.

The same may be said about the arrival of the Greeks in Egypt, almost a millennium earlier. The historian educated in the European tradition will inevitably view the changes through the eyes of the dominant power. If there is any excuse for this, it will have to be that the European historiographical tradition stands four-square on its Graeco-roman heritage. The interpretation of the history of Egypt between Alexander and the Arab conquest has been essayed – not only in this book – largely on the basis of a mass of written material the greater part of which is in Greek. The importance of the Egyptian traditions – in language, culture, religion and architecture – may stand in danger of being obscured; but they are there in the landscape, in the visible remains of the society, in the hieroglyphic, demotic and Coptic documents and even, if the trouble is taken to look for them, in the Greek.

If the preceding chapters have tried to make any particular point with emphasis, it is that no stark and rigid division between 'Greek' and 'Egyptian' can be useful in describing the development of this society after Alexander the Great. The various elements ebb and flow in their degrees of distinction, juxtaposition and fusion. But it is also essential not to go too far in the opposite direction and accord an equal importance to all of the various co-existing facets of Egyptian civilisation. The dominance of the Greek or Graeco-roman elements was the distinctive and most important feature of the period. How far they destroyed, eclipsed or altered something of value and importance is bound to be, to some extent, a subjective judgement. But it is hoped that the preceding pages have at least made a case for believing that their appearance in the Nile valley both contributed to and benefited from the development of Egyptian civilisation.

Appendix I

The Reigns of the Ptolemies

Some of the dates given in the table below are uncertain. For discussion of the technical problems involved see Samuel (1962), Skeat (1969). For a genealogy of the Ptolemaic family see *Cambridge Ancient History* (Second Edition), vol. VII, pt. I (ed. A. E. Astin, F. W. Walbank, 1984), 488–9.

All dates are BC

305 (November 7)
Ptolemy I Soter officially assumes kingship.

285 (December 28)
Joint reign of Ptolemy I Soter and Ptolemy II Philadelphus begins.

282 (January 7/summer)
Death of Ptolemy I Soter.

246 (January 29)
Death of Ptolemy II Philadelphus, accession of Ptolemy III Euergetes I.

222 (October 18/December 31)
Death of Ptolemy III, accession of Ptolemy IV Philopator.

205 (?October/November)
Death of Ptolemy IV (concealed until ? Sept. 204).

204 (summer/September 8)
Accession of Ptolemy V Epiphanes.

180 (September 2/October 6)
Death of Ptolemy V, accession of Ptolemy VI Philometor.

176 (April 8/October 14)
Cleopatra II, wife/sister of Philometor associated in rule.

164/3
Expulsion of Ptolemy Philometor VI by brother, later Ptolemy VIII Euergetes II Phsycon.

145 (spring/summer)
Association of Ptolemy VII Neos Philopator with Ptolemy VI.

145 (before September 19)
Accession of Ptolemy VIII Euergetes II Physcon.

130–1
Revolution of Cleopatra II begins.

116 (June 28)
Death of Ptolemy VIII.

115 (before April 6)
Reign of Cleopatra III with Ptolemy IX Soter II Lathyros begins.

110/9–108 (spring)
Ptolemy IX temporarily replaced by Ptolemy X Alexander I.

107 (autumn)
Ptolemy IX replaced by Ptolemy X Alexander I.

101 (before October 26)
Death of Cleopatra III, Ptolemy X ruling with Cleopatra Berenike III.
88 (just before September 14)
Death of Ptolemy X, return of Ptolemy IX.
80 (March)
Death of Ptolemy IX, rule of Cleopatra Berenike III for 6 months, the last 19 days in association with Ptolemy XI Alexander II.
80 (before September 11)
Death of Ptolemy XI, accession of Ptolemy XII Neos Dionysos Auletes.
58 (after September 7)
Departure of Ptolemy XII.
57 (by July 11)
Rule of Berenike IV and Cleopatra VI Tryphaena (died in 57).
55 (by April 22)
Return of Ptolemy XII.
51 (?March/April)
Joint rule of Ptolemy XII, Cleopatra VII Philopator and Ptolemy XIII begins.
51 (spring/summer)
Death of Ptolemy XII.
47 (before January 15)
Death of Ptolemy XIII, replaced by younger brother as Ptolemy XIV.
42–1
Temporary association with Caesarion.
36
Joint rule of Cleopatra and Caesarion begins.
30 (August 12)
Death of Cleopatra VII, followed by '18-day reign' of her children.

Appendix II

Metrology and Currency

The establishment of precise equivalents for units of measurement and currency is sometimes problematic, either because of unresolved technical difficulties or apparent variation in the units themselves.[1] The following list gives the standard definitions of terms used in the text:

Aroura
The universally used unit of land measurement in Egypt; 0.68 acres or 0.275 ha.

Measures of capacity

Artab
A dry measure whose capacity apparently varies. The 'standard' artab of Roman Egypt was probably 38.8 litres. An artab of milled wheat weighs approximately 30.2 kilograms. Some scholars believe that the 'standard' Ptolemaic artab was about 30 per cent larger.

Choinix
A dry measure, one fortieth of an artab.

Chous
Liquid measure, 1.5 litres.

Medimnus
The Attic measure, 52.5 litres, equivalent to 1.32 artabs or 6 *modii*.

Modius
Standard Roman measure; the *modius Italicus* is about 8.4 litres and the artab therefore contains approximately 4.5 *modii*.

Sextarius
Roman measure, one sixteenth of a *modius*.

Units of currency

Drachma
The basic standard unit of currency (and of weight) in Egypt. Minted as silver drachmas in the Ptolemaic period and as four-drachma pieces (tetradrachmas) in the Roman period. Despite the small silver content, these are normally referred to as 'drachmas of silver' in documents, whilst 'drachmas in bronze' indicates the drachma-equivalent in smaller coin. The drachma, like the three following units in the list, was also used as a weight measurement (about 3.5 grams).

Obol
One sixth of a drachma. Strict reckoning makes the tetradrachma of the Roman period worth 24 obols, but the actual equivalence created by a form of official surcharge was 28 or 29 obols.

Mina
100 drachmas.

Talent
6,000 drachmas.

Denarius
The standard Roman silver coin, minted officially at the rate of 96 to the pound of silver from the reign of Nero onwards; but financial difficulties in the second and third centuries involved a succession of debasements and devaluations of the *denarius*. The *denarius* and the tetradrachma were of equivalent value.

Sesterce
One quarter of a *denarius*, therefore equivalent to one drachma.

Solidus
The gold coin which became the standard unit of currency from the early fourth century AD. Minted at 72 to the pound of gold.

Keration (carat)
One twenty-fourth of a *solidus*.

The units themselves make no sense without some notion of their modern equivalents but this can only be given by reference to prices, wage-rates and subsistence levels and is, at best, a broad approximation. The calculations which follow use as a basis human calorie requirements in wheat equivalents; the assumption is that a man aged 20–39 weighing 62 kilograms requires 2,852 calories per day if he is moderately active, 3,337 if he is very active and 3,822 if he is exceptionally active.[2]

One artab of wheat supplies about 3,350 calories per day for a month. A very active male therefore needs twelve artabs of wheat, or its equivalent, per year for subsistence; a family consisting of husband, wife and three children, something of the order of 36–40 artabs per year. Discounting peripheral sources of food (fish, meat obtained from hunting, fruit, wild plants etc.), a hypothetical population of 8 million (about 1.6 million notional families) requires the equivalent of about 60 million artabs of wheat per year. If there were nine million arourae of land under cultivation, each aroura would probably have to produce an average of the equivalent of ten artabs of wheat per year to allow subsistence after payment of taxes. The standard sowing rate was one artab of seed corn per aroura and an average of ten-fold yield is a reasonable working hypothesis. It is worth noting the claim, made in papyrus of the late second century BC, that a plot of five arourae would provide a family (actual size unknown) with the means of subsistence.[3]

The value of money is difficult to calculate because of variation over periods of time. In general, commodity prices rose steadily during the Roman period but the exaggerated effects of market forces could be very localised and there were often violent fluctuations within small areas and short periods. The average price of an artab of wheat in the first and second centuries AD was in the region of eight drachmas and wage-rates for casual agricultural labour were about 20 drachmas per month. Documents from the Fayum in the mid-third century suggest an average price of about 18 drachmas per artab for wheat and wage-rates for agricultural labour of about 60–68 drachmas per month.[4] This income would buy about 40–45 artabs of wheat per year which, after deduction of tax-payments and the cost of clothing, accommodation etc., was probably not quite enough to support a notional family of five. But it will frequently have been supplemented by extra payment of rations or income from other sources.

In the Byzantine period, the gold *solidus* seems normally to have been capable of purchasing ten artabs of wheat and a soldier's rations in the mid-fifth century were worth approximately four *solidi*. A contract for an indentured domestic worker in the sixth century specifies allowances in wheat, barley, wine and oil which represent a value of about two-and-a-quarter *solidi* per annum.[5]

Notes to Appendix II　　1. See D.W. Rathbone, 'The
weight and measurement of
Egyptian grains,' *ZPE* 53
(1983), 265–75 with earlier
bibliography, Bagnall
(1985)

2 Foxhall, Forbes (1982),
41–90 at 48–9
3 Above, 100
4 Rathbone (1986),
Appendix 2
5 *P. Strassb*. 40 (569),
A.H.M. Jones (1964), 445–8

Appendix III

The Archaeological Evidence

In comparison with earlier periods in the history of Egypt, the archaeological evidence for the millennium which is the subject of this book is disappointing in quantity and quality, and difficult to exploit. The reasons are not hard to discover. The attention of early Egyptologists was mainly directed to sites of Pharaonic interest, and very few settlements with significant physical remains from the Greek, Roman and Byzantine periods were systematically excavated in the period before the Second World War. When excavation was undertaken, the discovery of papyri rather than the scrupulous recording of the topography and physical structures was the principal aim. In so far as the latter were examined at all, their study was often regarded as incidental and in some cases the evidence which was obtained has never been fully published. In recent decades, although interest in post-Pharaonic sites has increased and excavation has been more systematic, the opportunities and the resources to undertake large-scale excavations have been relatively limited. It is therefore not surprising that it proves extremely difficult fully to integrate the papyrological and the archaeological evidence for Egypt between 332 BC and AD 642. It remains true, regrettably, that the present state of archaeological knowledge and reporting offers us a series of isolated results, some of which must have broader significance; what we lack is a coherent framework into which they can be fitted.[1]

The one exception, and the site which offers the greatest potential for a fully integrated study, is the village of Karanis in the Fayum, excavated by an expedition from the University of Michigan in the 1920s and 1930s (cf. pp. 145, 148–50, 171–2). Much of the data (an astonishingly rich yield of glassware, coins, pottery and other artefacts, as well as detailed plans of streets, houses and public buildings) still remains unpublished, although it has evoked renewed interest in recent years.[2] It is worth emphasising that the evidence will allow a detailed reconstruction of the character and history of this community from the late Ptolemaic period down to the last quarter of the fourth century AD and that the combination of such quantities of archaeological and documentary evidence is unique, not merely in Egypt but in the ancient Mediterranean world as a whole.[3] Other village sites in the Fayum have attracted attention, but none has been as thoroughly excavated and none is as well represented in terms of the yield of written texts.[4] Detailed study of the Fayum, in which some basic topographical survey and identification remains an urgent necessity, will provide information for communities whose character was largely shaped and determined by the heavy influx of Greek settlers in the Ptolemaic period (as can be seen, for instance, in the characteristic rectilinear layout of the streets at Philadelphia).[5] There is at present little prospect of any further advance in our knowledge of village sites in Middle and Upper Egypt. Despite the large number of village names attested, for instance, in the Oxyrhynchite and Hermopolite Nomes, there has been no systematic attempt to locate and identify them, though it might be possible to make some progress by combining the topographical and papyrological evidence. Some topographical investigations have been carried out in the Delta, for which there is virtually no auxiliary papyrological evidence.[6] Recent archaeological work in the Dakleh Oasis has been somewhat more rewarding, offering evidence for village sites and farmstead settlements of varying sizes during the Roman period, as well as important examples of mural paintings on traditional Greek mythological themes.[7]

The situation in the larger towns and nome-capitals is somewhat less encouraging: none has been fully excavated.[8] The physical features of Oxyrhynchus, for which our documentary evidence is fullest, are almost totally unknown. Hermopolis is somewhat more promising and the pre-1939 German excavations have recently been supplemented by renewed activity. One result has been an improvement in understanding of the topography of the site. Another has highlighted the crucial importance of achieving a better appreciation of the articulation of public buildings and public space in the towns by revealing an impressively large building of the mid-second century AD which has been tentatively identified as a kōmastērion (a building in which religious processions formed before proceeding to the temple).[9] In other provinces, the growth or creation of public building complexes in town centres is a crucial feature of urbanisation. A greater understanding of such developments in the towns of Egypt, in relation to the pre-existing Pharaonic structures, would enable us to appreciate better the influence of the Greeks and Romans in this respect; an influence which is suggested by the eventual appearance of some of the characteristic features of local government and administration.[10]

It is in precisely this area that the excavations conducted by Polish archaeologists at Kom el-Dikka in Alexandria are most important (cf. p. 208). They reveal a group of late Roman and Byzantine buildings, which includes a theatre, a large bath-house, a three-room school or auditorium as well as a block of houses. There is also some evidence of a public park or recreation space. The alignment of these buildings and their relation to one another offers some hope of new evidence which will bear on the long-debated issue of the layout of the major arteries of the city.[11]

Excavation on the southern shore of lake Mareotis casts some indirect light on the economic importance of Alexandria by producing information about the port of Marea, through which cargoes were transported up and down the Nile.[12] The port itself appears to have possessed three separate harbours, and the limits of the town have been identified. Three important structures to the south of the port have been examined: a complex consisting of artisans' shops or offices combined with residential accommodation; an extremely well-preserved wine factory, which emphasises the reputation of the wines of this area; and a large Byzantine peristyle house, which also incorporates wine-making structures. Almost all these remains seem to belong to the Byzantine period, but some more accurate evidence for dating would be welcome.

The organisation of trade and commerce on the Red Sea coast in the Roman period is illuminated by the excavations at Quseir al-Qadim.[13] This area also promises to produce important new evidence for Roman control of the quarries at Mons Claudianus. The extent of military supervision of quarrying and the transport of stone via the routes which traversed the Eastern Desert is emphasised by the physical evidence for the presence of the Roman garrison; particularly valuable is the discovery of more than a thousand Greek and Latin texts on ostraka, which will yield information on the organisation and administration of this important activity.[14] Other military structures cast light on the internal security and the defence of the frontiers.[15] The great temple at Luxor was turned into a military camp in the Diocletianic period.[16] A new fort-site from the same period provides a comparison with the fort already known at Qaṣr Qarun.[17] Beyond the frontier, recent excavations at Qaṣr Ibrîm (Primis) show its strategic importance as an outpost in the Ptolemaic and early Roman Periods.[18]

Notes to Appendix III

1 These and other general points are made by R. S. Bagnall in a helpful and constructive review-article in the *Journal of Roman Archaeology 1* (1988), 'Archaeology and Papyrology', which suggests that a bibliographical survey might be a useful addition to this book. Bagnall provides a select bibliography, which is not repeated in full here, although I have cited some items which he does not include; even so, the combined selections are far from exhaustive

2 Boak, Peterson (1931); Boak (1933, 1955); Husselman (1979); id. 'The granaries of Karanis,' *TAPA* 83 (1952), 56–73; id. 'The dovecotes of Karanis,' *ibid.* 84 (1953), 81–91; E. Gazda, *Karanis: An Egyptian Town in Roman Times* (1983) (with further bibliography)

3 This is a projected study which the present author has undertaken to complete with the generous co-operation of the Director of the Kelsey Museum of Archaeology, University of Michigan

4 Soknopaiou Nesos: Boak (1935). Tebtunis: C. Anti, 'Un esempio di Sistemazione Urbanistica nel III secolo av. Cr.,' *Architettura e arte decorativa* 10 (1930–1), 97–107; id. 'Gli scavi della missione archeologica italiana a Umm el Breigat (Tebtunis),' *Aegyptus* 11 (1931), 389–91; Bagnani (1934); Philadelphia: Viereck (1928); Medinet Madi; E. Bresciani, *Rapporto preliminare delle campagne di scavo 1966 e 1967, Istituto della Università degli Studi di Milano, Missione de Scavo a Medinet Madi (Fayum, Egitto)* = *Testi e documenti per lo studio dell'Antichità* 20 (1968); id. *Rapporto preliminare delle campagne di scavo 1969 e 1969, ibid.* 53 (1976); Dionysias/Qaṣr Qarun: Schwartz (1969); J.-M. Carrié, 'Les *Castra Dionysiados* et l'evolution de l'architecture militaire romaine tardive,' *MEFRA* 86 (1974), 819–50

5 Viereck (1928), Tafel I

6 E. C. M. van den Brink, 'A geo-archeological survey in the North-eastern Nile Delta, Egypt; the first two seasons, a preliminary report,' MDAIK 43 (1987), 7–31

7 A. J. Mills *et al.*, 'The Dakleh Oasis project,' *Journal of the Society for the Study of Egyptian Antiquities* 9.4 (1979), 10.4 (1980)

8 For recent excavations at Naukratis see W. D. E. Coulson and A. Leonard, Jr., *Cities of the Delta I: Naukratis: Preliminary Report on the 1977–8 and 1980 Seasons* (*ARCE Reports* 4, 1981)

9 Roeder (1959); E. Baraize, 'L' "Agora" d'Hermoupolis,' *ASAE* 40 (1940), 741–60; A. J. Spencer, *Excavations at el-Ashmunein I: The Topography of the Site* (1983); D. M. Bailey, W. V. Davies, A. J. Spencer, *British Museum Expedition to Middle Egypt: Ashmunein (1980)* (*British Museum Occasional Papers* 37, 1982); for the seasons of 1981 and 1982 see A. J. Spencer and D. M. Bailey, *ibid.* 41 (1982); A. J. Spencer, D. M. Bailey, A. J. Burnett, *ibid.* 46 (1983) (the *kōmastērion*). See Plate 145

10 See L. Dabrowski, 'La topographie d'Athribis à l'époque romaine,' *ASAE* 57 (1962), 19–31, concluding that in the Roman period the town lost the religious character which it had had in the Pharaonic period and that the development of its architecture was determined by a new alignment along two main intersecting streets. It is notable that the recent work of A. Lukasiewicz, *Les édifices publics dans les villes de l'Egypte romaine* (1986) makes very little use of archaeological evidence

11 Rodziewicz (1984); *id.*, 'Excavations at Kom el-Dikka in Alexandria 1980–81 (Preliminary Report),' *ASAE* 70 (1984/5), 233–46

12 F. el-Fakharani (1983)

13 D. S. Whitcomb, J. H. Johnson, *Quseir al-Qadim 1978: Preliminary Report* (1979); eid., *Quseir al-Qadim 1980: Preliminary Report* (*ARCE Reports* 7, 1982)

14 Th. Kraus, J. Röder, 'Mons Claudianus: Bericht über eine erste Erkundungsfahrt im Marz 1961,' *MDAIK* 18 (1962), 80–120; J. Bingen, 'Première campagne de fouille au Mons Claudianus,' *BIFAO* 87 (1987), 45–52

15 H. Jaritz, 'The investigation of the ancient wall extending from Aswan to Philae: First Preliminary Report,' *MDAIK* 43 (1987), 17–74

16 J.-C. Golvin *et al.*, *Le camp romain de Louqsor* (*Mémoires IFAO* 83, 1986)

17 Mohi ed-Din Mustafa, H. Jaritz, 'A Roman fortress at Nag 'el Ḥagar. First Preliminary Report,' *ASAE* 70 (1984/5), 21–32

18 W. Y. Adams, 'Primis and the "Aethiopian" Frontier,' *JARCE* 20 (1983), 93–104

Appendix IV

Additional notes

The following notes cite some books and articles, most of which have been published since 1985 and are incorporated in the main bibliography, which make a substantive contribution to the issues and themes discussed in my text.

Chapter 1
The physical environment: Bagnall 1993a, ch. 1.
Cultivable land: Rathbone 1990.
Knowledge of quarrying operations in the Roman period is further increased by excavations and discoveries at Mons Claudianus and Mons Porphyrites: see *O. Claud.*, Peacock 1992, Peacock and Maxfield 1994.
Estimates of the size of the population are very hazardous and uncertain. For arguments in favour of a lower figure than that which I proposed, and for the distribution between towns and villages, see: Bagnall and Frier 1994, 53–6, Rathbone 1990, Thompson 1988, 32–6.
Urbanisation: see Bowman 1992, Rathbone 1990 and the notes on Chapter 5, below.
Evidence of the effects of the plague of the second century AD: *P. Thmuis*.
Papyri as an historical source: Bagnall 1995.

Chapter 2
The nature of the monarchy and the Ptolemaic dynasty: Mooren 1983, Whitehorne 1994a.
Ptolemaic naval power and the empire: Hauben 1983.
Political history and relations with Rome: Bianchi *et al.* 1988, 13–20, Gruen 1984, ch. 18, Thompson 1994a.
Court titles and hierarchy: Mooren 1975.
The Augustan annexation and Egypt under Roman rule: Bowman 1996.
The date of the Jewish revolt 116–17 rather than 115–17: Barnes 1989.
Role of cities and magistracies in local government and administration, Bowman and Rathbone 1992.

The southern frontier: Speidel 1988.

Byzantine Egypt: Keenan 1993.

Politics, Christianity and the Church: Bagnall 1993, 278–89, Barnes 1993, chs. 4, 7, 10, Pearson and Goehring 1986, Trombley 1994, 205–46.

Chapter 3

Government in Ptolemaic Egypt: Lewis 1986.

The Ptolemaic army: Van 't Dack 1988, ch. 1.

The mention of a 'pro-Persian king' in the demotic ostrakon has been eliminated by a re-reading of the text: Bresciani 1983, Zauzich 1984.

For the Ptolemaic census see Clarysse and Thompson forthcoming.

The character of the Roman government: Bowman 1996, Bowman and Rathbone 1992, Montevecchi 1988.

The advent and effect of Roman law: Mélèze-Modrzejewski 1990, chs. 1, 9. The application of law in the villages: Hobson 1993.

The role of military personnel: Alston (1995).

The census: the establishment of a seven-year cycle superseded by a fourteen-year cycle, Bagnall 1991; survey and catalogue of census returns, Bagnall and Frier 1994.

Taxation: Rathbone 1989, 1993.

Government of Byzantine Egypt: Bagnall 1993a, 62–7, Keenan 1993, MacCoull 1988.

Military personnel as bureaucrats and landowners on a moderate scale: Bagnall 1993a, 72–80, Keenan 1994.

An important demonstration of the role of the 'great houses' of Byzantine Egypt in taking over governmental responsibilities: Gascou 1985.

Distribution of land and wealth: Bagnall 1992, 1993a, 68–78.

Chapter 4

A survey of the economic structures: Rathbone 1989.

The use of money: Howgego 1992.

Land, ownership and labour: Bagnall 1993a, ch. 3, Rowlandson 1996.

For the distribution of wealth, see above on ch. 3.

Investment, economic and financial organisation of agricultural estates in the Roman period: Kehoe 1992, Rathbone 1991; in the Byzantine period, Gascou 1985.

The character of agriculture in Ptolemaic Egypt: Thompson 1984.

Some Ptolemaic farmers and landholders: Lewis 1986. Economic opportunities for women: Rowlandson 1995.

A general account of import/export trade in the Roman period: Sidebotham 1986. An important document of the mid-second century AD illustrating the trade in nard, ivory and textiles from India: *SB* 13167 with Casson 1986, Thür 1987, 1988.

Manufacture and craft: Van Minnen 1987.

Chapter 5

There has been a very great deal written about ethnic identity, cultural interaction and insularity, especially from the point of view of Greeks and Egyptians. Particularly note-worthy are: Ethnicity: Bilde *et al.* 1992, Goudriaan 1988, La'da 1993, Lewis 1986, chs. 6, 8, Clarysse 1985, 1992.

Literacy, education: Thompson 1992a, 1992b, 1994b, Maehler 1983, Hanson 1991, Bagnall 1993a, ch. 7.

Language, literature, cultural patterns: Ray 1994, Clarysse 1993, Tait 1992, 1994, Frandsen ed. 1991 (a remarkable range of demotic literature from the village of Tebtunis),

Whitehorne 1994, MacCoull 1988, Trombley 1994 (the effect of Christianity).
Jews: Kasher 1985, Clarysse 1994, Bagnall 1993a, 275–8.
Legal status: Mélèze-Modrzejewski 1990.
Use of the census documents as a basis for determining the social and demographic patterns:
Bagnall and Frier 1994.
Contraception more effective than generally believed: Riddle 1991, 1992, ch. 7.
Exposure of infants: Harris 1994.
Brother-sister marriage: Shaw 1992.
Slavery: Bagnall 1993a, 208–14, 1993b.
Towns: Bailey 1991 (Hermopolis), Krüger 1990 (Oxyrhynchus), Thompson 1988 (Memphis), cf. Bowman 1992.

Chapter 6
A collection of evidence for religious festivals: Perpillou-Thomas 1993.
Temple of Jupiter Capitolinus at Arsinoe: Glare 1994.
For an excellent discussion of the Egyptian and Greek context and antecedents of the Corpus Hermeticum see Fowden 1986.
Magical practices and folk-religion: Gager 1992, Bagnall 1993a, 273–5.
Mummy-portraits: Corcoran 1992.
For the very uneven and complex developments surrounding the advent of Christianity and the decline of paganism see Pearson and Goehring 1986, Bagnall 1993a, ch. 8, Trombley 1994 (with a very good discussion of the activities of Shenute). My text (pp. 194–5) perhaps fails to emphasise sufficiently the differences between anchorite monks and coenobitic communities (on the latter see especially Rousseau 1985).
Coptic art: Thomas 1992.
A very important discovery of Manichaean texts at Dakleh Oasis: Gardner 1993.

Chapter 7
Buildings and physical development of the city: el-Abbadi 1990 (library), Burkhalter 1992 (the gymnasium); Kolotaj 1992 (the baths), Rodziewicz 1988 (domestic buildings).
Government and administration: Bowman and Rathbone 1992, Delia 1991, Barnes 1993.
Literary and intellectual life: Fowden 1986, 161–7.

Appendix I
Discussion of the evidence of demotic texts: Pestman 1967.

Appendix III
It is impossible to cite all the reports of archaeological activities in recent years. For a good survey of problems and possibilities see Rathbone 1994.
On specific sites mentioned in the text, note particularly: Tebtunis: Gallazzi 1989.
Hermopolis: Bailey 1991.
Dakleh Oasis: Hope *et al.* 1989, Gardner 1993, Whitehorne 1994.
Karanis: for the archaeological context of some papyri see Van Minnen 1994.
Mons Claudianus: *O. Claud.*, Peacock 1992.
Mons Porphyrites: Peacock and Maxfield 1994.
An important excavation of the monastery at Naqlun is currently being carried out by Polish archaeologists, see Derda 1994.
For an account of the monastery of St. Phoibammon on the site of the Temple of Hatshepsut at Deir el-Bahari see Godlewski 1986.

145 Hermopolis, buildings of the Roman period. A reconstruction of the area of the Komasterion (procession house) built in the second century AD. The Komasterion fronts the paved area and the Dromos of Hermes flanks the latter. To the right are the Great Tetrastylon and the Western Nymphaion.

Footnotes

Note: In order to keep the annotation minimal, the footnotes give references almost exclusively to the works of classical authors, publications of documents or of primary evidence specifically cited in the text. Modern works relevant to the subjects discussed in each chapter are listed, by author and year of publication, before the numbered annotations. The bibliographical list does not contain publications of texts on papyrus, which are cited frequently in the following footnotes. Such volumes, for which there is no single standard method of abbreviation, are cited by the abbreviations used in one or other of the following lists: E.G. Turner, *Greek papyri, an Introduction* (2nd ed. 1980, Oxford University Press), 154–79, J.F. Oates, R.S. Bagnall, W.H. Willis, and K.A. Worp, 'Checklist of Greek papyri and Ostraca,' (4th ed. 1992, Scholars Press, Atlanta). A few annotated editions of works of classical authors are included in the bibliographical list, but the forms of reference to standard texts may be found in the lists in Liddell-Scott-Jones, *Greek Lexicon* (9th edition) and the *Oxford Latin Dictionary*. The following abbreviation should be noted: *HM = Historia Monachorum in Aegypto*, ed. A.-J. Festugière (*Subsidia Hagiographica* 34, 1961), translated in B. Ward, N. Russell, *The Lives of the Desert Fathers* (1980, A.R. Mowbray, London).

Notes to chapter 1
Bibliography:
Bagnall (1982b); Baines and Malek (1980); Berry, Berry, Ucko (1967); Boak (1959); Bonneau (1964); Butzer (1976); Crawford (1971); Johnson (1936); Meredith (1952–3); Trigger, Kemp, O'Connor, Lloyd (1983); Turner (1980); Walek-Czernecki (1941)

1 Herodotus, 2.20–7, Strabo 17.1.5
2 Strabo 17.1.4
3 Herodotus 2.14
4 Butzer (1976), 108
5 Butzer (1976), 82
6 Ch. 4, 98ff.
7 Pliny, *NH* 18.121, 13.107, Strabo 17.1.15
8 Ammianus 22.15.19
9 Ammianus 22.15.24
10 Trigger, Kemp, O'Connor, Lloyd (1983), 12
11 Ammianus 22.16.23
12 F. Petrie, *Roman Portraits and Memphis (IV)* (1911, School of Archaeology in Egypt, London), 14; Berry, Berry, Ucko (1967)

13 *BJ* 2.385
14 Walek-Czernecki (1941)
15 E. W. Lane, *Manners and Customs of the Modern Egyptians* (1981 repr. of 1895

ed., East-West Publications, London), 34
16 Appendix II
17 Ammianus 22.15.3

Notes to chapter 2

Bibliography:
Bagnall (1976); Baynes (1955), ch. 6; Bell (1956); Bevan (1927); Bowman (1976); Butler (1978); Heinen (1966); A. H. M. Jones (1964); Kirwan (1937), (1977); Lewis (1970), (1983), ch. 1, (1984); Maehler (1983); Milne (1924); Mitteis and Wilcken (1912); Montevecchi (1973); Préaux (1978), vol. I; Rostovtseff (1953); Trigger, Kemp, O'Connor, Lloyd (1983); ch. 4; Turner (1984); Walbank (1981), ch. 6; Will (1966–7)

1 Herodotus, Book 2
2 Translation in Bevan (1927), 28–32
3 Plutarch, *Antonius* 27
4 Rice (1983), 11–3; below, 216
5 Koenen (1977)
6 Manetho, *Aegyptiaca*
7 Austin (1981), no. 222
8 *Ibid.*, no. 226
9 *Ibid.*, no. 231
10 *Commentary on the Book of Daniel*, 11.5
11 Préaux (1978), 364 n. 1
12 Shear (1978)
13 Austin (1981), no. 227
14 Speigelberg (1914), Johnson (1974)
15 *P. Oxy.* 2332
16 Polybius 29.27
17 Ray (1976), no. 2
18 Austin (1981), no. 230
19 Plutarch, *Antonius* 26
20 Dio Cassius 51.16
21 *Res Gestae* 27
22 *Sel. Pap.* III, 113
23 Rea (1982a)
24 Below, 68ff.
25 Ovid, *Tristia* 4.4.15
26 Aurelius Victor, *Epit. de Caes.* 1.6
27 Tacitus, *Ann.* 3.54
28 *Acts of the Apostles*, 27.27ff.
29 *Historia Augusta, Quad. Tyr.* 3
30 Below, 92
31 Butler (1978), 197
32 Pliny, *NH* 6.184
33 *I. Phil.* II.128
34 Seneca, *Dial.* 12.19.6
35 Suetonius, *Vespasian* 7
36 Philostratus, *VS* 563
37 *CPJ* II, pp. 225ff.

38 *P. Oxy.* 705
39 *CPJ* II, 159, see below, p. 213
40 *P. Oxy.* 2435 recto
41 *P. Col.* VI
42 Van Groningen (1957)
43 *P. Oxy.* XL, p. 15
44 *P. Oxy.* 1413 (?271/2)
45 John Malalas, *Chronographia* (ed. Dindorff), 308–9
46 Procopius, *Hist.* 1.19.27–35
47 *P. Beatty Panop.* 1
48 *FIRA* II, pp. 580–1
49 Lactantius, *DMP* 34.48, Eusebius, *HE* 8.17, 10.5
50 Below, 81
51 *Corpus Iuris Civilis* III, 783; below, 93f.
52 Averil Cameron, *Continuity and Change in Sixth Century Byzantium* (1981, Variorum Press, London), V, p. 16
53 Bagnall (1982a)
54 R. Pococke, *A Description of the East and some other Countries* (1743–5, London), Bk. V, ch. 17, 279ff.
55 Stevenson (1989), no. 101
56 *P. Lond.* VI, 1914
57 Below, 214
58 Stevenson (1989), no. 220
59 *WChr.* 6 (425/50), *Corpus Scriptorum Christianorum Orientalium* vol. 42, §22, p. 69 (*Scriptores Coptici*, series secunda, tom. IV, 1908)
60 Procopius, *Hist.* 1.19.36–7, *P. Cair. Masp.* 67004 (*c.* 552)
61 Jansen (1950), John of Nikiou (Charles, 1916), 51.59–60
62 Butler (1978), pp. xlviff.
63 *Patrologia Orientalis* III, p. 220; Winlock

and Crum I (1916), 101; *Patrologia Orientalis* I, p. 486

64 Winlock and Crum I (1916), 227ff.

Notes to chapter 3

Bibliography:

Bell (1944), (1956); Bonneau (1971); Bowman (1971), (1976), (1978); Brunt (1975); Cockle (1984); Crawford (1971); Hardy (1931), (1968); Johnson (1936); Johnson and West (1949); A. H. M. Jones (1940); chs. 10–18, (1964), (1971), ch. 11; Keenan (1973–4), (1975), (1977), (1981); Lesquier (1911), (1918); Lewis (1970), (1982a), (1983); Maehler (1983); Maspero (1912); Mitteis and Wilcken (1912); Parassoglou (1978); Peremans and Van't Dack (1950–); Préaux (1939); Price (1976); Rowlandson (1985); Speidel (1982); Thomas (1975), (1975–82), (1978), (1983); Turner (1952), (1979), (1984); Wallace (1938)

1   Austin (1981), no. 236 (259 BC)
2   Bresciani (1978), Turner (1984), 135
3   Below, Ch. 4
4   *C.Ord.Ptol.* (2nd ed., 1980)
5   *Sel.Pap.*II, 273.28–37 (259 BC)
6   Austin (1981), no. 258 (156 BC)
7   *Sel.Pap.*II, 268 (220 BC)
8   Austin (1981), no. 256
9   *P.Teb.*24
10 Pestman (1981)
11 Austin (1981), no. 245 (*c.* 256/5 BC)
12 *P.Col.*66 (161/0 BC)
13 Austin (1981), no. 231
14 *P.Oxy.*3285, Mattha (1975)
15 *P.Teb.*60–88, 1116–23
16 Boswinkel and Pestman (1982)
17 *Ibid.*, no. 9 (*c.* 139 BC)
18 *Ibid.*, no. 11 (108 BC)
19 Austin (1981), no. 250
20 Suetonius, *Augustus* 18
21 *BGU* 1835
22 *BGU* 1210, *proem.* (150/61), below, 127
23 *SB* 7696.82–6, 100–05
24 *In Flaccum* 3
25 Turner (1973), 44–5
26 *P.Oxy.*41 (III/IV)
27 *P.Oxy.*1415
28 *P.Oxy.*1416
29 *P.Yale* 61
30 *FIRA* III, 171
31 *Sel.Pap.*II, 219
32 Chalon (1964), 27–39 (ll.47–8)
33 *P.Ryl.*595
34 *P.Bouriant* 42, *WChr.*341
35 *P.Beatty Panop.* 1.167–79
36 *Edict* XIII (ch. 2, n. 50)
37 *P.Coll.Youtie* 66 (253–60), see below, 160
38 *P.Cair.Masp.*67024 (*c.* 551)
39 *Ibid.*, 15–6
40 *P.Cair.Masp.*67002
41 *P.Abinn.*
42 *P.Abinn.*18
43 *P.Cair.Masp.*67002 (567)
44 *P.Abinn.* 44 (342), 45 (343), 49 (346), 50 (346)
45 Winlock and Crum I (1916), 227
46 *P.Lond.* 1674.33ff., 93ff. (*c.* 570)
47 *P.Cair.Masp.*67057 (?554/9), Justinian, *Edict* XIII (ch. 2, n. 50)
48 Below, 194f.
49 *P.Landlisten*, see Bowman (1985)
50 *C.Theod.*11.24.6
51 Schiller (1964), 118–9 and (1968)

Notes to chapter 4

Bibliography:

Bagnall (1985); Bingen (1978); Boak and Peterson (1931); Boak (1933), (1937); Bonneau (1964), (1971); Bowman (1980), (1985); Brewster (1927); Crawford (1971); Duncan-Jones (1976); el-Fakharani (1983); Gascou (1985); Hardy (1931); Hobson (1983); Johnson (1936); Johnson and West (1949); Keenan (1980), (1981); Lewis (1982b), (1983), chs. 6–7; Parássoglou (1978); Préaux (1939), (1983); Raschke (1978); Rathbone (1986); Rostovtseff (1922), (1953); Rowlandson (1996); Thompson (Crawford) (1983); Wallace (1938); West and Johnson (1944); Wipszycka (1972)

1 Diodorus 1.31.7–8, Josephus *BJ* 2.385, see above, 17
2 Below, 218–23
3 Below, 93
4 Austin (1981), no. 238
5 *P.Oxy.*1411
6 T.Frank, *Economic Survey of Ancient Rome* V (1940, Johns Hopkins University Press, Baltimore), 314
7 *P.Coll.Youtie* 81.15 note (= *P.Oxy.*3265) (326)
8 Above, 27, Strabo 17.1.13
9 Velleius Paterculus 2.39, Josephus, *BJ* 2.385–6
10 Justinian, *Edict* XIII.8 (ch. 2, n. 50), Aurelius Victor, *Epit.de Caes.*1.6
11 *HM* 18
12 *P.Soterichos*, see Bagnall (1980)
13 See above, 86, 100
14 *P.Flor.*171
15 *P.Landlisten*, see above; *P.Cair.Masp.*67002 (567)
16 *P.Teb.* 56
17 Keenan (1980)
18 *Itin.Eg.*9.4–5 (Wilkinson (1971), 103)
19 *P.Ryl.*143 (38)
20 *P.Oxy.*2783 (III)
21 Pliny, *NH* 5.58
22 *P.Cair.Zen.* 59155
23 *P.Oxy.* 2681 (III)
24 Johnson (1936), no. 105
25 *P.Lond.*2007 (?248 BC)
26 Herodotus 2.141, 164
27 Rea (1982b)
28 Below, 146
29 *P.Oxy.* 1461
30 *P.Oxy.* 520 (143), 1727 (II/III)
31 *P.Petaus* 30 (II)
32 *P.Got.* 7
33 *P.Oxy.* 2727, 527 (II/III)
34 H.I.Bell. *Aegyptus* 2 (1921), 281–8
35 *P.Oxy.* 3595 (243)
36 *P.Oxy.* 1668
37 *SPP* 22.35 (58)
38 *P.Oxy.*724 (155)
39 *P.Mich.*245 (47)
40 Austin (1981), no. 256
41 *P.Oxy.*3624–6 (359)
42 *P.Oxy.*3192 (307)
43 *BGU* 1133 (19 BC)
44 *P.Mich.*237–42
45 *P.Oxy.*319 (37), 269 (57), 304 (55), 318 (59), 320 (59)
46 *P.Lond.*193 recto (II), *Sel.Pap.*I, 131 (II or III)
47 *P.Oxy.*705
48 *P.Oxy.*1274
49 *P.Mich.Zen.*28 (256 BC)
50 *P.Oxy.*1153 (I)
51 Below, 220
52 *NH* 6.101
53 *P.Cair.Zen.*59012
54 *P.Oxy.*3593–4 (238–44), *P.Holm.*152, *P.Oxy.*1924 (V/VI), *P.Oxy.*1851 (VI/VII)
55 Above, 17 and Appendix II

Notes to chapter 5

Bibliography:
Bagnall (1982b); Baines (1983); Barns (1978); Bell (1944), (1956); Bingen (1951); Boak and Peterson (1931); Boak (1933), (1935), (1955), (1959); Braunert (1964); Cameron (1965), (1976); Crawford (1971), (1979); Drew-Bear (1979); Duncan-Jones (1977); Hobson (1985); Hopkins (1980); Husselman (1979); Keenan (1973–4), (1975); Lewis (1983) chs. 2–4, 10; Lichtheim (1980); MacCoull (1981); Matthews (1970); Nelson (1979); Pack (1965); Parsons (1980); Pomeroy (1990); Porten (1968); Rémondon (1964); Roeder (1959); Rostovtseff (1953); Samuel (1971), (1983); Schwartz (1969); Spencer (1982), (1984); Thomas (1975); Trigger, Kemp, O'Connor, Lloyd (1983), ch. 4; Turner (1952), (1975), (1980); Viereck (1928); West (1969); Westerman (1924); Youtie (1973–5), (1975)

1 Porten (1968)
2 Above, 32
3 *Papyrologica Lugd.-Bat.* 19, pp. 30–6
4 *CPJ* 141; for Alexandria see below, 212
5 *CPJ* 19 (226 BC), 23 (182 BC), 26 (172/1 BC)
6 Peremans and Van't Dack (1950–), III
7 Boswinkel and Pestman (1982), 1–7

(110/106 BC) (demotic); *Papyrologica Lugd.-Bat.* 19, 1, 2 (109 BC), (demotic); 3 (109 BC), 25 (?46 BC) (Greek and demotic), 5 (118 BC) (demotic and Greek)

8 *UPZ* 148, see Rémondon (1964)

9 *WChr.* 50 (III BC)

10 *WChr.* 51 (244/221 BC)

11 *OGIS* 49 (III BC)

12 Above, 68

13 *Sel.Pap.*II, 215

14 *Sel.Pap.*I, 152

15 *P.Oxy.*237.VII.37–8

16 Pliny, *Ep.*10.6

17 *BGU* 1210, sections 8, 9, 14, 18, 23, 38, 39, 43 (150/61)

18 *In Flaccum* 78

19 *HM* 14.13

20 *HM* 8.30–1

21 *BGU* 706

22 *P.Petaus* 11

23 *CPJ* 436

24 *Sel.Pap.*I, 120 (II)

25 *Sel.Pap.*I, 125 (II)

26 *Sel.Pap.*I, 133 (early III)

27 *WChr.*131 (IV)

28 *P.Oxy.*237.VI.16–9

29 *P.Oxy.*903

30 *Sel.Pap.*I, 87

31 Dzierzykray-Rogalski (1983)

32 *P.Osl.*1.321–32 (IV)

33 *CPJ* 1510 (?5 BC)

34 *Sel.Pap.*I, 105 (1 BC)

35 *P.Osl.*1.110–14 (IV)

36 *HM* 22.1

37 *HM* 1.34

38 *Sel.Pap.*I, 174 (IV)

39 *P.Oxy.*3313 (II)

40 *Sel.Pap.*I, 4 (66)

41 *Sel.Pap.*I, 6 (13 BC)

42 *P.Ross-Georg.*III.2 (III), *Sel.Pap.*I, 103 (95 BC)

43 *Sel.Pap.*I, 168 (VI)

44 *Sel.Pap.*I, 157 (III/IV)

45 E.g. Plate 78, above

46 *Sel.Pap.*I, 12 (91 or 109)

47 *P.Cair.Isid.*81, 97, 125, 91, 8

48 *CPJ* 473, *P.Coll.Youtie* 92 (569)

49 *HM* 14.3

50 *HM* 13.3–4

51 Above, 83

52 Porphyrius, *Vita Plot.* 1

53 *P.Oxy.*2476

54 *HM* 5.4

55 Drew-Bear (1979), 351ff.

56 *HM* 5.2

57 *P.Köln.*52 (263)

58 *P.Oxy.*2718

59 *Sel.Pap.*II, 269 (220 BC)

60 *Sel.Pap.*II, 406 (113)

61 *P.Oxy.*2707

62 *P.Hib.*54

63 *Sel.Pap.*I, 20 (206)

64 *P.Oxy.*475 (182)

65 *P.Oxy.*2719 (III)

66 *P.Osl.*111

67 *Sel.Pap.*I, 123

68 *P.Oxy.*2406 (II)

69 Husselman (1979), maps 2–3

70 *P.Oxy.*3365 (241)

71 Diodorus, 1.80.5–6

72 *Sel.Pap.*I, 186 (*c.* AD 1)

73 E.g. *P.Oxy.*3245 (297)

74 *Sel.Pap.*I, 158

75 *P.Oxy.*1088 (early I)

76 *Sel.Pap.*I, 182 (*c.* 257 BC)

77 136

78 *P.Ryl.*127 (29)

79 Above, 107

80 *PSI* 1248 (235)

81 *P.Oxy.*1772 (late III), *P.Oxy.*3069 (III/IV)

82 *Sel.Pap.*III, 109

83 Above, 117

84 *Sel.Pap.*I, 134 (III)

85 *P.Oxy.*2680

86 *P.Oxy.*1773 (III)

87 *P.Strasb.*233 (second half of III)

88 *Sel.Pap.*II, 220 (104)

89 *P.Sakaon* 44 + 35, *P.Turner* 44 (331/2)

90 Above, 88

91 Bowman and Thomas (1977) (211), *P.Oxy.*1119 (254)

92 Bowman (1970)

93 Below, 209, 219, 232

94 *P.Oxy.*283 (45)

95 *Sel.Pap.*I, 149

96 *P.Cair.Zen.*59242 and 59251 (253/2 BC), *CPJ* I, pp. 115ff.

97 *P.Cair.Masp.*67024

98 *P.Ryl.*IV, pp. 104ff.
99 Strabo 2.3.5
100 *P.Oxy.*1271 (246)
101 *P.Oxy.*3312 (II)
102 Above, 127
103 *Sel.Pap.*I, 112
104 Ch. 6
105 *P.Oxy.*1029
106 Griffith (1937), 126, Ph.436
107 *P.Mich.*467–71, 476–80 (II); *P.Oxy.*2193–4 (V/VI), *P.Köln* 160 (I/II)
108 *HM* 6, Pack (1965), 3009 (VI)
109 *SB* 5117 (55), see Youtie II (1973), 162–3
110 *P.Oxy.*2892–2922
111 *Sel.Pap.*II, 305 (263)
112 *P.Petaus* 121 (II), see Youtie II (1973), 677–93; on Isidorus see above 138 and n. 47
113 Youtie II (1973), 629–51
114 Below, 222–33
115 Pack (1965), 2642–2751
116 O. Guéraud, P. Jouguet, *Un livre d'écolier du IIIe siècle avant J.-C*

(1938, Publications de la société royale égyptienne de papyrologie, Textes et documents 2, Cairo)
117 *P.Bouriant* 1
118 *P.Coll.Youtie* 66 (253, 60)
119 Horsley II (1982), 138
120 *P.Teb.Tait, Papyrologica Lugd.-Bat.* 19, *O.Leid.dem.* etc.
121 Above, 124
122 *P.Oxy.*3069 (III/IV)
123 *P.Oxy.*2192 (II)
124 *P.Petaus* 30
125 Youtie II (1973), 1035–41
126 Pack (1965), see also below, 233
127 *P.Oxy.*519
128 *P.Oxy.*2891 (early II)
129 Herodotus 2.91 (using the name Chemmis)
130 Cameron (1965), 478
131 Lichtheim (1980), 125ff.
132 *Ibid.*, 159ff.
133 West (1969)
134 *P.XV Congr.* 22 (early IV)
135 *Letters from Egypt* (3rd ed., 1983 reprint, Virago Press, London), 67–8

Notes to chapter 6
Bibliography:
Bagnall (1982a); Bagnani (1934); Barns (1961); Bell (1948), (1953); Blackman (1911); Boak and Peterson (1931); Boak (1933), (1935); Bonneau (1964); Clarysse and Van der Veken (1983); Crawford (1980); Evans (1961); Foerster (1972–4); Frend (1972); Hardy (1952); Hornung (1982); A.H.M. Jones (1964); chs. 22–3; Judge (1977), (1981); Judge and Pickering (1977); Kakósy (1982); Kalavrezou-Maxeiner (1975); Koenen and Henrichs (1970), (1975); Lewis (1983); ch. 5; Nock (1929), (1972); Pagels (1979); Quaegebeur (1978); Rees (1950); Roberts (1979); Rousseau (1985); Schmidt and Polotsky (1933); Segal (1981); Smith (1974); Spencer (1982); Stevenson (1989); Turner (1952); Walters (1974); Winlock and Crum (1916); Wipszycka (1972)

1 Lucie Duff Gordon, *Letters from Egypt* (3rd ed., 1983 reprint, Virago Press, London), 56–7
2 Austin (1981), no. 222
3 Above, 61
4 Griffith (1937), 104, Ph. 370
5 *SB* 9016
6 *Sel.Pap.*II, 404
7 *P.Teb.*88 (115–4 BC)
8 *P.Teb.*39, 14 (114 BC)
9 Boak (1933), 3–55, Bagnani (1934)
10 *Sel.Pap.*II, 416 (112 BC)

11 *P.Teb.*I, p. vi
12 Ray (1976), pp. 136ff.
13 Diodorus 1.83, *Sel.Pap.*II, 329
14 *P.Mert.*73 (163–4)
15 *WChr.*116
16 *UPZ* 1 (late IV BC)
17 *WChr.*117 (II AD), *SB* 1060 (II BC)
18 *P.Oxy.*1380
19 Lucian, *Deorum concilium*, 10–11
20 Herodotus 2.47–64, Diodorus 1.12–27, Plutarch, *de Iside et Osiride*
21 *BGU* 362 (215), *P.Oxy.*3367 (272), *P.Fay.*119 (*c.* 100)

22 Above, 61
23 *P.Giss*.99
24 *P.Oxy*.1029
25 Johnson (1936), no. 397 (138),
   P.Oxy.1449 (213/7)
26 van der Horst (1984), frag.10
27 *BGU* 1210, section 71 (150/61)
28 Johnson (1936), no. 394 (108)
29 Thompson (1938), 498–9 (137 BC)
30 Johnson (1936), no. 397 (138)
31 *P.Teb*.44 (113 BC)
32 *BGU* 1210, section 86 (150/61)
33 *BGU* 362 (215)
34 *Sel.Pap*.II, 242
35 *Sel.Pap*.II, 403 (II)
36 Seneca, *NQ* 4a.2.7, Pliny *NH* 5.57
37 Carlo Levi, *Christ Stopped at Eboli*
   (1947, Farrar, Strauss and Co., New
   York), 116–7
38 *Corpus Hermeticum* I–IV (ed.
   A.D.Nock, A.-J.Festugière, 1945–54)
39 *P.Oxy*.1272 (144)
40 *Sel.Pap*.II, 413
41 *P.Giss*.20 (*c*. 116)
42 *Sel.Pap*.I, 94 (*c*. 255 BC)
43 *Sel.Pap*.I, 84
44 R.O.Faulkner, *The Ancient Egyptian
   Book of the Dead* (1985, British Museum
   Press, London)
45 Crawford (1980), 21
46 Herbert (1972), no. 22, see above, 69,
   plate 43
47 *P.Col.Zen*.I, 18 (257 BC), Austin (1981),
   no. 245 (*c*. 256/5 BC), *Sel.Pap*.II, 327
48 *P.Giss*.23 (*c*. 116)

49 *P.Oxy*.1758 (II)
50 Ray (1976), 17a (165 BC)
51 *Sel.Pap*.I, 193 (I)
52 *P.Vindob.Salomans* 1 (I/II)
53 Above, 134
54 Above, 112, plate 66
55 *PGM* (2nd ed.), IV.2447–55
56 Rea (1977), 151–6
57 *P.Ryl*. 457
58 *P.Oxy*.1464 (250)
59 Eusebius, *HE* 8.9.5
60 *P.Oxy*.2601 (early IV)
61 *P.Oxy*.2673, see Rea, *ZPE* 35 (1979),
   128
62 *P.Oxy*.3035 (256), 3119 (III)
63 Above, 47
64 Fakhry (1950), 60–5
65 *P.Oxy*.43 verso
66 Blackman (1911), 36–7
67 *CPR* V, II.11
68 *P.Lond*.VI, 1913–22
69 Above, 129
70 *P.Lond*.VI, 1913 (334)
71 Jerome, *Ep*.22.34
72 *P.Oxy*.2195 (VI), *P.Cair.Masp*.67138
   (VI)
73 *P.Wisc*.64 (480)
74 *WChr*.123
75 *P.Ryl*.469, *FIRA* II, pp. 580–1
76 Schmidt and Polotsky (1933), Henrichs
   and Koenen (1975, 1978)
77 Henrichs and Koenen (1975), 66
78 Foerster (1974), 3–120
79 *P.Oxy*.1 (II or III)
80 *P.Oxy*.1152

Notes to chapter 7
Bibliography:
Bagnall (1979); Bell (1946), (1956); Breccia (1922); Butler (1978), chs. 24–5; Cameron (1965), (1969), (1976); Chadwick (1966); Daszewski (1978), (1983); Dillon (1977); el-Fakharani (1983); Foerster (1972–4); Fraser (1951), (1972); Grimm, Heinen, Winter (1981); Hadas (1955); Hardy (1952); A.H.M.Jones (1940); C.P.Jones (1978); Kolotaj (1983); Lewis (1974), (1981); Lloyd (1984); Monks (1953); Musurillo (1954); Nock (1972); Pack (1965); Pfeiffer (1958); Préaux (1978); Raschke (1978); Rice (1983); Rodziewicz (1985); Samuel (1983); Smith and Hall (1983); Thompson (Crawford) (1983); Turner (1975), (1980), (1984); Walbank (1981), ch. 10

1 Diodorus, 17.52.5
2 Austin (1981), no. 7
3 Herodian 4.8.9, Dio Cassius 77.22–3

4 Dio of Prusa, *Or*.32.36
5 Austin (1981), no. 232
6 Philo, *Leg. ad Gaium*, 151

7 Diodorus 17.52
8 *Bellum civile* 4, *P.Hal.*1.88ff.
9 Fraser (1951), 103
10 Theocritus, *Idyll* 15.87–8
11 Dio, *Or.*32.40
12 *Sel.Pap.*I, 212 (41)
13 *P.Oxy.*3022
14 *CPJ* 150
15 *Idyll* 15.47–9
16 Strabo 17.1.53, Diodorus, 1.83.8
17 *Leg. ad Gaium*, 120–131
18 *Leg. ad Gaium*, 184–5
19 Above, 209f
20 Musurillo (1954)
21 *CPJ* 156
22 Above, 43
23 *P.Oxy.*3065
24 Socrates, *HE* 7.13–15
25 Dio, *Or.*32.62
26 *Ibid.* 55, 59
27 Suetonius, *Nero* 20
28 Herodas, *Mimiambi* (ed.
   I.C.Cunningham, 1971, Oxford
   University Press)
29 Philo, *In Flaccum*, 85
30 Dio, *Or.*32.45, 81
31 Athenaeus, *Deipnosophistae* 5.201E, Rice
   (1983), 21
32 Theocritus, *Idyll* 15.82–6
33 Gregory of Nazianzus, *Or.*21.29
34 Dio, *Or.*32.36
35 Strabo 17.1.7
36 Winstedt (1909), 104A–C
37 Pliny, *NH* 6.100–101
38 Schoff (1912)
39 Above, 39
40 Palladius, *Hist.Laus.* 14, Rufinus,
   *Hist.Mon.*16
41 Epiphanius, *Panarion* 76.1.4–7
42 *Historia Augusta, Quad.Tyr.* 8

43 Strabo 16.2.25
44 *P.Oxy.*3265 (326)
45 *Expositio totius mundi et gentium* 36
46 Pliny, *NH* 13.71ff., above, 161
47 Johnson (1936), 338
48 Pliny *NH* 12.59
49 Johnson (1936), no. 228, Pliny, *NH*
   33.131
50 Ammianus 22.16.17
51 Austin (1981), no. 232
52 Suidas, *s.v.* Theon
53 Aulus Gellius, 7.17.3, Seneca, *de
   tranquillitate* 9.5, Orosius 6.15.31–2
54 Plutarch, *Antonius* 58
55 *Idyll* 17.112ff.
56 Above, 163
57 Hadas (1955)
58 Diodorus 5.37.3
59 Above, 224
60 Tertullian, *de anima* 10, Celsus, *Medica,
   proem.*23–4
61 Plutarch, *Antonius* 80
62 *Or.*32.9
63 Above, 209
64 Eusebius, *HE* 6.8
65 Above, 140
66 Above, 199f.
67 Suidas, *s.v.* Proclus
68 *VS* 493
69 Above, 162
70 Suidas, *s.v.* Horapollon, Zacharias
   Scholasticus, *Life of Severus of Antioch,
   Patrologia Orientalis* II, pp. 22–3
71 Timon of Phlius quoted by Athenaeus,
   Deipnosophistae 1.22D
72 *Menander* (ed. A.W.Gomme,
   F.H.Sandbach, 1973, Oxford
   University Press), *P.Köln* 58 (I/II)
   (Archilochus)

Bibliography

Note 1: the following bibliography, which is confined largely to books and articles in English, makes no claim to be comprehensive and includes only selected works which have a direct bearing on matters discussed in the text. It may therefore be useful to preface the main list with some recent and more comprehensive bibliographical surveys. In addition to Bowman (1976), and the bibliographies in Montevecchi (1988), Préaux (1978) and Turner (1980) which are in the list below, note:

R. S. Bagnall, 'Papyrology and Ptolemaic history 1956–80', *Classical World* 76 (1982–3), 13–21

G. Geraci, 'Economia e società nei papiri greci d'epoca bizantina: linee di una problematica,' *Corsi di cultura sull'arte ravennate e bizantina* (1977), 197–222

P. Lemerle (ed.), *Traité des études byzantines ii, Les papyrus*, Ch. IV (A. Bataille), Presses universitaires de France, Paris, 1955

Cambridge Ancient History (Second Edition), Vol. VII, Part I, 554–74, Cambridge University Press, 1984

Note 2: Modern journals are cited, with a few self-explanatory exceptions, according to the abbreviations given in *L'année philologique*. *ANRW* = H. Temporini, W. Haase ed. (1972–), *Aufstieg und Niedergang der römischen Welt*, de Gruyter, Berlin.

Select Bibliography

M. A. H. el-Abbadi (1990), *The Life and Fate of the Ancient Library of Alexandria*, UNESCO, Paris

W. Y. Adams (1983), 'Primis and the "Aethiopian" frontier,' *JARCE* 20, 93–104

R. Alston (1995), *Soldier and Society in Roman Egypt*, Routledge, London

C. Anti (1930–1), 'Un esempio di sistemazione urbanistica nel III secolo av. Cr.,' *Architettura e arte decorativa* 10, 97–107

C. Anti (1931), 'Gli scavi della missione archeologica italiana a Umm el Breigat (Tebtunis),' *Aegyptus* 11, 389–91

M. M. Austin (1981), *The Hellenistic World from Alexander to the Roman Conquest*, Cambridge University Press

R. S. Bagnall (1976), *The Administration of the Ptolemaic Possessions outside Egypt*, E. J. Brill, Leiden

R. S. Bagnall (1979), 'The date of the foundation of Alexandria,' *AJAH* 4, 46–9

R. S. Bagnall (1980), 'Theadelphian archives,' *BASP* 17, 97–104

R. S. Bagnall (1982a), 'Religious conversion and onomastic change in early Byzantine Egypt,' *BASP* 19, 105–23

R. S. Bagnall, (1982b), 'The population of Theadelphia in the fourth century,' *BSAC* 24, 35–57

R. S. Bagnall (1985), *Currency and Inflation in Fourth Century Egypt* (*BASP*, Supplement 5)

R. S. Bagnall (1988), 'Archaeology and papyrology,' *JRA* 1, 197–202

R. S. Bagnall (1991), 'The beginnings of the Roman census in Egypt,' *GRBS* 32, 255–65

R. S. Bagnall (1992), 'Landholding in late Roman Egypt: the distribution of wealth,' *JRS* 82, 126–49

R. S. Bagnall (1993a), *Egypt in Late Antiquity*, Princeton University Press

R.S.Bagnall (1993b), 'Slavery and society in late Roman Egypt,' in Halpern ed. (1993), 220–40

R.S.Bagnall (1995), *Reading Papyri, Writing Ancient History*, Routledge, London

R.S.Bagnall, B.W.Frier (1994), *The Demography of Roman Egypt*, Cambridge University Press

G.Bagnani (1934), 'Gli scavi di Tebtunis,' *Aegyptus* 14, 3–13

D.M.Bailey, W.V.Davies, A.J.Spencer (1982), *British Museum Expedition to Middle Egypt: Ashmunein (1980) (British Museum Occasional Papers* 37)

D.M.Bailey (1991), *Excavations at El-Ashmunein IV. Hermopolis Magna: Buildings of the Roman period*, British Museum Press, London

J.Baines, J.Malek (1980), *Atlas of Ancient Egypt*, Phaidon, Oxford

J.Baines (1983), 'Literacy and ancient Egyptian society,' *Man* n.s. 18, 572–99

E.Baraize (1940), 'L'"Agora" d'Hermoupolis,' *ASAE* 40, 741–60

T.D.Barnes (1989), 'Trajan and the Jews,' *JJS* 40, 145–62

T.D.Barnes (1993), *Athanasius and Constantius. Theology and Politics in the Constantinian Empire*, Harvard University Press, Cambridge Mass.

J.W.B.Barns (1961), 'Shenute as a historical source,' *Actes du Xe congrès internationale de papyrologues, Warsaw–Cracow, 1961*, 151–9

J.W.B.Barns (1978), *Egyptians and Greeks (Papyrologica Bruxellensia* 14)

N.H.Baynes (1955), *Byzantine Studies and Other Essays*, Athlone Press, London

H.I.Bell (1944), 'An Egyptian village in the age of Justinian', *JHS* 44, 21–36

H.I.Bell (1946), 'Alexandria ad Aegyptum', *JRS* 36, 130–2

H.I.Bell (1948), 'Popular religion in Graeco-Roman Egypt,' *JEA* 34, 82–97

H.I.Bell (1953), *Cults and Creeds in Graeco-Roman Egypt*, Liverpool University Press

H.I.Bell (1956), *Egypt from Alexander the Great to the Arab Conquest*, Oxford University Press

A.C.Berry, R.J.Berry, P.J.Ucko (1967), 'Genetical change in ancient Egypt,' *Man* n.s. 2, 551–68

E.Bevan (1927), *A History of Egypt under the Ptolemaic Dynasty*, Methuen, London

R.S.Bianchi *et al.* (1988), *Cleopatra's Egypt: Age of the Ptolemies*, Brooklyn Museum

P.Bilde *et al.* ed. (1992), *Ethnicity in Hellenistic Egypt*, Aarhus University Press

J.Bingen (1978), 'Économie grecque et société égyptienne au IIIe siècle,' in Maehler and Strocka ed. (1978), 211–19

J.Bingen (1981), 'L'Egypte gréco-romaine et la problématique des interactions culturelles,' *Proceedings of the XVI International Congress of Papyrology (American Studies in Papyrology* 22), 3–18

J.Bingen (1987), 'Première campagne de fouille au Mons Claudianus,' *BIFAO* 87, 45–52

A.M.Blackman (1911), *The Temple of Dendur*, IFAO, Cairo

Blue Guide (1993), *Egypt*, by V.Seton-Williams and P.Stocks, A. & C.Black, London

A.E.R.Boak, E.Peterson (1931), *Karanis: Topographical and Architectural Report of Excavations . . . 1924–8 (University of Michigan, Humanistic Studies* 25)

A.E.R.Boak (1933), *Karanis: the Temples, Coin Hoards, Botanical and Zoological Reports, Seasons 1924–31 (University of Michigan, Humanistic Studies* 30)

A.E.R.Boak (1935), *Socnopaiou Nesos: the University of Michigan Excavations at Dime in 1931–2 (University of Michigan, Humanistic Studies* 39)

A.E.R.Boak (1937), 'The organisation of gilds in Greco-Roman Egypt,' *TAPA* 63, 212–20

A.E.R.Boak (1955), 'The population of Roman and Byzantine Karanis,' *Historia* 4, 157–62

A.E.R.Boak (1959), 'Egypt and the plague of Marcus Aurelius,' *Historia* 8, 248–50

D.Bonneau (1964), *La crue du Nil, divinité égyptienne à travers mille ans d'histoire*, C.Klincksieck, Paris

D. Bonneau (1971), *Le fisc et le Nil*, Editions Cujos, Paris

D. Bonneau (1993), *Le régime administratif de l'eau du Nil dans l'Egypte grecque, romaine et byzantine*, E. J. Brill, Leiden

E. Boswinkel, P. W. Pestman (1982), *Les archives privées de Dionysius, fils de Kephalas* (*Papyrologica Lugd.-Bat.* 22)

A. K. Bowman (1971), *The Town Councils of Roman Egypt* (*American Studies in Papyrology* 11)

A. K. Bowman (1976), 'Papyri and Roman imperial history, 1960–75' *JRS* 66, 153–73

A. K. Bowman (1978), 'The military occupation of Egypt in the reign of Diocletian,' *BASP* 15, 25–38

A. K. Bowman (1980), 'The economy of Egypt in the earlier fourth century,' in C. E. King ed., *Imperial Revenue, Expenditure and Monetary Policy in the Fourth Century AD* (*British Archaeological Reports*, International Series 76)

A. K. Bowman (1985). 'Landholding in the Hermopolite Nome in the fourth century AD,' *JRS* 75, 137–63

A. K. Bowman (1992), 'Public buildings in Roman Egypt,' *JRA* 5, 495–503

A. K. Bowman (1996), 'Egypt,' *Cambridge Ancient History*, Volume X (Second Edition), Ch. 14b, Cambridge University Press

A. K. Bowman, D. W. Rathbone (1992), 'Cities and administration in Roman Egypt,' *JRS* 82, 107–27

A. K. Bowman, J. D. Thomas (1977), 'P.Lond.inv.2506: a reconsideration,' *BASP* 14, 59–64

A. K. Bowman, G. D. Woolf ed. (1994), *Literacy and Power in the Ancient World*, Cambridge University Press

H. Braunert (1964), *Die Binnenwanderung: Studien zur Sozialgeschichte Ägyptens in der Ptolemäerzeit und Kaiserzeit* (*Bonner Historische Forschungen* 26)

E. Breccia (1922), *Alexandrea ad Aegyptum: a Guide to the Ancient and Modern Town and its Graeco-Roman Museum*, Istituto Italiano d'Arti Grafiche, Bergamo

E. Bresciani (1968), *Rapporto preliminare delle campagne di scavo 1966 e 1967, Istituto della Università degli Studi di Milano, missione di Scavo a Medinet Madi (Fayum, Egitto)* (= *Testi e documenti per lo studio dell' Antichità* 20)

E. Bresciani (1976), *Rapporto preliminare delle campagne di scavo 1968 e 1969* (*Testi e documenti per lo studio dell' Antichità* 53)

E. Bresciani (1978), 'La spedizione de Tolomeo II in Siria in un ostrakon demotic inedito da Karnak,' in Maehler and Strocka ed. (1978), 31–6

E. Bresciani (1983), 'Registrazione catastale e ideologia politica nell'Egitto tolemaico. A completamento di la "Spedizione di Tolomeo II in Siria" in un ostrakon demotico inedito di Karnak,' *Egitto e vicino oriente* 6, 15–31

E. Brewster (1927), 'A weaver of Oxyrhynchus,' *TAPA* 58, 132–54

P. A. Brunt (1975), 'The administrators of Roman Egypt,' *JRS* 65, 124–47

A. Bülow-Jacobsen ed. (1994), *Proceedings of the 20th International Congress of Papyrologists, Copenhagen, 22–29 August 1992*, Museum Tusculanum Press, Copenhagen

F. Burkhalter (1992), 'Le gymnase d'Alexandrie: centre administratif de la province romaine d'Egypte,' *BCH* 116, 345–73

A. J. Butler (1978), *The Arab Conquest of Egypt and the Last Thirty years of the Roman Dominion* (2nd ed., rev. P. M. Fraser), Oxford University Press

K. W. Butzer (1976), *Early Hydraulic Civilisation in Egypt*, University of Chicago Press

A. Cameron (1965), 'Wandering poets: a literary movement in Byzantine Egypt,' *Historia* 14, 470–509

A. Cameron (1969), 'The last days of the Academy at Athens,' *PCPS* n.s. 15, 7–29

A. Cameron (1976), *Circus Factions*, Oxford University Press

J.-M. Carrié (1974), 'Les *castra Dionysiados* et l'évolution de l'architecture militaire romaine tardive,' *MEFRA* 86, 819–50

L. J. Casson (1986), 'P. Vindob. G40822 and the shipping of goods from India,' *BASP* 23, 73–9

H. Chadwick (1966), *Early Christian Thought and the Classical Tradition*, Oxford University Press

G. Chalon (1964), *L'édit de Tiberius Julius Alexander*. Urs Graf-Verlag, Olten-Lausanne

R. H. Charles (1916), *The Chronicle of John, Bishop of Nikiou*, Text and Translation Society, London

W. Clarysse (1985), 'Greeks and Egyptians in the Ptolemaic army and administration, *Aegyptus* 65, 57–66

W. Clarysse (1993), 'Egyptian scribes writing Greek,' *CE* 68, 186–201

W. Clarysse (1992), 'Some Greeks in Egypt,' in J. H. Johnson ed. (1992), 51–6

W. Clarysse (1994), 'Jews in Trikomia,' in Bülow-Jacobsen ed. (1994), 193–203

W. Clarysse, D. J. Thompson (forthcoming), *Counting the People*, Leuven

W. Clarysse, G. Van der Veken (1983), *The Eponymous Priests of Ptolemaic Egypt* (*Papyrologica Lugd.-Bat.* 24)

W. H. Cockle (1984), 'State archives in Graeco-Roman Egypt from 30 BC to the reign of Septimius Severus,' *JEA* 70, 106–22

L. H. Corcoran (1992), 'A cult function for the so-called Faiyum mummy portraits,' in J. H. Johnson ed. (1992), 57–60

W. D. E. Coulson, A. Leonard Jr. (1981), *Cities of the Delta I: Naukratis: Preliminary Report on the 1977–8 and 1980 Seasons* (*ARCE Reports* 4)

D. J. Crawford (1971), *Kerkeosiris: an Egyptian Village in the Ptolemaic Period*, Cambridge University Press

D. J. Crawford (1979), 'Food: tradition and change in Hellenistic Egypt,' *World Archaeology* 2, 136–46

D. J. Crawford (1980), 'Ptolemy, Ptah and Apis in Hellenistic Memphis,' *Studies on Ptolemaic Memphis* (*Studia Hellenistica* 24), 1–42

L. Criscuolo, G. Geraci ed. (1989), *Egitto e storia antica dall'ellenismo all'età araba. Bilancio di un confronto. Atti del colloquio internazionale, Bologna 31 Agosto – 2 Settembre, 1987*, Cooperativa Libraria Universitaria Editrice Bologna

L. Dabrowski (1962), 'La topographie d'Athribis à l'époque romaine,' *ASAE* 57, 19–31

W. A. Daszewski (1978), 'Some problems of early mosaics from Egypt,' in Maehler and Strocka ed. (1978), 121–36

W. A. Daszewski (1983), 'An old problem in the light of new evidence,' in Grimm, Heinen, Winter ed. (1983), 161–5

D. Delia (1991), *Alexandrian Citizenship during the Roman Principate* (*American Classical Studies* 23)

T. Derda (1994), 'Deir el-Naqlun 1986–91: Interdependence of Archaeology and Papyrology,' in Bülow-Jacobsen ed. (1994), 124–30

J. Dillon (1977), *The Middle Platonists*, Duckworth, London

M. Drew-Bear (1979), *Le Nome Hermopolite: sites et toponymes* (*American Studies in Papyrology* 21)

R. P. Duncan-Jones (1976), 'The price of wheat in Egypt under the Principate,' *Chiron* 6, 241–62

R. P. Duncan-Jones (1977), 'Age-rounding, illiteracy and social differentiation in the Roman empire,' *Chiron* 7, 333–53

T. Dzierzykray-Rogalski (1983), 'Aspects paléo-démographiques et paléo-pathologiques de l'influence de l'entourage sur la population de Gabbari-Alexandrie,' in Grimm, Heinen, Winter ed. (1983), 205–7

J. A. S. Evans (1961), 'A social and economic history of an Egyptian temple in the Greco-roman period,' *YCS* 17, 145–283

F. el-Fakharani (1983), 'Recent excavations at Marea in Egypt,' in Grimm, Heinen, Winter ed. (1983), 175–86

A. Fakhry (1942–50), *Bahria Oasis* I–II. American University in Cairo Press

W. Foerster (1972–4), *Gnosis: a Selection of Gnostic Texts* I–II (trans. R. McL. Wilson), Oxford University Press

G. Fowden (1986), *Egyptian Hermes*, Cambridge University Press

L. A. Foxhall, H. A. Forbes (1982), 'Σιτομετρεία: the role of grain as a staple food in classical antiquity,' *Chiron* 12, 41–90

P. J. Frandsen ed. (1991) *The Carlsberg Papyri I: Demotic Texts from the Collection*, Museum Tusculanum Press, Copenhagen

P. M. Fraser (1951), 'A Syriac Notitia Urbis Alexandrinae,' *JEA* 37, 103–8

P. M. Fraser (1972), *Ptolemaic Alexandria*, Oxford University Press

W. H. C. Frend (1972), *The Rise of the Monophysite Movement*, Cambridge University Press

W. H. C. Frend (1978), 'The Christian period in Mediterranean Africa,' *Cambridge History of Africa* II, Ch. 7, Cambridge University Press

J. G. Gager (1992), *Curse Tablets and Binding Spells from the Ancient World*, Oxford University Press

C. Gallazzi, G. Hadji Minaglou (1989), 'Fouilles anciennes et modernes sur la site de Tebtynis,' *BIFAO* 89, 180–202

I. Gardner (1993), 'A Manichaean liturgical codex found at Kellis,' *Orientalia* 62 (1993), 30–59

J. Gascou (1985), 'Les grands domaines, la cité et l'état en Egypte byzantine,' *Travaux et Mémoires* 9, 1–90

E. Gazda (1983), *Karanis: an Egyptian Town in Roman Times*, Ann Arbor, Kelsey Museum of Art and Archaeology

P. Glare (1994), 'The temple of Jupiter Capitolinus at Arsinoe and the imperial cult,' in Bülow-Jacobsen ed. (1994), 550–4

J.-C. Golvin *et al.* (1986), *Le camp romain de Louqsor* (*Mémoires IFAO* 83)

W. Godlewski (1986), *Deir el-Bahari V, Le monastère de St. Phoibammon*, Centre d'archéologie méditerranéenne de l'Académie Polonaise des Sciences, Warsaw

K. Goudriaan (1988), *Ethnicity in Ptolemaic Egypt*, J. C. Gieben, Amsterdam

F. Ll. Griffith (1937), *Catalogue of the Demotic Graffiti of the Dodecaschoenus* I, Oxford University Press

G. Grimm, H. Heinen, E. Winter ed. (1981), *Alexandrien* (*Aegyptiaca Treverensia* 1)

G. Grimm, H. Heinen, E. Winter ed. (1983), *Das römisch-byzantinisch Ägypten, Akten des internationalen Symposions 26–30 September 1978 in Trier* (*Aegyptiaca Treverensia* 2)

B. A. van Groningen (1957), 'Preparatives to Hadrian's visit to Egypt,' *Studi in onore de A. Calderini, E. R. Paribeni* II, 253–6, Casa Editrice Ceschina, Milan

E. Gruen (1984), *The Hellenistic World and the Coming of Rome*, University of California Press, Berkeley

M. Hadas (1955), *Aristeas to Philocrates*, Harper, New York

B. Halpern ed. (1993), *Law, Politics and Society in the Ancient Mediterranean*, Sheffield University Press

A. E. Hanson (1991), 'Ancient Illiteracy,' J. H. Humphrey ed. (1991), 159–98

E. R. Hardy (1931), *The Large Estates of Byzantine Egypt*, Columbia University Press, New York

E. R. Hardy (1952), *Christian Egypt, Church and People*, Oxford University Press, New York

E. R. Hardy (1968), 'The Egyptian policy of Justinian,' *Dumbarton Oaks Papers* 22, 23–41

W. V. Harris (1994), 'Child-exposure in the Roman empire,' *JRS* 84, 1–22

H. Hauben (1983), 'Arsinoé II et la politique extérieure de l'Égypte,' in Peremans ed. (1983), 97–127

H. Heinen (1966), *Rom und Ägypten von 51 bis 47 v. Chr.*, University of Tübingen

K. Herbert (1972), *Greek and Latin Inscriptions in the Brooklyn Museum*, Brooklyn Museum

D. W. Hobson (1983), 'Women as property owners in Roman Egypt,' *TAPA* 113, 311–21

D. W. Hobson (1985), 'House and Household in Roman Egypt,' *YCS* 28, 211–29

D. W. Hobson (1993), 'The impact of law on village life in Roman Egypt,' in Halpern ed. (1993), 193–219

C. E. Hope *et al.* (1989), 'Dakleh Oasis Project: Ismant el-Kharab 1991–2,' *JSSEA* 19, 1–26

K. Hopkins (1980), 'Brother-sister marriage in Roman Egypt,' *CSSH* 22.3, 303–54

E. Hornung (1982), *Conceptions of God in Ancient Egypt* (trans. J. Baines), Cornell University Press, Ithaca, N.Y.

G. H. R. Horsley (1981–92), *New Documents Illustrating Early Christianity* I–VI, Ancient History Documentary Research Centre, Macquarie University, North Ryde

P. W. van der Horst (1984), *Chaeremon, Egyptian Priest and Stoic Philosopher* (*Etudes préliminaires aux religions orientales dans l'empire romain* 101), E. J. Brill, Leiden

C. J. Howgego (1992), 'The supply and use of money in the Roman world, 200 BC to AD 300,' *JRS* 82, 1–31

J. H. Humphrey ed. (1991), *Literacy in the Roman world*, *JRA* Suppl. 3

E. M. Husselman (1952), 'The granaries of Karanis,' *TAPA* 83, 56–73

E. M. Husselman (1953), 'The dovecotes of Karanis,' *TAPA* 84, 81–91

E. M. Husselman (1979), *Karanis: Excavations of the University of Michigan in Egypt, 1928–35, Topography and Architecture* (*University of Michigan, Kelsey Museum of Archaeology, Studies* 5)

H. L. Jansen (1950), 'The Coptic story of Cambyses' invasion of Egypt,' *Avhandlinger utgitt av det Norske Videnskaps-Akademi i Oslo. II. Hist.-Filos. Klasse 1950*, no. 2

H. Jaritz (1987), 'The investigation of the ancient wall extending from Aswan to Philae: first preliminary report,' *MDAIK* 43, 17–74

A. C. Johnson (1936), *Roman Egypt to the reign of Diocletian* (T. Frank, *Economic Survey of Ancient Rome*, vol. II), Johns Hopkins University Press, Baltimore

A. C. Johnson, L. C. West (1949), *Byzantine Egypt, Economic Studies*, Princeton University Press

J. H. Johnson (1974), 'The Demotic Chronicle as an historical source,' *Enchoria* 4, 1–19

J. H. Johnson ed. (1992), *Life in a Multi-cultural Society. Egypt from Cambyses to Constantine and Beyond. Studies in Ancient Oriental Civilisation*, no. 51, Oriental Institute of the University of Chicago

A. H. M. Jones (1940), *The Greek City from Alexander to Justinian*, Oxford University Press

A. H. M. Jones (1964), *The Later Roman Empire*, 284–602, B. H. Blackwell, Oxford

A. H. M. Jones (1971), *Cities of the Eastern Roman Provinces* (Second edition), Oxford University Press

C. P. Jones (1978), *The Roman World of Dio Chrysostom*, Harvard University Press, Cambridge Mass.

E. A. Judge (1977), 'The earliest use of "monachos" for monk and the origins of monasticism,' *JAC* 20, 72–89

E. A. Judge, S. R. Pickering (1977), 'Papyrus documentation of Church and community in Egypt to the mid-fourth century,' *ibid.*, 47–71

E. A. Judge (1981), 'Fourth century monasticism in the papyri,' *Proceedings of the XVI International Congress of Papyrology* (*American Studies in Papyrology* 22), 613–20

L. Kakósy (1982), 'The Nile, Euthenia and the Nymphs,' *JEA* 68, 290–8

I. Kalavrezou-Maxeiner (1975), 'The imperial chamber at Luxor,' *Dumbarton Oaks Papers* 29, 225–51

J. G. Keenan (1973–4), 'The names Flavius and Aurelius as status designations in later Roman Egypt,' *ZPE* 11, 33–63; 13, 283–304

J. G. Keenan (1975), 'On law and society in later Roman Egypt,' *ZPE* 17, 237–50

J. G. Keenan (1977), 'The provincial administration of Egyptian Arcadia,' *Museum Philologum Londiniense* 2, 193–202

J. G. Keenan (1980), 'Aurelius Phoibammon, son of Triadelphus; a Byzantine Egyptian land entrepreneur,' *BASP* 17, 145–54

J. G. Keenan (1981), 'On village and polis in Byzantine Egypt,' *Proceedings of the XVI International Congress of Papyrology* (*American Studies in Papyrology* 22), 479–85

J. G. Keenan (1993), 'Papyrology and Byzantine historiography,' *BASP* 30, 137–44

J. G. Keenan (1994), 'Soldier and civilian in Byzantine Hermopolis,' in Bülow-Jacobsen ed. (1994), 444–51

D. P. Kehoe (1992), *Management and investment on estates in Roman Egypt during the early empire. Papyrologische Texte und Abhandlungen* 40

L. P. Kirwan (1937), 'Studies in the later history of Nubia,' *Liverpool Annals of Archaeology and Anthropology* 24, 69–105

L. P. Kirwan (1977), 'Rome beyond the southern Egyptian frontier,' *PBA* 53, 13–51

L. Koenen, A. Henrichs (1970), 'Ein griechischer Mani-codex,' *ZPE* 5, 97–216

L. Koenen, A. Henrichs (1975), 'Der kölner Mani-codex,' *ZPE* 19, 1–85

L. Koenen (1977), *Ein agonistische Inschrift aus Ägypten und frühptolemäische Königsfeste* (*Beiträge zur klassischen Philologie* 56)

W. Kolotaj (1983), 'Recherches architectoniques dans les thermes et le théâtre de Kom-el-Dikka à Alexandrie,' in Grimm, Heinen, Winter ed. (1983), 187–94

W. Kolotaj (1992), *Imperial baths at Kom el-Dikka* (Centre d'archéologie méditerranéenne de l'Académie Polonaise des Sciences, Warsaw)

Th. Kraus, J. Röder (1962), 'Mons Claudianus: Bericht über eine erste Erkundungsfahrt im Marz 1961,' *MDAIK* 18, 80–120

J. Krüger (1990), *Oxyrhynchos in der Kaiserzeit. Studien zur Topographie und Literaturrezeption*, Peter Lang, Frankfurt am Main

C. La'da (1993), 'One stone, two messages,' *Acta Demotica. Acts of the Fifth International Congress for Demotists, Pisa, 4–8 September 1993*, Giardini Editori, Pisa

J. Lesquier (1911), *Les institutions militaires de l'Egypte des Lagides*, E. Leroux, Paris

J. Lesquier (1918), *L'armée romaine d'Egypte d'Auguste à Dioclétien* (*IFAO, Mémoires* 41)

N. Lewis (1970), 'Graeco-roman Egypt: fact or fiction?' *Proceedings of the Twelfth International Congress of Papyrology, Ann Arbor 1968* (*American Studies in Papyrology* 7), 3–14

N. Lewis (1974), *Papyrus in Classical Antiquity*, Oxford University Press

N. Lewis (1981), 'Literati in the service of Roman emperors,' in L. Casson, M. Price ed., *Coins, Culture and History in the Ancient World*, 149–66, Wayne State University Press, Detroit

N. Lewis (1982a), *The Compulsory Public Services of Roman Egypt* (*Papyrologica Florentina* 11)

N. Lewis (1982b), 'Soldiers permitted to own provincial land,' *BASP* 19, 143–8

N. Lewis (1983), *Life in Egypt under Roman Rule*, Oxford University Press

N. Lewis (1984), 'The romanity of Roman Egypt: a growing consensus,' *Atti del XVII Congresso Internazionale di Papirologia*, 1077–84

N. Lewis (1986), *Greeks in Ptolemaic Egypt*, Oxford University Press

M. Lichtheim (1980), *Ancient Egyptian Literature* III, University of California Press, Berkeley

G. E. R. Lloyd (1984), 'Hellenistic Science,' *Cambridge Ancient History* (Second Edition), Vol. VII, Part I, Ch. 9a, Cambridge University Press

A. Lukasiewicz (1986), *Les édifices publics dans les villes de l'Egypte romaine*, University of Warsaw

L. S. B. MacCoull (1981), 'The Coptic archive of Dioscorus of Aphrodito,' *CE* 56, 185–93

L. S. B. MacCoull (1988), *Dioscorus of Aphrodito. His Work and his World*, University of California Press, Berkeley

H. G. T. Maehler, V. M. Strocka ed. (1978), *Das ptolemäische Ägypten, Akten des internationalen Symposions 27–29 September 1976 in Berlin*, Philip Von Zabern, Mainz

H. G. T. Maehler (1983a), 'Egypt under the last Ptolemies,' *BICS* 30, 1–16

H. G. T. Maehler (1983b), 'Die griechische Schule im ptolemäischen Ägypten,' in Peremans ed. 1983, 191–203

J. Maspero (1912), L'organisation militaire de l'Egypte byzantine (*Bibl. de l'école des hauts-études*, 201)

G. Mattha (1975), *The Demotic Legal Code of Hermopolis West* (*IFAO, Bibl. d'étude* 45)

J. F. Matthews (1970), 'Olympiodorus of Thebes and the history of the west (AD 407–25),' *JRS* 60, 79–97

D. McBride (1988), 'Egyptian Manichaeism,' *JSSEA* 18, 80–98

J. Mélèze-Modrzejewski (1990), *Droit impérial et traditions locales dans l'Egypte romaine*, Variorum Press, Aldershot

D. Meredith (1952–3), 'The Roman remains in the eastern desert of Egypt,' *JEA* 38, 94–111; 39, 95–106

A. J. Mills (1979–80), 'The Dakleh Oasis project,' *JSSEA* 9.4, 10.4

J. G. Milne (1924), *A History of Egypt under Roman Rule*, Methuen, London

L. Mitteis, U. Wilcken (1912), *Grundzüge und Chrestomathie der Papyruskunde*, B. G. Teubner, Leipzig/Berlin

Mohi ed-Din Mustafa, H. Jaritz (1984/5), 'A Roman fortress at Nag 'el Hagar. First preliminary report,' *ASAE* 70, 21–32

G. R. Monks (1953), 'The Church of Alexandria and the city's economic life in the sixth century,' *Speculum* 28, 349–62

O. Montevecchi (1988a), *La Papirologia* (Revised Edition), Vita e Pensiero, Milan

O. Montevecchi (1988b), 'L'amministrazione dell'Egitto sotto i Giulio-claudi,' *Aufstieg und Niedergang der römischen Welt*, II.10.1, 412–71, de Gruyter, Berlin

L. Mooren (1975), *The Aulic Titulature in Ptolemaic Egypt. Introduction and Prosopography. Verhandelingen van de Koninklijke Akademie voor Wetenschappen, Letteren en Schone Kunsten en België. Klasse der Letteren*

L. Mooren (1983), 'The nature of the Hellenistic Monarchy,' in Peremans ed. (1983), 205–40

H. A. Musurillo (1954), *The Acts of the Pagan Martyrs*, Oxford University Press

C. A. Nelson (1979), *Status Declarations in Roman Egypt* (*American Studies in Papyrology* 19)

A. D. Nock (1929), 'Greek magical papyri,' *JEA* 15, 219–35

A. D. Nock (1972), *Essays on Religion and the Ancient World* I–II (ed. Z. Stewart), Oxford University Press

R. A. Pack (1965), *The Greek and Latin Literary Texts from Greco-roman Egypt* (Second Edition), Ann Arbor, University of Michigan Press

E. H. Pagels (1979), *The Gnostic Gospels*, Weidenfeld and Nicolson, London

G. M. Parássoglou (1978), *Imperial Estates in Roman Egypt* (*American Studies in Papyrology* 18)

P. J. Parsons (1980), 'The papyrus letter,' *Didactica Classica Gandensia* 20, 3–19

D. P. S. Peacock (1992), *Rome in the Desert, a Symbol of Power*, University of Southampton

D. P. S. Peacock, V. Maxfield (1994), *The Roman Imperial Porphyry Quarries: Gebel Dokhan, Egypt. Interim Report, 1994*, Southampton and Exeter Universities

B. A. Pearson, J. E. Goehring ed. (1986), *The roots of Egyptian Christianity*, Fortress Press, Philadelphia

W. Peremans ed. (1983), *Egypt and the Hellenistic World. Proceedings of the International Colloquium, Leuven 24–26 May, 1982 (Studia Hellenistica* 27)

W. Peremans, E. van't Dack (1950–81), *Prosopographia Ptolemaica* I–IX (*Studia Hellenistica* 6, 8, 11, 12, 13, 17, 20, 21, 25)

F. Perpillou-Thomas (1993), *Fêtes d'Egypte ptolémaïque et romaine d'après la documentation papyrologique grecque (Studia Hellenistica* 31)

P. W. Pestman (1967), *Chronologie égyptienne d'après les textes démotiques 332 av. J.-C. – 453 ap. J.-C. (Papyrologica Lugd.-Bat.* 15)

P. W. Pestman (1981), *A Guide to the Zenon Archive (Papyrologica Lugd.-Bat.* 21)

R. Pfeiffer (1958), *History of Classical Scholarship*, Oxford University Press

S. B. Pomeroy (1990), *Women in Hellenistic Egypt* (Second Edition), Wayne State University Press, Detroit

B. Porten (1968), *Archives from Elephantine*, University of California Press, Berkeley

C. Préaux (1939), *L'économie royale des Lagides*, Fondation Egyptologique Reine Elisabeth, Brussels

C. Préaux (1978), *Le monde hellénistique: la Grece et l'orient de la mort d'Alexandre à la conquête romaine de la Grèce (323–146 av. J.-C.)* I (*Nouvelle Clio* 6), Presses Universitaires de France, Paris

C. Préaux (1983), 'L'attache à la terre: continuités de l'Egypte ptolémaïque à l'Egypte romaine,' in Grimm, Heinen, Winter ed. (1983), 1–5

R. M. Price (1976), 'The limes of Lower Egypt,' *British Archaeological Reports*, Supplement 15, 143–54

J. Quaegebeur (1978), 'Reines ptolémaïques et traditions égyptiennes,' in Maehler and Strocka ed. (1978), 245–62

M. G. Raschke (1978), 'New studies in Roman commerce with the east,' H. Temporini, W. Haase ed., *Aufstieg und Niedergang der römischen Welt* II.9.2, 604–1378, de Gruyter, Berlin

D. W. Rathbone (1983), 'The weight and measurement of Egyptian grains,' *ZPE* 53, 265–75

D. W. Rathbone (1990), 'Villages, land and population in Graeco-Roman Egypt,' *PCPS* n.s. 36, 103–42

D. W. Rathbone (1991), *Economic Rationalism and Rural Society in Third-century AD Egypt. The Heroninus Archive and the Appianus Estate*, Cambridge University Press

D. W. Rathbone (1993), 'Egypt, Augustus and Roman taxation,' *Cahiers du Centre G. Glotz* 4

D. W. Rathbone (1994), 'Settlement and society in Greek and Roman Egypt,' in Bülow-Jacobsen ed. (1994), 136–45

J. D. Ray (1976), *The Archive of Hor (Egypt Exploration Society, Texts from Excavations, Memoir* 2)

J. D. Ray (1994), 'Literacy and language in Egypt in the Late and Persian Periods,' in Bowman and Woolf ed. (1994), Ch. 4

J. R. Rea (1977), 'A new version of P. Yale inv. 299,' *ZPE* 27, 151–6

J. R. Rea (1982a), 'Lease of a red cow called Thayrris,' *JEA* 68, 277–82

J. R. Rea (1982b), 'P.Lond.inv. 1562 verso: market taxes in Oxyrhynchus,' *ZPE* 46, 191–209

B. R. Rees (1950), 'Popular religion in Graeco-roman Egypt II,' *JEA* 36, 86–100

R. Rémondon (1964), 'Problèmes du bilinguisme dans l'Egypte lagide,' *CE* 39, 126–46

E. E. Rice (1983), *The Grand Procession of Ptolemy Philadelphus*, Oxford University Press

J. M. Riddle (1991), 'Oral contraceptives and early-term abortifacients during classical antiquity and the middle ages,' *Past and Present* 132, 3–32

J. M. Riddle (1992), *Contraception and Abortion from the Ancient World to the Renaissance*, Harvard University Press, Cambridge, Mass.

C. H. Roberts (1979), *Manuscript, Society and Belief in Early Christian Egypt*, Oxford University Press

M. Rodziewicz (1984), *Les habitations romaines tardives d'Alexandrie*, Centre d'archéologie mediterranéenne de l'Académie Polonaise des Sciences, Warsaw

M. Rodziewicz (1984/5), 'Excavations at Kom el-Dikka in Alexandria 1980–1 (Preliminary Report),' *ASAE* 70, 233–46

M. Rodziewicz (1988), 'Remarks on the domestic and monastic architecture in Alexandria and surroundings,' in Van den Brink (1988), 267–77

G. Roeder (1959), *Hermopolis, 1929–39*, Verlag Gebrüder Gerstenberg, Hildesheim

M. Rostovtseff (1922), *A Large Estate in Egypt in the Third Century* BC, University of Wisconsin Press, Madison

M. Rostovtseff (1953), *The Social and Economic History of the Hellenistic World* (Second Edition), Oxford University Press

P. Rousseau (1985), *Pachomius, The Making of a Community in Fourth Century Egypt*, University of California Press, Berkeley

J. L. Rowlandson (1985), 'Freedom and subordination in ancient agriculture: the case of the basilikoi georgoi of Ptolemaic Egypt,' Crux, Essays Presented to G. E. M. de Ste Croix on his 75th Birthday, History of Political Thought 5.1/2, 327–47

J. L. Rowlandson (1995), 'Beyond the polis: women and economic opportunity in early Ptolemaic Egypt,' A. Powell ed. (1995), *The Greek World*, ch. 13, Routledge, London

J. L. Rowlandson (1996), *Landowners and Tenants in Roman Egypt: the Social Relations of Agriculture in the Oxyrhynchite Nome*, Oxford University Press

A. E. Samuel (1962), *Ptolemaic Chronology* (*Münchener Beiträge zur Papyrusforschung und antiken Rechtsgeschichte* 43)

A. E. Samuel et al. (1971), *Death and Taxes: Ostraka in the Royal Ontario Museum, Toronto, 1* (*American Studies in Papyrology* 10)

A. E. Samuel (1983), *From Athens to Alexandria: Hellenism and Social Goals in Ptolemaic Egypt* (*Studia Hellenistica* 26)

C. H. O. Scaife (1953), 'The origin of some Pantheon columns,' *JRS* 43, 37

A. A. Schiller (1964), 'The interrelation of Coptic and Greek papyri,' H. Braunert ed., *Studien zur Papyrologie und antiken Wirtschaftsgeschischte F. Oertel . . . gewidmet*, 17–19, Rudolf Habelt, Bonn

A. A. Schiller (1968), 'The Budge Papyrus of Columbia University,' *JARCE* 7, 79–118

C. Schmidt, H. J. Polotsky (1933), 'Ein Mani-fund aus Ägypten,' *Sitz. preuss. Akad. der Wissenschaften, phil.-hist. Klasse* 1933.1

W. H. Schoff (1912), *The Periplus of the Erythraean Sea*, Longmans, Green & Co., New York

J. Schwartz (1969), *Fouilles franco-suisses, Rapports ii. Qasr-Qarun/Dionysias, 1950* (*IFAO, Publications*)

A. F. Segal (1981), 'Hellenistic magic: some questions of definition,' in R. van der Broek, J. Vermaseren ed. *Studies in Gnosticism and Hellenistic Religions* (*Etudes préliminaires aux religions orientales dans l'empire romain*, 91), E. J. Brill, Leiden

B. Shaw (1992), 'Brother-sister marriage in Graeco-Roman Egypt,' *Man* 27, 267–99

T. L. Shear jr. (1978), *Kallias of Sphettos and the Revolt of Athens in 286* BC (*Hesperia*, Supplement 17)

S. E. Sidebotham (1986), *Roman economic policy in the Erythra Thalassa, 30 BC–AD 217*, E. J. Brill, Leiden

T. C. Skeat (1969), *The Reigns of the Ptolemies* (Second Edition, *Münchener Beiträge zur Papyrusforschung und antiken Rechtsgeschichte* 39)

H. S. Smith (1974), *A Visit to Ancient Egypt: Life at Memphis and Saqqara c.500–30 BC*, Aris and Phillips, Warminster

H. S. Smith, R. M. Hall (1983), *Ancient Centres of Egyptian Civilisation*, Egypt Education Bureau, London

M. Speidel (1982), 'Augustus' deployment of the legions in Egypt,' *CE* 57, 120–4

M. Speidel (1988), 'Nubia's Roman Garrison,' H. Temporini, W. Haase ed., *Aufstieg und Niedergang der römischen Welt* II.10.1, 767–98, de Gruyter, Berlin

A. J. Spencer (1982), *Death in Ancient Egypt*, Penguin, Harmondsworth

A. J. Spencer (1984), *Excavations at El-Ashmunein I: the Topography of the Site*, British Museum Press, London

A. J. Spencer, D. M. Bailey (1982), *British Museum Expedition to Middle Egypt': Ashmunein (1981)* (*British Museum Occasional Papers* 41)

A. J. Spencer, D. M. Bailey, A. J. Burnett (1983), *British Museum Expedition to Middle Egypt: Ashmunein (1982)* (*British Museum Occasional Papers* 46)

W. Spiegelberg (1914), *Die sogenannte demotische Chronik des Pap.215 der Bibliothèque nationale zu Paris*, J. C. Hinrichs, Leipzig

J. Stevenson (1989), *Creeds, Councils and Controversies* (Second Edition, revised by W. H. C. Frend), SPCK, London

W. J. Tait (1992), 'Demotic literature and Egyptian society,' in Johnson ed. (1992), 303–10

W. J. Tait (1994), 'Some notes on demotic scribal training in the Roman period,' in Bülow-Jacobsen ed. (1994), 188–92

J. D. Thomas (1975), 'A petition to the prefect of Egypt,' *JEA* 61, 201–21

J. D. Thomas (1975–1982), *The Epistrategos in Ptolemaic and Roman Egypt*: I, *The Ptolemaic Epistrategos*, II, *The Roman Epistrategos* (*Papyrologica Coloniensia* 6)

J. D. Thomas (1978), 'Aspects of the Ptolemaic civil service: the dioiketes and the nomarch,' in Maehler and Strocka (1978), 187–94

J. D. Thomas (1983), 'Compulsory public service in Roman Egypt,' in Grimm, Heinen, Winter ed. (1983), 35–9

T. K. Thomas (1992), 'Greeks or Copts? Documentary and other evidence for artistic patronage during the late Roman and early Byzantine periods at Herakleopolis Magna and Oxyrhynchus, Egypt,' in Johnson ed. (1992), 317–20

D. J. Thompson (Crawford) (1983), 'Nile grain transport under the Ptolemies,' in P. Garnsey, K. Hopkins, C. R. Whittaker ed., *Trade in the Ancient Economy*, 64–75, Chatto and Windus, London

D. J. Thompson (1984), 'Agriculture,' *Cambridge Ancient History* (Second edition), VII, Part 1, Ch. 9c, Cambridge University Press

D. J. Thompson (1988), *Memphis under the Ptolemies*, Princeton University Press

D. J. Thompson (1992a), 'Language and literacy in early Hellenistic Egypt,' in Bilde *et al.* ed (1992), 39–52

D. J. Thompson (1992b), 'Literacy and the administration in early Ptolemaic Egypt, in Johnson ed. 1992, 323–6

D. J. Thompson (1994a), 'Egypt, 146–31 BC,' *Cambridge Ancient History*, Vol. IX (Second Edition), Ch. 8c, Cambridge University Press

D. J. Thompson (1994b), 'Literacy and power in Ptolemaic Egypt,' in Bowman and Woolf ed. (1994), Ch. 5

H. Thompson (1938), 'Self-dedications,' *Actes du Ve congrès internationale de papyrologie*, 497–504

G. Thür (1987), 'Hypotheken-Urkunde eines Seedarlehens für eine Reise nach Muziris und Apographe für die Tetarte in Alexandria,' *Tyche* 2, 229–45

G. Thür (1988), 'Zum Seedarlehen κατα Μουζειριν. P. Vindob.G40822,' *Tyche* 3, 229–33

B. E. Trigger, B. J. Kemp, D. O'Connor, A. B. Lloyd (1983), *Ancient Egypt, a Social History*, Cambridge University Press

F. R. Trombley (1994), *Hellenic Religion and Christianization c.370–529* II, E. J. Brill, Leiden

E. G. Turner (1952), 'Roman Oxyrhynchus,' *JEA* 38, 78–93

E. G. Turner (1973), *The Papyrologist at Work (Greek, Roman and Byzantine Monograph* 6)

E. G. Turner (1975), 'Oxyrhynchus and Rome,' *HSCP* 79, 1–24

E. G. Turner (1980), Greek Papyri, an Introduction (Second Edition), Oxford University Press

E. G. Turner (1984), 'Ptolemaic Egypt,' *Cambridge Ancient History* (Second Edition) Vol. VII, Part I, Ch. 5, Cambridge University Press

E. C. M. Van den Brink (1987), 'A geo-archaeological survey in the north-eastern Nile Delta, Egypt; the first two seasons, a preliminary report,' *MDAIK* 43, 7–31

E. C. M. Van den Brink (1988), *The Archaeology of the Nile Delta*, Netherlands Foundation for Archaeological Research in Egypt, Amsterdam

P. Van Minnen (1987), 'Urban Craftsmen in Roman Egypt,' *Munstersche Beiträge zur antiken Handelsgeschichte VI.I*, 31–88

P. Van Minnen (1994), 'House-to-house enquiries: an interdisciplinary approach to Roman Karanis,' *ZPE* 100, 227–52

E. Van't Dack (1988), *Ptolemaica Selecta (Studia Hellenistica* 29)

P. Viereck (1928), *Philadelpheia: die Gründung einer hellenistischen Militärkolonie in Ägypten*, J. C. Hinrichs, Leipzig

F. W. Walbank (1981), *The Hellenistic World*, Fontana, London

T. Walek-Czernecki (1941), 'La population de l'Egypte a l'époque saïte,' *Bull. de l'institut de l'Egypte* 23, 37–62

S. L. Wallace (1938), *Taxation in Egypt from Augustus to Diocletian*, Princeton University Press

C. C. Walters (1974), *Monastic Archaeology in Egypt*, Aris and Phillips, Warminster

L. C. West, A. C. Johnson (1944), *Currency in Roman and Byzantine Egypt*, Princeton University Press

S. West (1969), 'The Greek version of the legend of Tefnut,' *JEA* 55, 161–83

W. L. Westerman (1924), 'The castanet dancers of Arsinoe,' *JEA* 10, 134–46

D. S. Whitcomb, J. H. Johnson (1979), *Quseir al-Qadim 1978: Preliminary Report*

D. S. Whitcomb, J. H. Johnson (1982), *Quseir al-Qadim 1980: Preliminary Report (ARCE Reports)*

J. Whitehorne (1994a), *Cleopatras*, Routledge, London

J. Whitehorne (1994b), 'A postscript about a wooden tablet book (P. Kellis 63),' in Bülow-Jacobsen ed. (1994) 277–83

J. Wilkinson (1971), *Egeria's Travels*, SPCK, London

E. Will (1966–7), *Histoire politique du monde hellénistique* I–II, Université de Nancy

H. E. Winlock, W. E. Crum (1916), *The Monastery of Epiphanius at Thebes* I–II, Metropolitan Museum of Art, New York

E. O. Winstedt (1909), *Cosmas Indicopleustes, Christian Topography*, Cambridge University Press

E. Wipszycka (1972), *Les ressources et les activités économiques des églises en Egypte du Ve au VIIIe siècle (Papyrologica Bruxellensia* 10)

H. C. Youtie (1973–5), *Scriptiunculae* I–III, A. M. Hakkert, Amsterdam

H. C. Youtie (1975), 'ΑΠΑΤΟΡΕΣ: law vs. custom in Roman Egypt,' J. Bingen, G. Cambier, G. Nachtergael ed., *Le monde grec. Hommages à Claire Préaux*, 723–40, Université de Bruxelles

K.-Th. Zauzich (1984), 'Von Elephantine bis Sambehdet,' *Enchoria* 12, 193–4

Index